Conversations with John Edgar Wideman

Literary Conversations Series

Peggy Whitman Prenshaw
General Editor

News Office, University of Massachusettts, Amherst

Conversations
with John Edgar Wideman

Edited by
Bonnie TuSmith

University Press of Mississippi
Jackson

Books by John Edgar Wideman

A Glance Away (novel). New York: Harcourt, Brace & World, 1967.

Hurry Home (novel). New York: Harcourt, Brace & World, 1970.

The Lynchers (novel). New York: Harcourt Brace Jovanovich, 1973.

Damballah (short stories). New York: Avon Books, 1981; Vintage, 1988.

Hiding Place (novel). New York: Avon Books, 1981; Vintage, 1988.

Sent for You Yesterday (novel). New York: Avon Books, 1983; Vintage, 1988.

Brothers and Keepers (nonfiction). New York: Holt, Rinehart and Winston, 1984; Vintage, 1995.

The Homewood Trilogy (includes *Damballah, Hiding Place,* and *Sent for You Yesterday.*) New York: Avon Books, 1985.

Reuben (novel). New York: Henry Holt and Company, 1987; Penguin, 1988.

Fever (short stories). New York: Henry Holt and Company, 1989; Penguin, 1990.

Philadelphia Fire (novel). New York: Henry Holt and Company, 1990; Vintage, 1991.

The Homewood Books (hardbound reprint of *The Homewood Trilogy*). Pittsburgh: University of Pittsburgh Press, 1992.

All Stories Are True (short stories). New York: Vintage, 1993.

Fatheralong: A Meditation on Fathers and Sons, Race and Society (nonfiction). New York: Pantheon Books, 1994; Vintage, 1995.

The Cattle Killing (novel). New York: Houghton Mifflin, 1996.

Copyright © 1998 by University Press of Mississippi

All rights reserved

Manufactured in the United States of America

01 00 99 98   4 3 2 1

The paper in this book meets the guidelines for permanence and durability of the Committee on Production Guidelines for Book Longevity of the Council on Library Resources.

Library of Congress Cataloging-in-Publication Data

Wideman, John Edgar.
    Conversations with John Edgar Wideman / edited by Bonnie TuSmith.
      p. cm. — (Literary conversations series)
    Includes index.
    ISBN 1-57806-053-2 (cloth : alk. paper). — ISBN 1-57806-054-0
(pbk. : alk. paper)
      1. Wideman, John Edgar—Interviews.   2. Afro-American
authors—20th century—Interviews.   3. Afro-Americans in literature.
I. TuSmith, Bonnie, 1951– . II. Title. III. Series.
PS3573.I26Z465   1998
813′.54—dc21   97-40961
                                               CIP

British Library Cataloging-in-Publication data available

Contents

Introduction

What John Wideman's books convey, above all, is love—love for family, for culture, for self—and the persistence it takes to "keep on keepin' on" against formidable odds. Now, thirteen books into his lifelong commitment as a creative writer, it is time to take stock of the artist. In interviews spanning over thirty-five years, with most taking place in the 1980s and 90s, *Conversations with John Edgar Wideman* represents one step in this direction. I am hopeful that, by perusing these interviews, the newcomer will be inspired to take a closer look at the creative output of this challenging writer, and Wideman fans and scholars will use the volume as a touchstone for their abiding interest.

"As I grow older and look at the world, I see art as a gift to people, certainly a gift to the artist," he tells an interviewer in 1989 (Rowell). As a serious, dedicated writer, he rarely squanders this gift. While it is appealing to think of him as the former UPenn basketball star, the Rhodes Scholar, or even the UMass English Professor, ultimately we must come to terms with the "astonishing Wideman"—as he was lauded in his first interview—as a consummate artist.

How love and caring translate into quality literature is one possible clue offered by these interviews. They tell us, for example, that the African Americans of Wideman's Homewood clan deserve complex treatment because their lives were rich and complex. As the writer puts it: "I have tried to cultivate a high degree of sophistication in the way I tell stories and try to learn a helluva lot about how stories are told" since, in writing about real-life black folk, "there was no simple set of techniques, no simple story form, which would contain them" (Sabatelli interview). Wideman's novels are among the most challenging in contemporary American literature, with daring artistic moves and surprising narrative twists that sometimes perplex even the most intrepid and experienced reader. The artist works hard at his craft to be true to his subject and vision of the world. It is this respect—respect for others and for oneself—combined with extraordinary linguistic ability and intellectual acumen that make reading a Wideman story a memorable event. "I want to empower folks to feel the intimacy and reciprocity of the language," Wideman tells the interviewer, and adds later, "that it's an expressive medium in which they can expand and learn things about themselves."

In a 1983 interview, Wideman identifies his grandfather John French's advice to "give them the benefit of the doubt!" as possibly "the most valuable inheritance I have" (Samuels). While the writer confesses that he is not sure he can live up to this inheritance, the interviews included here verify that, as artist and human being, John Wideman has certainly come close. The notion of taking a "longer, slower look at people and situations" before drawing conclusions reflects both the writer's interview style and artistic stance. There are no shortcuts, no "quick fixes." Just as he patiently writes out each word of his novels and stories in longhand—generating drafts and revisions with his trusty Bic pens and yellow pads—he also worries a question or issue from various angles and perspectives. Such an approach often results in complex thinking and open-ended narrations. Readers as well as interviewers must do their part for meaning to emerge. As the present volume shows, this cerebral and discursive style is quite demanding. Within the limits of his control Wideman avoids throwaway interviews.

Giving others the benefit of the doubt requires faith. Wideman's first nonfictional and possibly most well-known book to-date, *Brothers and Keepers*, actually confronts this issue in the person of his mother. In a seven-page discussion of his grandfather's legacy, the narrator offers a heart-rending analysis of how, after a lifetime of charity and compassion, his mother began to change when she realized that her son Robby was not going to be treated fairly by the law. As eyewitness to this "change inside" in the role model that he had "admired, envied, and benefited infinitely from," how was the stellar son affected? Along with his mother, did John Wideman lose faith in humanity and declare war on society as well? Keeping in mind that the autobiography *Brothers and Keepers* was published one year after the Samuels interview, I believe that the present collection is a helpful tool for assessing the writer's relation to his cultural inheritance. In drawing a parallel between his mother's loss of faith and the gradual deterioration of his hometown ("If I'd been alert enough . . . I might have understood sooner how desperate and dangerous Homewood had become"), Wideman's intense personal story might suggest that the values of an earlier Homewood—as epitomized by the generous, patient, and formidable John French—cannot be sustained in the grandson. And yet, if we pay close attention to his subsequent works and what he says about them in the interviews, we might reach a different conclusion.

"In a way, [*The Cattle Killing*] is a love story," Wideman says in a 1996 interview (McGinty). Given that his latest novel includes themes such as the self-destruction of an African people, the eighteenth-century plague in Philadelphia, and various other seemingly "bleak" storylines, this statement is intriguing. The writer explains that because the narrator's stories keep a very ill woman alive and her listening keeps him alive, this constitutes a love story—offering a "nice definition of love." Building this storytelling-as-love idea into his recent fiction suggests that, no matter how unconventional and complex readers may find his writing, Wideman has remained consistent in a simple faith. The belief in telling stories to save lives is deeply rooted in African American culture and its oral tradition. It suggests an understanding of human love that goes far beyond common or stereotypical notions. Support, trust, mutual aid in the face of adversity—these values feed into a definition of love that is thoroughly consistent with the meditations on love that have been presented in Wideman's works through the years.

In the award-winning 1983 novel *Sent for You Yesterday*, for example, there is an image of a man's love for his family that is profoundly moving in its simplicity and accuracy. Searching for a response to his friend's question "How come you a family man?" an image John French evokes is that of his little girl in a polka-dot dress "planted like a flower" in her daddy's faded work boots. All it takes is a couple of such memories for French to conclude that it is self-evident why he is a family man. Because these intimate experiences of love are difficult to reconstruct in so many words—especially to a "running buddy" who has chosen the singles lifestyle—French fails to communicate his feelings to his friend. John Wideman the writer, however, successfully conveys to his readers the family man's overflowing feeling of love.

Wideman once told me that there is a call-and-response between his work and that of Toni Morrison's. One notable connection, I believe, is each writer's exploration of the strengths and pains of love. From the interviews assembled here, the writer's abiding interest in family and community, historical and collective memory, individual and group identity, political and legal issues, sports, music, dance, art, and a host of other themes is apparent. Nevertheless, the overarching, persistent exploration of love—between father and son, father and daughter, husband and wife, friends, total strangers—is a pervasive strain in Wideman's writing that is little recognized. His sense of putting things on record for the benefit of his children (TuSmith interview); his concern over the black community's loss of children (Smith interview); his willingness to confront his fears ("Good writing is about . . . things that are scary to you, things that eat you up" [Rowell interview])—these qualities reflect a loving, caring, courageous individual. They serve as countervailing evidence for the image of the rageful menace that is too often imposed on African American men. As Wideman himself points out, a photograph of him squinting in the sun quickly became interpreted as the "rageful black writer" on a dustjacket (Reed interview).

In some of the more recent interviews, Wideman probes deeper and revises or extends his answers to questions that he has been asked before. As can be expected, one question of everlasting interest to interviewers is how the writer views himself in relation to his race and ethnicity. When asked about his reluctance to be labeled a "black writer," Wideman jokes that what he should have said was, "Well, look a little closer at me and ask me that question again." He goes on to explain: I mean, from the fact that I'm of African American descent, nothing follows. I could write mystery novels, I could write in Victorian English, I could write like the guys on the corner write now, I could write travel books. Nothing follows from the fact of my African American ancestry. Writing is not reflex, is not biologically-driven. Well, in some ways it is biologically-driven. But it's not determined by race. I want to make that clear. (McGinty interview)

The interviewers here frequently ask the author about his personal life—which is understandable when the interviewee is a writer who is known for his autobiographical explorations. Wideman generally responds to such questions indirectly, obliquely—especially when they touch on his personal grief and loss (which has caused a few interviewers to describe "the wall" they sometimes sensed with him). In drawing the line between autobiographical *art* and the personal side of his life that is off-limits to prurient interest, he makes a useful and necessary distinction. In telling us that his *books* are about loss, Wideman clearly suggests that the reader should look to the artist's creations for insight in this regard.

At times, the writer will put personal and family matters in a more general context. "It's a universal story," he says about his rendition of his brother Robby's life (Olander interview). Like any good storyteller, he offers personal anecdotes to make a point. It is in this way that tragic developments in his life surface in his art. Nevertheless, when Wideman chooses to incorporate his family history into his work—which he has done most movingly—he provides us with the social and historical context and thoughtful personal insight that is missing in most journalistic treatments on the subject. Fortunately, his own presentation of his family history and of African American experience in books and articles, as well as in the interviews collected here, greatly eclipses the narrow viewpoints expressed by eye-catching headlines.

Several interviewers comment on Wideman's physical appearance, especially his athleticism. This is more than incidental to his life and work. Basketball has played a prominent role from the beginning of Wideman's career up to the present. It made an appearance in the 1963 *Look* article; it was featured again in the brief 1983 *Sports Illustrated* profile on his coaching experience; and it surfaced once more in a 1996 interview regarding the pro-basketball player Dennis Rodman (McGinty). Arguably, the sport serves as a metaphor for individual expression in a communal context in works such as *Philadelphia Fire* and *Fever*. Then there is his daughter Jamila's budding career with the WNBA and Wideman's intentions of affording the sport fuller treatment in a future writing project (TuSmith interview). The flip side of the writer's connection to basketball, though, is once again the stigma of "race." As Ishmael Reed quotes Wideman to himself in an interview, "No reason for niggers to be at the University if they weren't playing ball or coaching ball. At least that's what white people thought, and since they thought that way, that's the way it was" (*Fever*). The interviews included here indicate that the writer brings both personal experience and intellect to bear when treating sports as a theme or issue.

A claim I will not make about the interviews collected here is that they give us the "real" or "true" John Wideman. The writer will be the first to deny such a claim for any book about any complicated subject. Commenting on the African proverb "all stories are true," Wideman says, "The other side of that phrase is that none of them are true." An author this consciously accepting of paradoxes will not provide simple conclusions about life. Yet, despite what sounds at first like relativism, one of the strongest impressions in Wideman's work is of a creative mind constantly probing—trying to figure things out, to get to the very bottom of an issue or idea or experience.

It would not be inaccurate to call John Wideman one of our most "philosophical" writers. In fact, it was no surprise to learn, as I did during my conversation with him, that he was reading Thomas Pynchon's newest novel. As the interviews show, recurrent themes in Wideman's works tend toward the philosophical. In the author's own words: "Two of my fascinations are time and identity. . . . And those two subjects are connected. I believe that the next real revolution in human consciousness . . . will be a readjustment of the notion of continuous personality" (Silverblatt 1993 interview). While notions of the self as unstable, fragmented, and multiple have been in currency among theorists for some time, Wideman's particular application of this understanding has triggered some of his most accomplished and innovative writing. There is also a pragmatic side to his thinking: "If we can face up to and acknowledge and begin to use the diversity we find inside ourselves, then maybe we'll be able to start to tolerate diversity in the world outside of ourselves" (Silverblatt 1993).

Some of the most useful comments in the interviews concern the author's writing technique. Wideman's ability to articulate difficult ideas in a conversational style corresponds to his approach to art. He talks about developing the necessary skill of linguistic improvisation in oral communication as a young black man growing up in the 1950s and 1960s. He compares "gangsta rap" style today to his experiments in fiction. He compares the self-referentiality of the narrator in *The Cattle Killing* to a blues singer who draws attention to himself in the middle of a song. About emotion and feeling in fiction, he borrows from Duke Ellington's motto: "It don't mean a thing if it ain't got that swing." For Wideman, the power of literature is to make us feel. The language of literature is an extension of the language of home. Words are accompanied by certain "codes"—a lesson with which he credits his childhood experience. He tells of listening to the women in his family talking in front of "Mr. Big Ears" (himself as a curious child), who was not supposed to understand everything that was said (Silverblatt 1995 interview). He acknowledges an early connection to Modernist writers—especially Eliot and Joyce—and stream-of-consciousness as a literary device, and says that he has never deliberately severed himself from these influences (Silverblatt 1995 interview). There are interesting connections for readers to make between watching Wideman think on his feet in the interviews, the virtuosity and playfulness in his written prose, and his comments about the joys of "playground" basketball.

It probably should not surprise us, as seen in the later interviews and in *The Cattle Killing*, that the fifty-six-year-old writer seems to have a more intense interest in spirituality than ever before. Wideman rejects the positivistic or materialistic view of history. Incidents of the oppression of marginalized peoples not only have recurred in history (the Ghost Dance, the cattle killing of the Xhosa, etc.), but, from his viewpoint, are part of a mythic cycle. By no means a traditional believer, Wideman discusses immortality in connection with storytelling and with the continuing influence, after death, of powerful voices—such as that of Martin Luther King, Jr. In this way, he demonstrates a connection with the traditional African belief that ancestors impinge on the present. Even in his bleakest analyses of contemporary society, Wideman professes profound admiration for the faith of religious believers like his mother.

Wideman continues to have to deal with the charge that he asks too much of his readers. One interviewer quite honestly admits that he missed much of the different layers of meaning in *The Cattle Killing* on his first reading (McGinty). He asks the writer whether he is afraid that "he will put off some readers" because he makes them work so hard. Obviously having thought seriously about this charge, Wideman gives a good accounting of himself by letting us in on the effort he puts into his research and writing. In explaining the sources of *The Cattle Killing* he says that he drew on his three years studying eighteenth-century literature and culture at Oxford as well as more recent research. He is unapologetic about making the reader work a bit. He has every intention of moving the reader outside of the familiar and the comfortable. He says that he reads serious literature to learn, to go outside of himself (TuSmith interview). *The Cattle Killing* is essential for understanding where Wideman is today as a creative writer. His comments here give us a good deal of guidance for understanding the novel. I believe that critics will be "catching up" to the writer for some time to come.

In many ways the title of the 1963 *Look Magazine* article, "The Astonishing John Wideman," is right on the mark. Thirty-five years later, John Wideman is still likely to astonish those who are exposed to him and his work. I would like to thank him for his support and cooperation in the preparation of this book. His acuity, engaging style, and genuine interest in the project have made this a pleasurable undertaking for all of us. Drawing from my own experience I have concluded that, if anyone feels "intimidated" by John Wideman, it probably has more to do with misinterpreting his intensity than with anything else. Warmth, intellect, and a low-keyed sense of humor characterize Wideman in my mind. I was especially moved by his act of faith in loaning me his only copies of original materials from his files. In giving me the benefit of the doubt, Wideman has shown that a valuable part of the African American legacy continues in him. I sincerely hope that *Conversations with John Edgar Wideman* is worthy of his trust.

What follows is a collection of nineteen interviews spanning over three decades (with several years in the 1970s when Wideman did not publish books or give interviews). The majority of interviews have been previously published and are reprinted here as they originally appeared. Obvious errors of fact have been silently corrected. Interviews that were originally conducted for non-print media were edited for publication, with every effort made to preserve the content and form of the original. The reader will notice some redundancy across the interviews, although there are often meaningful variations on a theme. The interviews are presented here in the order in which they took place so that Wideman's entire career is represented and the evolution of his thought and literary output can be discerned.

Without the hard work and intellectual acumen of my husband and research associate Dr. Gerald Bergevin, I would not have been able to complete this book within the prescribed time. I thank Jerry for his dedicated labor and loving support. I would also like to express my appreciation to Seetha A-Srinivasan at the University Press of Mississippi for her commitment to the project and overall sound judgment. Finally, I would like to thank Aaron Kuntz for his technical assistance.

BT
August 1997

Chronology

1941 On June 16th John Edgar Wideman is born to Edgar and Betty French Wideman in Washington, DC. Within a year the family moves to Homewood, a black neighborhood in Pittsburgh, Pennsylvania.

1951–59 The family moves to the predominantly white upper-middle-class neighborhood of Shadyside. John attends Peabody High School, becomes captain of the basketball team, and is class valedictorian. He wins the Benjamin Franklin Scholarship to attend the University of Pennsylvania in Philadelphia.

1959–63 Begins as psychology major and switches to English. Earns membership in Phi Beta Kappa, competes in track, and wins all-Ivy status as a forward on basketball team. In senior year, decides to become a writer.

1963 Receives BA in English. Wins Rhodes Scholarship to attend Oxford University. Profiled in *Look* magazine article entitled "The Astonishing John Wideman."

1965 Marries Judith Ann Goldman. Teaches American literature at Howard University in Washington, DC (summer course).

1966 Awarded a bachelor of philosophy degree at Oxford University in England.

1966–67 Attends University of Iowa's Writers' Workshop and completes his first novel, *A Glance Away* (1967).

1967–74 Teaches at University of Pennsylvania.

1968–72 Assistant basketball coach, University of Pennsylvania.

1968 At students' request, teaches a course in African American literature.

1970 Publishes second novel, *Hurry Home*.

1971–73 Director of Afro-American studies program.

1973   Publishes third novel, *The Lynchers*.

1973–81   His "woodshedding phase" during which he "forges a new language for talking about the places I'd been, the people important to me."

1973–74   He attends the funerals of his editor and his grandmother. At his grandmother's wake, he listens to family stories told by his Aunt May which he credits as inspiration for his books about life in Homewood.

1974   Earns rank of Professor of English, University of Pennsylvania. Named member of Philadelphia Big Five Basketball Hall of Fame. Accepts teaching position at the University of Wyoming at Laramie and moves west with his wife and three children (Daniel Jerome, Jacob Edgar, Jamila Ann).

1975–86   Professor of English, University of Wyoming.

1976   His brother, Robby Wideman, is sentenced to life imprisonment for armed robbery and murder.

1981   Publishes *Damballah* and *Hiding Place*.

1983   Publishes *Sent for You Yesterday*, which wins the PEN/Faulkner Award.

1984   Publishes *Brothers and Keepers*, which is nominated for the National Book Award.

1986   His middle child, Jacob, confesses to the murder of his roommate at summer camp and, at 18-years-old, is sentenced to life imprisonment.

1986   Accepts teaching position at University of Massachusetts-Amherst.

1987   Publishes *Reuben*.

1989   Publishes *Fever*.

1990   Publishes *Philadelphia Fire*, which wins a second PEN/Faulkner Award.

1993   Publishes *All Stories Are True*.

1993   Awarded MacArthur "Genius" Fellowship totalling $315,000.

1995   Publishes *Fatheralong: A Meditation on Fathers and Sons, Race and Society*, which is nominated for the National Book Award.

1996   Publishes *The Cattle Killing*. Edits *The Best American Short Stories 1996*.

Conversations with John Edgar Wideman

The Astonishing John Wideman

Gene Shalit / 1963

From *Look Magazine* 27.10 (May 21, 1963): 30–36. Reprinted with
permission from Hobby-Catto Properties, L.L.C.

Anyone who didn't know better would assume that John Wideman has it
made. At 21, he is about to be graduated with honors from the academically
tough University of Pennsylvania in Philadelphia. He has been elected to Phi
Beta Kappa, writes poetry and plays, and is captain of Penn's basketball
team. More than one member of the faculty has referred to him as a genius.
Girls call him up for dates, professors invite him to their home for dinner,
and soon he will sail to Britain for two years of study at Oxford on a Rhodes
Scholarship. Obviously, the world is his plaything.

Obviously, it is not. John Wideman is a Negro, and those who assert that
nothing in this world is black and white had better check again, because John
Wideman's world is. For him, as a sign in his room starkly states, there may
be "No exit."

"John has apparently come to grips with the color of his skin and with all
the hideous foolishness about Negroes," says a Pennsylvania professor who
admires Wideman and has closely observed him during his four years at the
university. "But skin color is nothing he can hide, so in everything John ever
does, he is going to have to be careful. Now, he is a symbol."

Prof. Richard G. Bozorth recalls, "Shortly after he won the Rhodes, John
came in and said he wanted to talk to Dr. Mark Longaker about Oxford. Then
he gave me a lovely smile, and he said, 'Oddly enough. I mean Oxford,
England—not Oxford, Mississippi.' The fact that he could smile about it, the
fact that he could make a purposeful joke about it when he didn't have to—
this charmed me."

John Wideman has been showered with so many academic and athletic
honors, awards and "firsts" that he is unable to enumerate them. He sometimes forgets that he won a prize that another student would consider the high
point of a college career.

Prof. Maurice Johnson, chairman of graduate English at Penn, teaches a
class for undergraduates. John is one of some 35 students enrolled. "I sprang
a surprise test on them the other day," Johnson reports. "I can confess that,

if I had been confronted by this quiz without warning, I couldn't have answered all the questions right. And all but one of my students didn't, either. John Wideman got 100 percent. He not only knew all the answers, he knew all the right reasons—he *understood*. It was an astonishing performance."

And yet a campus friend insists that Wideman is no "grind." "He can write an 'A' theme in half an hour, standing up," the friend says.

"The really good 'A' student you run into," Bozorth says, "is the boy with the fine high-school background who's been lucky in his teachers and has used his time well. It's clear that John had teachers who cared." Wideman's parents were determined that he get a good education, and always managed to live in a good district with integrated schools, although they were never well off. John's extraordinary record at Penn won him membership in Sphinx, the men's senior honor society. One of the few Negroes ever invited to join, he is the Pharisee (treasurer) of the organization. He is proud of the honor, but speaks of it lightly: "Sometimes, I find it hard to collect dues, especially from myself."

"John seems not to be race- or class-conscious," Professor Longaker has said. "Although he is certainly aware of the complex problems that beset Negroes, he himself seems to be on an eminence looking down."

"I've never been confronted with any big problem as far as racial prejudice goes," says Wideman. "I can't say I'm completely unconscious of the problem, because, to me, being Negro is only a physical fact.

"If there were something I wanted very badly that being Negro prevented me from doing, then I might have the confrontation of a racial problem, and I would be driven to do something about it. I'm sure I *would*. But so far, the things that I've wanted to do haven't been held back from me because of my being a Negro. So the problem is not my own problem, not something I feel I have to cope with or resolve.

"At college, I've found that there's no cleavage beyond the physical fact, although in a way—socially, I suppose—I've often wondered if things would have gone along the same way if I'd had a white girl friend on campus. There's a fine line there, a line that is a kind of threat, something that even in the most liberal circles isn't talked about, and that's the idea of . . . well, probably sex. The actual fact of a Negro-white relationship—an interracial or interreligious marriage—is always the last thing to go. Because then there is complete equality, and there's nothing that would actually separate the races anymore. Anything that goes toward that direction creates a tension.

And that's a psychological situation that can't be remedied by any amount of constitutional reforms.

"The only thing that I'm really concerned about in the racial problem is that the legal barriers be removed. After that, assimilation will either take place or not take place in the usual way that social reforms occur, through time and patience. You can't legislate sociological change.

"Being Negro has actually provided me with some advantages. If I'm the only Negro in a discussion group, and they want to find out a few things, I automatically have a certain focus, and I might command the floor sooner than the others, just because I am different in one sense. And occasionally I might be able to get a job because the company would like to have a Negro working there. Of course," he adds with a rueful smile, "it can also work out just the opposite."

John Wideman is no militant on the race problem. He says, "I probably could not have done what James Meredith did at Mississippi. I have a passive role myself. I feel passive about it. I can support fully any movement that will effect legislation and make it meaningful, not just paper legislation, and I say, 'Go to it!' but leave me here. My major concern is something else. Whether that's good or bad, that's the way it is."

It wasn't always so easy for John to live in a white world. Betsy Ward, who was part of that white world, remembers her student days with him at Peabody High School in Pittsburgh: "I think I knew him very well. We sat next to each other in homeroom, and we talked a lot. But we never talked about what it meant to him to be a Negro. Once when we were working on a play together, he said that he wouldn't want to be seen on the street alone with a white girl. Another time, when we accidentally met on the street, he said, 'Let's go somewhere else to talk.'

"When class breaks came, he would seldom walk to the next class with the white students. Instead, he would go off to talk with the other Negroes in the corridor. Then, just as the bell rang, he'd slip into his seat at the next class. I was exceptionally aware of this because of our close homeroom situation. All Negroes in the school liked him very much, I'm sure, and so did the white students. After all, he was elected senior-class president. He was always careful about people's feelings. Beneath his pleasantness was a profound philosophical person."

Dr. Howard Mitchell of the university's Department of Psychiatry is one of the persons closest to Wideman. Himself a Negro, Mitchell has carefully discussed the problem of being a Negro in an academic world.

"There's a tremendous issue facing the Negro community," Dr. Mitchell says. "It centers on this question: If a Negro achieves in the total community and really integrates (as Wideman has done at Penn, where he lives in a house with nine whites), does it mean that he is unsympathetic to Negroes, that he is a traitor? I think the mission of any of us as men and as Americans is to take advantage of our opportunities, and to move as our talents, desires and motivations dictate. If you do that, you'll recognize that, along with your other attributes, you're also a Negro. But you should be a man first, with certain strengths and certain weaknesses, who is also a Negro, rather than a Negro who is also a man. I think that John has learned that lesson."

Wideman hopes to teach in one of the better Eastern universities after his years at Oxford. "If I'm any good at all," he says, "I've got to succeed in the toughest league of all, and I've got to end up being as good as anybody up there."

John Wideman

John O'Brien / 1972

After studying literature at Oxford as a Rhodes scholar, John Wideman published his first novel, *A Glance Away*, in 1967. His second novel, *Hurry Home*, came out three years later, and his third novel, *The Lynchers*, was published in 1973. His academic training shows up in allusions to and imitations of the literary figures he admires, especially T. S. Eliot. *A Glance Away* echoes the early poetry of Eliot both in mood and style and has a central character who—Wideman admits—resembles Prufrock. His second novel uses an Hieronymus Bosch painting as a controlling metaphor and structural device, as well as employing surrealistic techniques in its narrative method.

The Lynchers continues his thematic concern with race, identity, and the workings of the imagination, and reflects his earlier formal interest in myth, ritual, and symbol; yet this novel is very different in many ways. Whereas the first two novels mirrored Wideman's European influences, *The Lynchers* turns to wholly American themes, myths, diction, and locale. The novel revolves around the aborted effort of a group of young blacks to lynch a policeman in the South, an action which the author describes as the most ritualistic and symbolic in portraying racial relations in America. Though the lynching fails, its planning alters the lives of all those involved. It causes less a political upheaval than an imaginative one. And exploration of the imagination is the recurring and pervasive concern in all three novels. Out of necessity his characters are forced to push the imagination to its limits in an effort to order their lives and free themselves from the threatening experiences of the past. At the same time we are made aware that Wideman is as interested in solving the problems of life as he is in solving the problems of the novel, especially the experimental novel. His imagination, like his characters, is being tested to see whether it can reshape the inherited form of the novel or invent a new one.

At the time of the interview, which was conducted in a series of phone conversations in October of 1972, Wideman was at work on a series of interrelated short stories and a novel about the most native of American rituals—athletics. Currently, he teaches black literature and creative writing at the University of Pennsylvania.

Interviewer: Your first two novels, *A Glance Away* and *Hurry Home*, are very differently conceived one from the other. The second experiments rather radically with the form of the novel.

Wideman: Well, each book presented different kinds of problems. I would say in the first book, with a close reading, that you would see pretty quickly that I am interested in the formal aspects of the novel. I am doing apprenticeship work, I am going to school to various other writers, using other's techniques, but also trying out some things that I hope are original. I had a real interest in experimenting, in expanding the form of the novel even in the first book. I think then that the second book continues that. The first book was much less self-consciously organized; in the second book I thought a lot about what precisely I wanted to do from page one to the very last page. There was a progression in technique and craft in *Hurry Home*, so that I had a little more certainty about what I could do. I could set up goals or objectives far more consciously in it and I think this is even more true in *The Lynchers* because there I began the book with a completed plot. I could write a section and know that it was something that would be near the end of the novel.

Interviewer: Is it more difficult when you are just beginning a novel to know how the parts will relate to the whole?

Wideman: When you're beginning, even though you may be telling yourself otherwise, the process is very much in bits and pieces. You think there might be connections, but you're not really sure. You never really can be sure until the last word is written and you see what you have. For instance, *A Glance Away* didn't begin as a novel. I wanted to write something long but it didn't come. I kept writing shorter pieces. I had maybe fifteen or twenty shorter pieces just lying around. Then I began to re-read them and I suddenly found that two or three main characters emerged if I cut out about ten of the stories. So it became very natural to think of ways of putting these bits and pieces together. But I tried with all three books to set up a regular work-schedule. In that way, whether or not you have an idea, you're producing something. There is a lot of brute work involved in getting several thousand words down on paper. It takes time, but you have to do that at some stage, whether the words are very polished or not. You have to get the raw material down.

Interviewer: Do you think of *A Glance Away* as being a realistic novel?

Wideman: It starts off with a warning that it is not going to be totally realistic. The Prologue uses many poetic rather than traditional prose devices for organization. It warns any reader that he is not going to be able to effect a traditional kind of relationship to the material following the Prologue. So it moves pretty quickly away from realistic convention. By the end it attempts to orchestrate on the page the inner thoughts of people and treat those in the same way a conventional novel would treat dialogue; and there are levels of interaction between the character's minds that permit them to roll over time and place. All of that makes it not at all a realistic novel.

Interviewer: There seems to me to be a tension in both novels, perhaps most pronounced in *Hurry Home*, between traditionally realistic content and your interest in innovative forms.

Wideman: There were contradictions in my own experience that meant that on the one hand I had a great concern for and a great store of realistic material from which I could draw in a very concrete way. On the other hand, I had quite a bit of formal training in literature so that I just couldn't sit down and write a book that didn't show some consciousness of my literary as well as my actual experience.

Interviewer: One of those literary voices that keeps echoing in *A Glance Away* is that of T. S. Eliot. What has been Eliot's influence on you?

Wideman: As with most complex relationships there are various stages. The first stage was when I was a sophomore or junior in high school. I read *The Waste Land* and there was no way in the world that I could get through the ramifications of the poem. Ten or fifteen years later I read in an interview with Ellison that he had had a similar reaction to Eliot. As I grew older I came to understand the whole texture of the poem, its tonal qualities, the effects of the movement from vernacular to high literary speech, the echoes of foreign languages. But I think that I share some of Eliot's vision as well, particularly in *Hurry Home* and now in *The Lynchers*, because one of the themes that Eliot is dealing with is cultural collapse.

Interviewer: Have there been more recent influences upon your writing?

Wideman: About five years ago I began to read other black writers and I began teaching a course in black literature. This whole exposure has been crucial in my development as a writer. It awakened in me a different sense of self-image and the whole notion of a third world. The slave narratives, folklore, and the novels of Richard Wright and Ralph Ellison have been most important to me. And these things are just beginning to become embodied in the things that I write. Toomer's *Cane* as an individual work was very important to me because of its experimentation and open form and also because of Toomer's vision. But actually I go back to the eighteenth century and the beginning of the novel when I talk about influences of experimentalists—to Defoe, Fielding, and particularly Laurence Sterne. If there is any single book I learned a hell of a lot from, it's *Tristram Shandy*. My scholarly work at Oxford was on the development of the novel in this period. It's interesting that the novel began by imitating facts or what passed itself off as fact, and now we have novels imitating novels.

Interviewer: Do you think that this preoccupation of the contemporary writer with form is changing?

Wideman: There are indications that the pendulum is swinging back again. Someone like John Fowles gives you story, plot, and a lot of the old nineteenth-century trimmings. *The Lynchers* is also in a very realistic tradition. I hope that I have learned from the nonrepresentational school about fantasy and playing around with different forms. The novel started out with these two tendencies—realism and fantasy. *The Lynchers* is in part plot-oriented; I wanted to create drama and get the reader involved with it. On the other hand, the subject of the book is imagination. The novel absorbs some of the philosophical assumptions that caused experiments in form over the last several years, and attempts to merge them with a more traditional plot-line.

Interviewer: Is it a safe generalization to say that the processes of the imagination is the underlying thematic consideration that pervades all three of your novels?

Wideman: (laughing) That's a valid enough generalization. In various conversations you recreate the books you've written and at different times you understand different things about them; it is tied up with your perceptions at the moment. In my last two books I had imagination on my mind, I had notes in my journals and wrote about how to capture some of the ambiguities about imagination. It's a unifying theme in the novels and it's something that is very much on my mind at the moment. It's a natural preoccupation because the imagination plays such a powerful role in the relationship between blacks and whites in America, which is also a predominant theme in my work. It's not what we are, it's what we think we are. From the very beginning Western civilization has an idea of what black men are, and that idea has come down to us generation after generation, has distorted and made impossible some kinds of very human and basic interaction. The mechanics of that are both very frightening and very fascinating. I'm sure that it comes out in my work all the time. In *The Lynchers* it doesn't make any difference whether the conspirators pull their plot off or not, it doesn't make any difference whether we have an Armageddon in America or not; what does matter is what certain social realities have pushed these characters to, what attitudes are taken by both blacks and whites. In fact, a subterranean apocalypse does come to pass because people are changed more by their imagination than they are by actual external events.

Interviewer: The first several pages of *The Lynchers* are made up of quotations from various sources about slavery and racism. Was your purpose for using these to break down the distinction between the "real" and the "fictional"?

Wideman: All the quotations are actually taken from newspapers and documents. I wanted to immerse the reader in a reality that for one reason or another he wasn't ready to accept, one which under normal circumstances would seem fantastic to him. I thought this might be a traumatic way of introducing him into a different kind of world. Somehow documents have a different kind of resonance from fiction. I do not have to try to convince anybody that those things happened. They happened, that's all. So when the reader gets involved in the other imaginative world that the novel comprises, perhaps some of his defenses are down.

Interviewer: Can you remember what the genesis was for *Hurry Home*?

Wideman: My best friend in Pittsburgh lived with an aunt and uncle and I noticed that the uncle had a lot of framed documents on the wall. I never payed much attention to the uncle. Then one day I was waiting for my friend and I looked at these things and they were really quite prestigious credentials. One of them was a law degree. Who he was and what he was stuck in my mind. Why would a black man who went through law school and made all the sacrifices one must make to do that, then just disappear, just decide to go down a different path altogether? I attempted to answer that question in the book.

Interviewer: The last line of *Hurry Home* is "So Cecil dreamed." There are suggestions throughout the second and third sections of the novel that all that transpires may be taking place in Cecil's mind or fantasy. Does this line invite us to wonder whether any of this has really happened except in a kind of dream? In what sense might it be a dream?

Wideman: I don't want the ending to be a trick. I don't want it to negate what's come before. Rather than that, I hope that the reader sees that what was specifically Cecil's experience becomes conflated with the whole collective history of his race, that there is a thin line between individual and collective experience which permits one to flow into the other. It has to do with imagination. Cecil can suffer because somebody centuries ago suffered on a slave ship. In the novel this happens through an imaginary voyage, but I feel very strongly that people have this capacity to move over time and space in just such an empathetic way. It's almost silly to talk about whether it's a fantasy or whether it's happening because all of our experience has that same collapsible quality. It's a question of trying to blur that line between dream and reality.

Interviewer: Then, as with Stephen Dedalus, history is a dream?

Wideman: History is a spiraling process. "So he dreamed" follows a metaphor about the garbage cans and how in the moonlight there seemed to be circles going around the cans and they seemed to be endless. The question of "So he dreamed" and this metaphor go together. They recapitulate the way the book has been moving and they pose again the question that Cecil asks throughout the book, "Why did you do that?" To go back into one's past is in fact dreaming. What is history except people's imaginary recreation? In one generation you have Charlemagne the hero, and in the next he's the villain. You have Christians writing history, you have Muslims writing history, you have blacks writing history. Each will create a myth. And so too if you're asking about somebody's life. You will find various versions, you will get various dreamers. It's appropriate to look at Cecil's attempt to go back into his past and to create an identity as also an attempt to create a dream. There is an arbitrariness in meaning that is somehow close to the logic of dreams. The line between Cecil's actual past and his dream past— what is it? Where is it?

Interviewer: The only way that he can find an answer to who he is and what he has done is by returning to the past?

Wideman: In attempting to answer the question that is formulated at the beginning of the novel, "Why did you do that?" Cecil realizes he must go back very far and he also realizes that in an essential way he didn't have a past, that he was surrounded by certain versions of himself, that he had no history, or at least he was presumed to have no history. So he sets out to find whether that's true. That's one of the imperatives—"Why did you do that?"—"Why did you throw that can down the steps early in the morning and wake people up?" Well, he doesn't know the answer. He just picked up the kind of ethic that says, "Go to law school, pull yourself up by your bootstraps, hustle, get ahead." So, he had made tremendous personal sacrifices and cut himself off from so many things. He had gotten his law degree but he didn't understand why he had done any of the things he had done. In that sense his past was invisible to him as well as it was invisible to the culture. He just decided that, after having made so many decisions in the dark, he had to limn out some of his background, he had to delineate it, he had to understand why he was doing what he was doing, he had to make sense of the present.

Interviewer: Does that question change in its meaning each time it occurs?

Wideman: I hope that "Why did you do that?" has a symphonic effect, that it accrues meaning with each instance. At first it might be the very specific question of why he threw the can down the steps; but it is also "Why did you go to law school?" "Why did you go to Europe?" "Why did you go to Africa?" "Why have you chosen the kind of life you've chosen?" I hope that this question spirals. As you go deeper and deeper into it you find out that it has ever-widening circles of significance. You will remember that when Cecil throws the can down the stairwell, it unfolds in a spiral movement.

Interviewer: Is part of Cecil's journey into the past made possible through racial memory?

Wideman: Racial memories exist in the imagination. I believe that there are certain collective experiences that get passed on. I don't know whether through the genes, but there may be other processes that science doesn't have the slightest idea about. Certain things have been repeated generation after generation so that there are archetypes. A man like Cecil is not simply a product of a family; his family reaches out toward larger and larger circles. One can read what an African said about slavery and if he's a sensitive reader then that may strike something in his memory. Once that happens you have a synthesis so that the individual memory becomes larger. The individual identity becomes merged with someone else's from a past generation.

Interviewer: Were you consciously working with certain myths in the novel? Did they—as much as the plot—help to structure Cecil's experiences?

Wideman: I'm sure that to some degree these things are conflated in my own mind, but I can list for you any number of informing myths that relate to various episodes. Cecil's passage through the black section of town on his way to get a haircut, after he has returned home, more or less parallels the Passion, and he is in fact crucified by his own people just as Christ was crucified by the Jews. That archetype is there. The shoeshine boy corresponds to a specific character in the Biblical story; there is a crowd there and the whole episode is structured around Saint John's version of the Passion. And I had in mind the tone and music of both Bach and Heinrich Schütz. In fact part of the narrative is a direct statement from the Schütz *Saint John Passion*. When Cecil goes back to Africa his Uncle Otis tells him the story about Roderic and the Visigoths and the Moors. All that is based upon an actual story. Otis also repeats the story of Tarik, the Moorish warrior who led the invasion of Spain. There are innumerable other legends and myths that act as an underpinning, that give plot to the specific plot that the novel has. Of course, on another level there are much larger kinds of informing myths— Cecil is questing for his own identity, the return to the womb, the return to his birthplace, man's cyclical journey.

Interviewer: Cecil sees a relationship between his experience and what he sees in Bosch's paintings. Did Bosch have an influence upon you as you were writing *Hurry Home*? Were the last two sections of the novel in any way a novelistic imitation of a Bosch painting?

Wideman: I used Bosch for tone, exaggeration, and the surrealistic manner that I sometimes employed. But also for specific details. Under a picture of Bosch is where two of the characters meet, and the pretext for going to Europe is to see the real thing. The picture is used again outside The Prado where Cecil meets a friend and they talk about Bosch. So, it's a narrative thread as well as being a tonal influence. I don't think that it's necessary for anyone to have a great familiarity with the painter to understand the book, but I think that if you are acquainted with his work, then you share some of the visual excitement.

Interviewer: The last question I want to ask is how the title of *A Glance Away* is related to the novel as a whole?

Wideman: I wanted to take a character who was in pretty bad shape and lift him out of his environment and place him back in again and see if in fact he could start fresh. That means that one of the things the book is concerned with is time. At one point a character becomes conscious in looking at his mother's face that she has aged. The way time passes sometimes makes time seem like no more than a "glance" and a "glance away." When you look away from somebody you open up this immensity of time, this gap that is almost impossible to talk about in terms of years or days or seconds. That's a rather terrifying idea. If you look away from somebody you really don't know what is going to be there when you look back. This has to do with history, it has to do with the relationship of the two people, and some strange thing about time. In your own life you see this arbitrariness of time; ten years can seem much less important than ten seconds.

Going Home: A Conversation with John Edgar Wideman

Wilfred D. Samuels / 1983

Reprinted by permission. Wilfred D. Samuels. "Going Home: A Conversation with John Edgar Wideman." *Callaloo* 6.1: 40–59. Copyright © 1983. The Johns Hopkins University Press.

John Edgar Wideman published his first novel, *A Glance Away* (1967), at the age of twenty-six. He immediately won accolades from critics who marvelled at the creative talents of this former Rhodes Scholar and Captain of the University of Pennsylvania basketball team. After the appearance of *Hurry Home* (1970) and *The Lynchers* (1973), he was identified as "perhaps the most gifted black novelist of his generation." Since 1973, Wideman has published two books of fiction: *Hiding Place* (1981), a novel; and *Damballah* (1981), a collection of short stories—both of which are Avon paperback originals. His earlier work demonstrated an interest in family and culture, and he now reveals that he has found in Homewood, his boyhood community, a reservoir of subject matter for fiction. Most important is Sybela Owens, one of Homewood's earliest settlers and Wideman's great, great, great grandmother. We begin our conversation with a discussion of his family history.

Wideman: According to the family history, my great, great, great grandmother was one of the first people to settle in Homewood.

Samuels: Does she become the Sybela in your short stories?

Wideman: Yes, Sybela is based on that female ancestor. My Aunt May, who lives in Pittsburgh, is the only family member left who actually saw Sybela. The way I spell it in the stories is "Sybela." But I have never seen it written; I have only heard people say her name. If two relatives are sitting around, one will say "Sybela" and the other will say "Sivela." So who knows?

Samuels: The one remaining relative, May, did you say?

Wideman: Yes, May.

Samuels: May. Again, there is a character like her in your short stories. And the one thing that struck me about her is that she is a kind of *griot*, in the African sense: she is the story teller, the family historian who knows the lore of the family. Did you have this in mind when you created that character and placed her in the stories (and novel), or is May based on your family member?

Wideman: There is always the reciprocity between fictional and real characters, but certainly the actual May came first and there are all sorts of close linkages between the actual Aunt May and the Aunt May in the stories. But the Aunt May in the stories is very definitely based on a particular human being I've known all my life.

Samuels: How old is she now?

Wideman: May is about seventy-five now. When she saw Sybela Owens, Aunt May was a tiny girl; and Sybela Owens, a very old woman. But they did meet. There is another woman in Homewood who remembers Sybela. This woman is not a member of the family, but she is very close to us. Her name is Elizabeth Lewis, and she, also, has memories of Sybela Owens. She said that Sybela Owens always wore a black cape.

Samuels: Is that right?

Wideman: Interestingly enough, my grandfather, Harry Wideman, who migrated to Pittsburgh from South Carolina when he was a young man, actually climbed Bruston Hill and did some work for Sybela Owens. The incident occurred long before my father was born, long before my mother was born. Harry Wideman climbed up the hill and saw Sybela.

Samuels: So Homewood and Bruston Hill are real, physical places, not just a fictional community that you have created for your work?

Wideman: Oh, no. Homewood is very real. As I said, the family history coincides with the history of the actual community. Aunt May claims that the first tree was chopped down by her great grandfather, Charlie Owens. When May was going to public school, there was a day set aside, a holiday, for celebrating the beginning of Homewood. May and her sisters would get mad because, in the story she was told in school, a man she'd never heard of was credited with founding the community by chopping down a tree. May knew better. She knew that it was Charlie Owens who cut down the first tree.

Samuels: And Charlie was Sybela's husband.

Wideman: Yes. Sybela's husband, the father of her children, anyway. He was white, but he was May's relative.

Samuels: That is interesting. This is a good place to talk about *Hiding Place* and *Damballah*. It seems to me that the major difference between the later works, these two pieces that I have just mentioned, and the earlier works is that there is a greater emphasis (in the last works) on community, on history, on past, and specifically on Black community, Black history, Black past. . . .

Wideman: Well, yes and no. The first book, *A Glance Away*, is very auto-biographical, and characters correspond to people in my family. Of course, a lot of the book is given over to the character of the schoolteacher, the white man. . . .

Samuels: Thurley.

Wideman: Thurley. Yes. He had a big role in *A Glance Away*, but the point of the book was to bring him into the world of the other characters—the Black world.

Samuels: But is it still not possible to argue that his life parallels that of the main character's, Eddie's, in many ways? What you have are two individuals who are in search of self; their quests do not necessarily have to do with race, not directly, anyway. For me, Eddie's search in the novel does not have to do with race.

Wideman: He is rooted in a particular family in a particular place, but I guess you can say that his problems have universal dimensions. But I had to plant him someplace. I planted him in the place I knew best: Homewood.

Samuels: As a critic, I would say that, from reading your last two works and from reading your earlier works, I find what could be called a "turning point": you've gone from a novel that is, in a way, raceless to one that speaks to and celebrates a particular experience. But what you are saying is that this doesn't mean that the experience becomes limited, that it is less meaningful to the human experience.

Wideman: I don't have any problems with the argument that says the emphasis of my fiction has changed, that there is a more explicit concern with Afro-American life. I am not interested in investigating family and community in a generalized, universal context. My subject is a Black family, a Black family in America, in a particular city. On the other hand, if you're lucky and writing well, the more specific you become, the more you root what you are doing in a particular environment, the more general resonance it has. If you capture absolutely what happened to you, then other people read it and say, "Yes, I recognize myself in that," no matter what their backgrounds are. . . . I hope that is what is happening in my last two books. I hope by examining the particularity of my past that I am making it exist on its own terms—but, that at the same time, giving it a greater accessibility.

It is hard to talk in abstract terms because the abstract word, for me anyway, can lead in several directions at once. You make a statement that sounds good, and you test it against the work and the statement loses what seemed to be its concreteness. At a certain point in my writing career (if you want to call it that), I made a decision. I had done three books, worked very hard, as hard as I could, and they represented my ability to think through certain problems; they represented my concerns as I wrote them. Also they were for me a real laboratory. I was learning how to write. But after those three books, I decided that I wanted to include other dimensions in my writing. I wanted to do some things that I had not accomplished before. I wanted, number one, to reach out to levels of audience that perhaps the earlier works had excluded.

Samuels: That is a very good point because, if I may just enter a comment here, it seems to me that the introduction to *Damballah* calls to attention a particular audience. Did you intend for that to be the case?

Wideman: Oh, I wanted to get everybody's ear, but if you've read T. S. Eliot, James Joyce, or William Faulkner, you aren't excluded from *Damballah*. But those are not the only "keys to the kingdom." If you have grown up Black, you also have some "keys" to what this book has to offer. Ideally, I had in mind a book that people familiar with America, with the technique and history of the novel—a book that the audience could appreciate and applaud and relate to the great traditions, if there are such things. But at the same time a book my brother, sister, aunts, uncles, cousins, mother and father could read. And in my mind it became quite clear that to do a book like that would not be writing down to a black audience, because my people have had the full range of human experience. Their feelings, thoughts, intelligence— all have been tested and been refined—so it wasn't a question of writing down to a less educated set of readers but rather to expand my own frames of reference. And my ambition still is to write as well as anybody has ever written. I am sure now that for a long time I didn't know what really counted—what would really count as legitimate subject matter, legitimate language, for such an enterprise. To write the very best, didn't you have to cheat a little, didn't you have to "transcend Blackness"? Didn't you have to ground yourself in an experience that was outside . . . Homewood? Didn't you have to show you were part of a larger world? Didn't you have to show continually your credentials with allusions to the "great writers"—the "great traditions"?

Samuels: And you consciously sought to do these things in your first two works?

Wideman: Not altogether consciously. I would not give myself that much credit. I was university trained, university educated; and as you go through as an English major at schools like the University of Pennsylvania and Oxford University, you get a value system imposed on you. You don't just guess what the best is: people tell you what the best is . . . and you see yourself on this hallowed ground; you stare and compare, and the messages are pretty clear. And a lot of that is not altogether conscious. It seeps in, just like when you learn to walk and talk. As you grow up, a value system seeps in, and so I was not consciously turning my back on Blackness; I was just getting acculturated, and the acculturation pushed my writing in certain directions.

Samuels: That, again, raises an important question. I have seen criticism which said you were influenced by such writers as Eliot, Joyce, and Faulkner. I think I can see a Hemingwayian influence in *Hurry Home*. I don't know whether this is true or not. But, in addition to the white writers, were there any Black writers who influenced you in your development as a writer?

Wideman: Well, absolutely. They came late because of the kind of academic training I had, but about 1967 or 1968 I was solicited by a group of students at the University of Pennsylvania to do a course in Afro-American literature. At that point, I guess I had read some of Richard Wright and some of Ellison. I was your typical traditional academic—as far as my knowledge of Afro-American literature went. But then I got involved in a project with Norton; they wanted to integrate their famous *Norton Anthology of American Literature*. Integrate it or publish a separate volume of Afro-American writings. So I took a summer and part of a year to develop a course in Afro-American literature and at the same time put together this anthology for Norton. I went from a very superficial acquaintance to an absolute immersion in Black literature. Now, you can only do so much in a year and a half, but I read fast and I concentrated, even spent time in the Schomburg. It was not just a question of reading the novels that were easily available. I did my homework for the anthology and the course, and then I continued teaching the course. It became a special love. I continue to teach Afro-American literature. So, it has now been over fourteen years—fifteen years—that I have been thinking about Black writers and my interest has burgeoned to Caribbean and African literature. I even taught myself a little linguistics so that I could understand what people were talking about when they were making distinctions between Black speech and American mainstream speech. Afro-American writing was a serious academic concern, on the one hand; on the other hand, it was a kind of great celebration, an eye opener, an awakening, a feast. As I explored these writers, no one was really more important than the others. I was exposed to the whole range, and I have pretty eclectic taste; I am a pretty eclectic reader. When I was reading Richard Wright, reading about Wright, I was taken with what he was doing. There are very few books that I have ever "closed down" or that I don't care about at all because a book is another mind talking to you and there is always something to learn. In the past fourteen or fifteen years, my writing has absolutely been transformed by the exposure I am talking to you about.

Samuels: Does this in any way explain the long break between the third novel and the last two works?

Wideman: Well, it partially explains it because I was exploring voice; I was trying to learn to use a different voice; I was doing a lot of studying. I was "woodshedding," as the musicians would say—catching up. I was constantly writing and I produced a lot of manuscripts, none of which were satisfactory. Some of them were sent out, and people either didn't like them or wanted more, or liked them but didn't want to publish them. I was engaged in that kind of business constantly, but as far as having a finished manuscript, for about six or seven years, I did not. Just bits and pieces. I was learning a new language to talk about my experience.

Samuels: Why did you publish the two books together? Do you expect your audience to read them in concert? There seems to be, of course, the link: Homewood, Bruston Hill, The Brass Rail Bar, Hamilton Avenue. These are scenes and people and names that permeate both works. Do you want your audience to read them together as a pair?

Wideman: Oh, sure! I would like them to read all five together, but those two make a natural pair. And there is a third book—I can call the three of them a fancy name, a trilogy. I am revising the third book now. Avon has purchased it.

Samuels: Do you have a title for it, so that we can look for it?

Wideman: The working title is *Brother Hall*, but I think I am going to have to change the name because there was a "Brother Hall," and his sister is still alive. I don't say anything nasty about Brother, but there is no sense in putting anybody in the dozens. I'll probably change the title. But I would like the title to have something to do with this character, Brother, who is an albino. He appeared before in *A Glance Away*.

Samuels: How do you arrive at a character? I find, for example, in *Hiding Place*, Bess. I am fascinated with that lady. You mentioned Richard Wright a few minutes ago. One day, while reflecting on Bess's characterization, I saw a little of the mother in one of Wright's stories—you know, the one where the mother takes the gun and goes to rescue her son who is being held captive.

Wideman: Yes, he is being held by some Klansmen.

Samuels: I also thought of the mother in "River Niger." Fundamentally, this character is the woman who for years has been somewhat isolated. She is quiet, but she is ebullient with action and conviction—with energy. At the right moment, she acts. How do you arrive at someone like Bess? I know that she is partially biographical, but then, there are the creative and imaginative processes that come to bear here. How do you fashion or mold a Bess?

Wideman: I can give you a general answer here. That is, the writers you are talking about and the characters you are talking about are drawing from a common source. From Sojourner Truth on down, there have been Black women who have been strong, who had incredible fortitude, and whether we knew them as our grandmother or as an Aunt May is not the point; probably all of us have been exposed to that archetype. And if we read we've probably seen them in other people's writings, too. Miss Jane Pittman is a skinny little thing, but she shares that strength and courage. So that is the general answer. Specifically, something happened with *Hiding Place* that had never happened before. I saw the ending of the novel just as clear in my mind as I see images on television or in the movies. It came to me with just such direct, vivid clarity. I saw a little angel flying around, I saw an old house going up in smoke, I saw the angel touching places in it, and I saw an old woman walking out of the burning house; not scared nor frightened. The walls had come tumbling down because she "called in the trumpets." It was her special triumphant moment, and I saw everything. In a space of about ten minutes, the whole story was in my mind.

Samuels: Sounds somewhat like a vision.

Wideman: We can call it that. The whole story was in my mind, beginning to end . . . you know how dreams are, they can compress so much information, so much understanding in a short amount of time? Well, that is the way the novel came to me. And I knew it. I just knew that it was just a question of setting it down, of going from page one to page whatever . . . that the story was there; that it existed in my mind; that I understood it. As a matter of fact, I went out to lunch that day with a friend—a good friend but not a person with whom I'd ever talked about my writing. But I sat there and told her the whole story. What the book was going to be about. I don't know whether she was bored, fascinated, or what; but she was a good listener that day. And she heard the whole thing. She mentioned similarities to *Great Expectations*, but I had never read *Great Expectations*. I've read a lot of Dickens, but I'd never read that particular novel and still haven't. Anyway, the book came to me like that. That is how Bess appeared; she appeared as a vision.

Samuels: You had the ending, and then you went back and created the work around it?

Wideman: Well, the ending was the first thing revealed to me, but it wasn't a question of trying to figure out how to get to the ending at all. That would distort what happened. The ending just happened to be the first flash. Then, other flashes came quickly. Sequence was arbitrary. I knew the story.

Samuels: The interesting thing about your comments is that, for me, the ending is one of the most powerful endings I have ever read. When I got to the end, I immediately went back ten pages to catch the beginning of the final action, the move up the hill. So, I am already convinced. I believe in what Carl Jung calls the "collective unconscious," and in one's ability to tap into it, see future experiences, and know outcomes.

Wideman: In a lot of stories, I try to deal with that, and the whole rationale of the stories presumes certain kinds of narrative license or imagination, which allows one person to get inside another person's skin. The first story in *Damballah* is about transformation of consciousness, about passing on experience from generation to generation, about the mysterious way such sharing takes place. The old woman in the "Chinaman Story" sees a China-man. In one sense the Chinaman is imaginary, yet she knows he is going to get her. And that story is almost literal. It happened to my grandmother. She had a stroke but hung on for many, many years. She began to believe she was being attacked by an evil spirit. She started muttering a word, and my uncle figured out it was "Chinaman." A little while after that, they took her to the hospital. My mother met a young Asian woman in the hospital. The young woman would sit in the lounge talking with my people because her father, like my grandmother, was bedridden in one of the hospital rooms. Her father got well, and on the way out of the hospital, she decided to stop to say goodbye to my folks who were in with my grandmother. The Asian woman took her little Chinese father into the room to peek at my grandmother who was sleeping. She never woke up again. She had a premonition that a China-man would come to her. And he did.

Samuels: So what would you tell critics who might say, as is often said about Toni Morrison, that the more you immerse yourself in the Black experience the more strains of mysticism and magic appear? For example, the title of your collection of short stories might lead someone to believe that you are bringing to your work more Black or Afro-American folklore or culture, and again, might lead him to argue that there is evidence of a kind of "turning point" in your recent work. For example, I am not certain whether or not critics will be able to continue to make references to your direct or indirect influences—say an Eliot or a Joyce—because your works speak to unique aspects and elements of Afro-American culture, specifically its folk culture.

Wideman: Oh, yes. But see, the terrible thing is that as writer or critic we are forced into these kinds of choices, and we are forced into them because there are values attached. You can say that "Wideman is a good writer; he uses Afro-American folklore, he knows this, that, or the other thing about his heritage and culture." You can make that argument, and show it in the work, and pat me on the back, but that doesn't get me out of the ghetto. It should, but it doesn't. If I do all that, I mean that is enough, but there is always an implied, invidious comparison: "OK, Wideman does fine with Afro-American stuff, but on the other hand the real writers are doing so and so. . . ." To protect ourselves as critics and artists, we are forced to jump back and forth, measure ourselves against an imaginary mainstream, define what we are doing in somebody else's terms. It's almost like making excuses. It is a terrible bind.

Samuels: It is unfortunate, but what you've said is true. I think, though, that what I find most pleasing when I look at your work, when I look at Toni Morrison's work and at James Baldwin's work, is a beautiful validation of the Afro-American experience as a vehicle for understanding what is called "the human experience." For me that is enough. I don't need the comparisons. Why can't the blues be recognized as an art form that speaks about alienation? Why can't the blues be accepted as a viable and valuable vehicle for understand the "human experience"?

Wideman: Yes, I agree, but we don't have to convince each other. The historical problem is there and how you solve it creates a sort of "out of the frying pan into the fire." There is an Afro-American tradition. There are Afro-American writers working right now; it makes sense to talk about them as a group, or about certain ways that their work relates. It is natural; it is enlightening; it is intelligent to do it that way, but, at the same time, to do that perpetuates the "bad side" of the whole notion of looking at things in black and white ways. You almost can't have one without the other. You see it in Academia. You have someone get up to argue. If things were perfect, American literature would include writings by Baldwin. That sort of sounds good, but it is also bullshit, too, because the individual strains in the tradition are really what the tradition is. Culture is a house of cards. The parts are

more tangible than the whole. A house of cards is dependent on the relationships among the cards. Its existence depends on the individual cards. The
sort of shape and form that you arrive at when you pile the cards together is
interesting, per se, and you can talk about it; you can analyze it; you can say
this, that, and the other, but if you pull one of those cards out, the whole
thing collapses. The parts are bigger than the whole. So, I like that metaphor
to talk about culture, particularly American culture.

    Samuels: So, how do you define yourself as a writer? Do you consider
yourself an Afro-American writer? An American Writer? A Writer?

    Wideman: Well, that is almost like asking: "Which name do I prefer?"
When I play basketball, some of the young guys call me "Doc." I like that.
Some of the old guys call me "Spanky." That's okay, too. But, now, I don't
want other people to call me by those names. Names are contextual. They
make sense in certain situations. And all these literary labels are okay with
me, as long as people don't get confused and call me out of my name; that is
the important thing.

    Samuels: In the past, you seem to have had a definite interest in experi-
menting with the form of the novel. Does that remain true today? Your collection of stories, for example, is written in the form of letters. You have an
introduction in which you address a certain character and tell him that you
are sending him these letters. At the end, there is a sense that you have
concluded—that you have finished your letters. How would you describe
your concern with form at this stage of your development?

    Wideman: Form for me is a kind of adventure. Any writing is a form of
adventure, a form of play, a form of fun. Very serious play, and very difficult
and involving play. The idea of writing a fairly conventional narrative, a plot
that requires a fairly straightforward development, a novel that could be used
as a model in bogus creative writing courses—that has no interest for me. I
have always been fascinated by chance, by possibility, by what one can do to
make a unique statement about anything. This goes for all kinds of expressive
activities. I think it's an Afro-American cultural inheritance. "Dr. J" plays
basketball very well, but he also uses basketball as a means of self-expression. He has mastered the techniques. So not only do you see basketball (the
game) being played, but you see "Dr. J." Ideally, that is how I would like to
play basketball, the way I would like to write a novel, and do anything else.
Very frankly, writing is a form of display, as well as a mastering of the craft.
And I think any writer, particularly this writer, can allow the desire to display
himself get a little bit out of hand. Until you really learn the fundamentals,

until you are very, very good, you can't afford to do too much jiving around.
But once you get those fundamentals mastered, then the whole point is to
jive around. You can call it experimentation, or you can call it ringing the
changes, or you can look at it as doing what Afro-American musicians do. I
value spontaneity, flexibility, a unique response to a given situation. Creating
little boxes for yourself and dancing out of them. Getting too close to the
edge but then recovering like the heroes of the Saturday matinee serials.
That's excitement. These are the things that draw me to writing in general. I
don't want to know exactly where I am going. I want to get there and then
deal with it. I want to set up situations that make me work in ways that maybe
I have never worked before in fiction. That is sort of my personal feeling,
and it goes along with the sort of reading taste I have. I said I like most
books, but the books that really get me are the ones in which somebody is
making a very personal statement without an egotistical, boring, intrusive
statement. They are doing their thing; they have mastered the fundamentals
but now they are going to take off; they are going to fly, and that is the kind
of excitement which writing holds for me. And when it stops holding that
kind of excitement, I'll probably stop.

Samuels: About making a statement. I think that the strongest statements
you make for me have to do with the Black man. I find that most Afro-
American writers are insensitive or unfamiliar with the complexity of the
Black man. You, on the other hand, in all your novels and stories, seek to
explore the joy and anguish or what it means to be Black, male, and American. And you do so to a degree that I don't find in many other works by
Black writers, male or female. Are you indeed trying to make a definite
statement about what it means to be Black, male, and American? Is this one
of your main concerns?

Wideman: I am not sure how to answer that, because it seems like it
could be . . . it seems like I lose either way. Not that it's a trick question, or
anything like that.

Samuels: No, it is not.

Wideman: But it is a complicated question. It just stops me in my tracks.
I shake my head, and say *how many skins of the onion do I have to peel to
get down to what this is all about?*

Samuels: Let's play with the question for a while. I think that your treatment of Cecil in *Hurry Home*, for example, reveals in a very real sense the
complexity of what it means to be a Black, a father, a husband, and a professional in American society. I was moved, for example, by his response to the

fact that his wife had lost their child. She had not been able to nourish the fetus to have a successful pregnancy. You probe his emotional response to this experience. Maybe I have not read enough, but I don't know of another work (perhaps with the exception of Baldwin's *If Beale Street Could Talk*), in which that kind of sensitivity and sensitive probing into the Black male psyche can be found. It is this probing that leads me to conclude that your presentation of the relationship between Cecil and Esther is real. The chaos and conflict that might exist between the Black man and woman transcend the superficial ones that we are most familiar with by now: the man is lazy, his problems emerge solely from the fact that society is on his back, he is politically and economically impotent. I don't mean to suggest that these are often not real issues in the lives of Black people, but you seem to go beyond the external to take a deeper look.

Wideman: I have seen more than that, and when I read the kinds of criticisms, the kinds of sociological studies, that you are talking about, I know that they aren't true, that they did not have the total picture. I have known that for a long time. I made some pretty prodigious economic leaps in my lifetime, so I have had the opportunity to observe many different kinds of people. Starting in a place like Homewood, and then going to Philadelphia to an Ivy League school, and then going abroad and studying at Oxford, and winding up in academia. Like those of many other Black people, my experiences encapsulate what often took generations of living. Imagine an immigrant family at the turn of the century. The father is a tailor; he does this and then he has kids, and they get to school and maybe they become businessmen of some sort, and maybe their kids get to school and to professional school. So, literally, in the classic American pattern it takes generations. But it happened to me in a lifetime. I was the first in my family—my extended family—to go to college. I've had a chance to observe lots of people and because the world was moving so fast around me, I was really thrown on my wits a lot. I was both participating but was also forced to take the posture of an observer because I didn't know what the hell was going on. It was best to keep quiet and sort of check it out before I exposed my game. The insider/outsider nature of my experience made me a listener. I have always listened to people and watched them closely and carefully. That habit is something I can fall back on as a novelist. Yet one of my biggest regrets is that moving fast caused me to miss so much. In the writing that I have been doing for the last three or four years, I have been trying to recover some of that lost experience, to re-educate myself about some of the things I missed because the world was moving so fast. Now, I have the returned to Homewood and have sort of settled in. I am trying to listen again. Fortunately, my people are being kind, compassionate, patient. They give me the benefit of the doubt. In spite of Thomas Wolfe, I can go home again; I listen again, I can learn again the things I heard and saw as a child and young man. There is a basic conservatism in any folk life. There are little sayings and phrases that I read in the WPA narratives from the thirties or in slave narratives. I'd heard them before in my living room. "Stomp down ugly." When I found that phrase in a slave narrative, I cracked up because I had been hearing that my whole life. Afro-American culture is conservative, and it does give you a chance to go back, and I have had that chance. Reading writers like Albert Murray, Leon Forrest, and of course Zora Hurston and Ellison and Richard Wright, I was reminded of things I had forgotten; books were also a way of returning.

Samuels: Well, I guess one of the reasons I make the point that I make is that I am certain some critics somewhere might argue that your male characters fall into the category of, as one critic calls it, "the black man in motion." I don't know if you are familiar with the concept. . . .

Wideman: Oh, yes; he is always running.

Samuels: Yes. He is always running; he is always moving. We see your major male characters in motion. Cecil is running; Eddie is running; Tommy is running. But for me to look at just that level, to look at a work and only see that is really to miss what lies beneath the surface. For example, I was moved by the scene in *Hiding Place* when Tommy comes home, goes to his wife, and is coldly received by her. Unhappy with the kind of husband he has been, she has decided to disregard his significance or importance. Though you show us this, you allow us to see Tommy from within. We see him standing there, looking at his son; you hold bare his innermost feelings and we come to know his internal conflicts, which are not very different from the ones that most married men feel while attempting to be husbands, fathers, lovers, and at the same time know a certain freedom. I consider your treatment here a very powerful revelation. It is one that is not found in the creative works of Blacks.

Wideman: Let me tell you a little anecdote, which I can relate, I hope, to what we are talking about. The book I am working on now is about a relationship between my brother and myself, my brother who is in prison. In one scene, I am visiting the prison with my family. My mother, my wife, our three kids are there, and my sister's kids; and we are going into the prison. We park in the prison lot and everybody gets out of the car. The kids had been cramped up in the car for a while, so they went running off. My mother and wife walked ahead of me, because I had to lock up the car. I see my family spread out in front of me. And, boy, it hit me. Here I am, responsible for these people. THESE ARE MY PEOPLE. Then I realized what the walls of the prison were saying to the Black men inside: you can't have a family; you can't have a profession; you can't make it in society. That is the message being forced upon them by stone and concrete and armed guards. I suddenly understood what an anomalous position I was in. Even today, even in 1982, it is rare for a black man to find himself in control, responsible. I felt like a gunfighter. I'm sure I sauntered because I wanted the guards to see me, and I wanted the prisoners to see me. I was alert; I was vigilant; and if I had to, I was ready to go to war. For a moment, I was in a position that gave the lie to so much that the society tries to force upon us. It was a powerful moment, and as I tried to remember it and write about it, it became even more so.

Samuels: You capture a little of that feeling in "Solitary," the story in *Damballah*, where the mother goes to visit her son, and she is thinking that her visits really destroy her. We literally see her fall apart, just crumble for a moment. We see the devastation as she takes the long walk from the bus stop to the prison gate; we see the mental and emotional experience that shakes her. Was this again partially biographical?

Wideman: Oh, yes. I have a brother in prison. My mother goes to visit him. She has talked to me about it, and I have gone with her. That is something that is shared.

Samuels: Is Tommy, the main character in *Hiding Place*, based on your brother's experience?

Wideman: Yes. Very much so, but Tommy is a fictionalized character as well.

Samuels: What about Clement from *Hiding Place*?

Wideman: Clement was fun. Clement is more pure invention than Tommy.

Samuels: What would you say if someone said to you, Clement reminds me a little of the deaf-mute in Faulkner's *The Sound and the Fury*?

Wideman: You know, someone has said that. Benjy.

Samuels: Yes, that is right, Benjy.

Wideman: Yes, and Dilsey is sometimes presented as not much more than a halfwit. I like Faulkner. I like what he does with his inarticulate characters: his ability to show the depth of their understanding. But I think Clement stands on his own feet. He is rooted in my experience. There were always

people like Clement around. Homewood was a place where it was bad taste
to put your people in Mayview, the state home. You knew how they'd get
treated there. And, so, a lot of people who might have been outcasts in some
other community had a perfectly comfortable place inside Homewood. I was
thinking the other day about a big guy I used to play with. All the other kids
played with him, too. He must have been 20 years old, huge, kind of a giant,
but a mentality of maybe five/six years old. And you'd think somebody that
big and that strong would really scare people, and they wouldn't want their
kids around him. But everybody knew he was okay. They knew the range of
what he would do. There are people like that. There are Clements all over the
world, people who are a comment on a community's flexibility, on its humanity, on its compassion. You don't have to kick people like that out.

Samuels: Yes, the community becomes an extended family.

Wideman: Amen. My grandfather's favorite statement was "give them
the benefit of the doubt!" That argues for a kind of longer, slower look at
people and situations. You can get really pissed off in certain situations, or
really angry at someone. But if you call on your better side and try to get
your ego out of it, that will allow you time to put things in perspective. That
might be the most valuable inheritance I have. I am not certain I can live up
to it; but if I could live up to it, I'd be happy, at least with one part of myself.
If I could always give people the benefit of the doubt and get that in return.
That philosophy lies behind the presence of a character like Clement. Also,
there is a surreal atmosphere and a dimension to Black experience. I talked
to you about my own life experiences, how so much was crammed into a
very short period. That creates dislocations. Crazy alienations, crazy juxtapo-
sitions. One day at home, I have to stomp on a roach; next day, I am eating
caviar and drinking Stolichnaya. Or maybe it's just the separation of a couple
hours. I go and meet a governor, or I am dealing with some ambassador, and
then I get a letter from my brother who is in prison. All these crazy juxtaposi-
tions. One world banging up against the other. That is everyday stuff in the
Black world. Thus, Clement is both everyman and no man. There are plenty
of people who live in that shadow world. We can't say for sure whether they
are demented or whether they are mystics; we really don't know. And they
are not going to tell us. They are like the classic fool, the jester, the trickster.

Samuels: There is so much more I wanted to talk about. I wanted to probe
more your exploration of the Black male theme, the importance of friendship.
You have mentioned that in passing. I again find very powerful the relationship between Brother and Eddie in *A Glance Away*. That is a powerful friend-

ship; it is often missing from Black fiction. Toni Morrison comes close to your exploration in her treatment of Sula and Nel in *Sula*. Within the last decade—certainly within the last five years—there have been so many negative treatments of Black males, so many negative stereotypes (fiction and non-fiction) and portrayals. I am thinking about Wallace's *Black Macho*, for example. I think here again what we have is a superficial view. The Black man is interested in his family, his children, his wife, and his internal concerns are multifarious and complex. Family is another important theme in your work. In "Solitary," there is a powerful scene where, near the end, the mother, after returning from the prison, is walking towards her home. She is alone, to a certain degree, but she is not lonely, because there is that history, there is family, there is a past that is always hers.

Wideman: Yes. She is walking back into her past. It is significant that she does get her flesh and blood brother to walk along with her. She goes to the bar and gets him out. She passes the ghosts of her men, but her brother is there, and they have a very symbiotic relationship. They don't have to say much. Lots of the things that he knows about her, she doesn't tell him. He just knows. That kind of unspoken communication is very important. "Solitary" was a very unusual story for me. The whole time I was writing it, I thought I was writing about a woman who had been so profoundly hurt that she had lost her faith. It had been her abiding characteristic, her religious faith. As I was writing the story, I thought I was writing about a woman who had lost faith because of a series of horrible events. She was going to lose her trust in God. I wrote the story thinking that was what I was showing, but I re-read it, maybe a week afterward, and I realized that she had gotten through. Her faith had been shaken but not broken. She glimpsed annihilation—the train coming down the track. For a moment she wasn't willing to face it, but then at the end of the story she was.

Samuels: She is different from Bess in that Bess does not have the interest in religion or God per se in the way that the mother in the story does.

Wideman: They are different. Bess is more of a pagan, an idolater almost. Her man is a god to her. Not that she has a slavish relationship to him. He is, in an African sense, a spirit. She has a whole panoply of spirits to which she relates. Bess wouldn't put all her trust in any "nigger" whether he was god or anybody else. She has to have all these different things that she can relate to, pull from, draw from. She is very much a pantheist, a traditional person. Elizabeth is more of a Christian. For her, God is a righteous essence in the sky.

Samuels: Equally important is Elizabeth's membership in the A.M.E. Church.

Wideman: Well, yes. She is a part of the community. And as you know, religion creates community, and communities create religion. They reciprocate. Church is where people find their being. I bet fully 70% of the things my mother does now have some relation to the church. Everything from meals to prayers, to trips to Atlantic City.

Samuels: Let me ask you something about critics. How important are they to your work? Do you listen to what they have to say? Do you respond in any way to what they have to say about your work? Just how important are critics to you as a writer?

Wideman: I have lots of answers to that question. Critics are extremely important if you want your stuff to be read, because they are a vehicle by which you are presented to the public. But I think very often critics frustrate this ideal function. I think that a lot of times, because of ego, because of their own limitations, they stand in the way of the work. That is frustrating, and I get furious. It's a very unfair competition because there is no real forum in which authors can answer critics' charges. If you said *Hiding Place* is a book about a guy who obviously hated his mother and wanted to destroy her by putting her up on a hill (he is afraid of women and such and such)—if you said that in an article, what could I do? Number one, anybody who reads that, the damage is done. You have gotten your word in, no matter how wrong. If a person has not read the book, then he will just assume you've reported the facts. A lot of people treat reviews that way, and it is not proper. There isn't an institutionalized way for me to answer you except to bitch at somebody in a letter to the editor, even if it is published. So it's a very one-sided kind of dialogue. That's a pain in the ass. I have had good reviews; some have been perceptive reviews. My things have gotten around to major publications, so I don't have any particular gripes. Personally, I have been treated pretty well. But as I said before, the whole vexed relationship of Black literature to the mainstream, the inability of critics to treat Black literature as technique, as art, the tendency of critics to use Black literature as a way of trying to put forward certain ideological concerns and points of view—that has been a disaster for all Black writers.

Samuels: That still remains true today?

Wideman: Sure.

Samuels: In spite of the fact there are such writers of quality work as yourself, Toni Morrison, Toni Bambara, and others. I think that the Afro-

American literary tradition is today in very healthy, stable shape. The quality of the works, the caliber of the writers, have never been better.

Wideman: I hope that's true, and I'd probably tend to agree with you. The trouble is (and it's always been the case), who is Afro-American writing getting to; who are the people we can trust to preserve it? I know there are some good spirits out there, black and white, who really appreciate Black writing for what it is worth. But the only way literature survives is through readers—because it has readers, because it has informed readers, because it has readers who love it and won't let it die. How much of our stuff is getting to black readers? Getting to the people? I know my black readership is minimal. I wish somebody would try to market Black literature the way records have been marketed in the Black community. Our people have always been willing to spend money for enjoyment, for entertainment, and that entertainment dollar is out there. Even when people are broke. If you could get the books in the same places that other consumer goods are, maybe the books can compete. That would make me very happy. That is why I wrote the way I did in the last two books and published them in paperbacks. I'm hoping that maybe someday one of these books will be accessible to a wide Black audience. Books should be a part of the Afro-American inheritance, as much as the music, as much as the oral culture. Books could provide ideas for raising consciousness, raising self-esteem, different models for how to live. Preservation of the past. But are good books available in most Black communities? The idea that books contain the wisdom of the people, the creativity of the people, has to get back to the community. That's your job.

Letter from the Publisher

Philip G. Howlett / 1983

During the mid-to-late 1950s, teachers at the Homewood Elementary and
then the Liberty School in Pittsburgh had an unusual option when it came to
class discipline. They could use a ruler to rap a rowdy class to attention, or
they could ask little John Wideman to come forward and tell a story. Borrowing from a book he'd read, a poem he'd written or, as Wideman says, "just a
child's imagination," he'd draw a quilt of quiet over the room.

Now 41, a former Rhodes scholar and author of five novels, Professor
Wideman—he has taught English for the last eight years at the University of
Wyoming—is still at home in front of a class. And he hasn't lost his touch
as a storyteller. One of his latest tales is a compelling combination of life,
literature and sport. Excerpted from his forthcoming book *Brothers and
Keepers*, it tells of Wideman's chance encounter with a part of his past and
the repayment of a lingering basketball debt to a man named Reds.

Basketball was as much the author's game as yarn-spinning. For three
years Wideman was a starter at Penn, averaging 12.0 points per game on
clubs that went 56-23 overall and won a Big Five co-championship in his
senior year, 1963. The "last of the 6' 2" forwards," Wideman was All Big
Five and team captain in 1962–63.

In 1974 Wideman was elected to the Big Five Hall of Fame, but his goals
have always been more hardcover than hardcourt. The Rhodes took him to
Oxford, where he received a degree in English and played guard on a basketball team that included an erstwhile Ivy League opponent and soon-to-be
Knick named Bradley. "I remember taking Bill to practice every day for two
years on the back of my raggedy motor scooter," said Wideman. "To think I
had a future Senator, maybe a future President, on the back of that old bike!"

Wideman's first novel, *A Glance Away*, was published by Harcourt Brace
and World in 1966, after he had completed his three years at Oxford and
accepted a fellowship at the prestigious Writers' Workshop in Iowa City.
Novels two and three, *Hurry Home* and *The Lynchers*, came out between

1967 and '73, while Wideman was teaching two subjects at Penn: English in the morning and basketball in the afternoon (assisting a freshman coach named Digger Phelps).

Wideman hooked up with Wyoming in 1973 when, while on a year's sabbatical, he and his wife, Judy, visited the West and decided to stay. It was in the following five or six years that two more novels were published, as well as a collection of short stories dealing with life in Homewood.

Today he tells his students that "sweat" has been his key to success, in writing as it was in basketball. "I've always been drawn to craftmen of language," he says. "The classical Greeks, Ralph Ellison, Norman Mailer. And I've learned from the oral tradition—from listening to my mother's stories, from the music of the blues, from slave narrations, from the magic of a preacher. I value the world. I respond to it as a writer."

John Edgar Wideman: Connecting the Truths

Sheri Hoem / 1984

From *Owen Wister Review* (Fall 1984): 4–9. Used by permission.

Interviewer: You were an honor student and basketball star at the University of Pennsylvania, a Rhodes Scholar, and you attended the University of Iowa Writers Workshop. Why did you decide to come to Wyoming to live?

Wideman: I wanted a change from an Eastern Ivy League University. I liked what I saw out here and I have good friends here in the English Department. It was a tentative choice; almost a "why not" rather than a very considered decision to come to Wyoming. It just kind of happened, and it worked out quite well.

Interviewer: Has the environment in Wyoming influenced your outlook in any way—either the community environment or the natural environment?

Wideman: I used to get bloody noses if that's what you mean! Wyoming is a small town and, in some ways, it's like the community I grew up in. Although I grew up in a city, the community was very well-defined. I knew everybody's name, and as a kid everybody knew me. There was sort of a collective family made up of all the members of the ten or twelve streets that we lived on. There was a nice coziness and feeling of community there in Homewood, which is part of Pittsburgh. Wyoming preserves some of those kinds of values as a small town. I found that refreshing, and it also helped me rediscover things about home. I liked the change of pace that Wyoming represented. One of the reasons that I left the East was because I felt that it was very difficult to write and maintain privacy in an environment where there is so much busyness, and so much pressure—somebody always wanting something, wanting you to do something, and something always needing to be done. Wyoming was an attempt to escape from some of those pressures and to find a place where I could write quietly—well, I hope that my writing is not quiet, but Wyoming was quiet and I could write what I felt I wanted to write, and that experiment more or less worked.

Interviewer: How about the consideration of space—more space in the West than in an urban environment. Can you feel that difference?

Wideman: I'm sure I'm not even conscious of all the ways in which I am aware of the space. When I first came to Wyoming, I started to keep a journal, and I thought that it might be interesting to see how this place, being so new and different physically, would impact itself—would actually affect me. I wanted to keep a record of that. I kept the journal for maybe two weeks, and then I gave up and did other things. But the space was certainly something I noted again and again. The space and the mountains—the cliches hit you first—the blue sky, the immensity of the sky. Then something like that settles into your mind and becomes a part of how you think, how you move, and how you see yourself. One of the most important effects is that the scale of things changes, both time scale and space scale. In a city, things that you see are man-made things—man-made structures, buildings, lamp posts, street lights—and you're circumscribed by those. They're on a man scale. Even a skyscraper is just a hundred floors; the same as one floor, only a hundred stacked on top of each other. There's also that temporary quality in spite of the density of a city and the number of people. Sometimes I can look straight through it—it doesn't exist. I get more of that sense of temporariness out here. I've conceived of Laramie many times as a kind of circle of wagons in the middle of the plains, and they're drawn together for protection against the imaginary Indians, or whatever. Laramie isn't really more substantial than that, if you think about it, in the sense that you can go five minutes in any direction and it's gone—absolutely gone; it doesn't exist. There is the scale of the town against the scale of the mountains, the scale of the country, and the fact that Laramie has been here not even a hundred years. The mountains, plains and animals have been here time out of mind. As a matter of fact, it's always been interesting to me that most of Wyoming was under water, that this was a sea, and a lot of the sculpturing of the country came from water. When you think of things in that geological sense of time, it opens up different kinds of perspectives, both personally, and in writing. So all that has happened, and I've absorbed the environment.

Interviewer: What advantages or disadvantages did you find at the Iowa Writers Workshop?

Wideman: Well, Iowa was somewhat unique because not only did it have a Ph.D. program in English for which you could do a creative thesis, but you could do a creative thesis in almost every area. So you had painters there who were getting academic degrees for their painting, and music people who, instead of writing about Bach, were actually composing music. It was a very lively environment. The geography is important. Iowa City is an island in the middle of immense corn fields. Right in the middle of this you had a big university with people from all over the place—very highly educated, very highly strung people, creative people in all disciplines, and all media. The university is like a hot house.

Interviewer: Stimulating?

Wideman: Yes, stimulating, but also crazy. Almost everybody I knew, for instance, who was married, either the marriage broke up, or it suffered some kind of traumatic experience. People committed suicide. People would ride motorcycles on the ice, not because it was fun, but the game was to see if it would break, or when it would break. Just madness . . . madness. If that's stimulating, then yes! But I met all sorts of people. For the most part, I found that there wasn't a lot of writing being down at Iowa. Even the professional writers who were there as teachers said Iowa was a place to come between books, but not a place to do serious writing. It was just too hyper. If a writer needs privacy, if a writer needs time to reflect, to meditate, etc., Iowa just had too many diversions. Maybe it was also the fact that too many people were trying to do those esoteric things. There was lots of posing, lots of talk about writing, and lots of peripheral activity that goes with writing, and that took the place of writing. On the other hand, many of my fellow students have since produced novels and have become fairly well-known. Some of the classes at Iowa were stimulating, so it was useful to me because I learned a lot about teaching writing. I also was lucky enough to spend some time with some published writers and became friendly with them. I learned to see the whole idea of a career in writing as something not so abstract, but, in reflection, turned to these people and their concrete experiences. I think that was very valuable for a young writer because it removed a lot of the myths—it removed a lot of the baloney. Also, I hope I learned from their experiences—the trauma, the mistakes, and the sidetracks that they had taken. I heard about them, and, hopefully, that helped me avoid them, although some of the traps and pitfalls sounded like fun—and I repeated them!

Interviewer: What are some of the myths about writers?

Wideman: I guess the main myth is that there is such a thing as "a writer," and that that activity can basically change who you are and what you are. When you are a kid, people ask you what you want to become. You never become anything. You continue along doing the things you've always done. Being a writer does not solve the problem of living. I think that's an important thing you have to learn, and you only learn it by actually experiencing it. Before you publish, you think "Wow, if I could ever get a book published, things will change and I'll become 'a writer.' " But you don't. You become a person who has published a book, and you still have to work on the next one—nothing goes away. You might gain some confidence, and you might gain a tremendous amount of satisfaction from publishing, but the satisfaction that counts most, and the only satisfaction that counts in the long run, is how much you get out of the activity. Is doing it pleasurable? Is doing it something that makes you want to get up in the morning? Is the craft something that's fascinating and fulfilling?

Some other myths are fame, fortune. You don't automatically get rich and you don't automatically get famous if you write books. And even if you do, those things, again, are just part of the routine. You handle them and deal with them and they can get in the way of your writing as much as help your writing. Kurt Vonnegut was one of the people at the workshop, while I was there, who I got to know, and his career was just taking off in a spectacular way. It was very instructive to me to find out that he was a person. That may sound simple-minded and corny, and I'm not saying that's all he was—a person, because he wasn't—but just seeing people in the flesh, going about the business of living, who were also writers, taught me a lot; many things probably I can't say in particular, but I know it was important.

Interviewer: Who was your mentor?

Wideman: My mentor, and one of my best friends at Iowa, was a man named José Donoso. He's a Chilean writer—absolutely world class in terms of reputation and talent. He had a very important novel called *The Obscene Bird of Night* which came out five or six years ago. He was the person I liked to show my writing to, and he was also an excellent teacher. José was European in terms of education and upbringing, and he brought a certain amount of freshness to my writing because of that European perspective. The fact that he wrote, and was being published in two languages, made him responsive to some of the things I was trying to do incorporating Afro-American speech and culture into a mainstream literature.

Interviewer: Tell me about your writing methods.

Wideman: I write everything out in longhand first, and I do lots of rewriting, not only sentence by sentence, but structurally. I think that's something I do pretty well, because I think I have the ability to improve things tremendously with rewriting, rethinking, and revising. Part of that rewriting is the

actual process of composition. In other words, when I'm composing something for the first time, I may go over and over and over a sentence so that
there's a sort of rewriting going on then. Of course, there's the stage of
getting this stuff that's scribbled all over yellow tablets into typed form, and
the script is revised in that stage. Then it comes back to me in typed form,
and I work on it again, and on and on and on.

Interviewer: Do you find that certain characters can lead in unplanned
directions, or do you have everything preplanned?

Wideman: Oh, it's been different with different books and different stories, but absolutely, characters can and do take over. There's a story in *Damballah* called "Solitary." It's about a woman going to visit her son in prison.
I conceived the story as a story about a crisis in faith. I thought that I would
have this woman, who had been a very religious person all her life, visit her
son. That experience would shake her so profoundly that she would ask questions, or feel something about her God, about her religion, that she had never
felt. I took the lady through the story and I made the visit a fairly devastating
experience. I brought her back to her town on a bus. She was crossing a
railroad bridge, and I thought that when she got to the center of that bridge a
train would come. It would be loud and noisy the way trains are, and just that
physical experience would literally shake her faith. But lo and behold, when
the lady got on the bridge, the train came, and she looked at it—she looked
at it real hard, and she was aware of the drama inside of her—but it didn't
shake her. It scared her. Her faith was stronger than the doubt and so she was
not changed by this visit. The solitary of the title, yes, she felt very solitary
and alone, but she didn't feel bereft of faith. In that sense the story wrote
itself—it took over.

Interviewer: Do you think that an important characteristic of effective,
great writing is for authors to concentrate on what they know best?

Wideman: That's circular. The answer has to be yes because good writing
has authority and authenticity which means that the writer knows it. Writing
is an expression of that knowledge, and the writing is a confirmation of the
writer's involvement and understanding of people and situations, etc. So you
probably, by definition, can't write well about something you cannot realize
in a powerful way.

Interviewer: Does that knowledge necessarily have to come from experience, or can it be something learned or understood from other sources?

Wideman: People ask that all the time, not only in interviews, but in critical works, and authors talking to one another. It seems fairly simple. I think it's basically irresolvable. It's probably because of the nature of experience. What does it mean to say that someone has experienced something? Well, it means a whole lot of things, obviously. If you tell me a story, and I feel very strongly about you—let's say you're my sister and you're telling me something very intimate and personal. I might get involved in that and know you so well that I, in a sense, experience what you've done. So now I'm writing a story, and I need to have a woman in it. I haven't experienced a woman's point of view, but because I know you, and because you are a good storyteller, and because I understand lots of things, and just simply because I have some kind of imaginative projection and we share some kind of imaginative terrain, I might be able to write about your experience very well from a woman's point of view. But it's a vexing question because, on the one hand, you believe in imagination which a writer almost has to do. That's what we're all about, imagination. Then you would think a black person ought to be able to write about a white person, and a woman about a man, and a dog about a horse—whatever. If the imagination works, it should work, and it should have no limits. On the other hand, if I want to write about war, I'd be very, very cautious. I've never been a soldier. I've seen countless war movies, I used to have ten million toy soldiers, I've read about every battle that's ever been fought, and I know a lot about it. But I'd be very careful because I haven't been there, so that's the other side of the question. The imagination is not God—it doesn't give the writer all the answers. It's a tool. It's a very encompassing, comprehensive tool, but I'm also sure it doesn't give you all the answers. The question is basically confused by the nature of experience, and both the limitlessness and the way the imagination works.

Interviewer: Do you think writing is a form of communication that goes deeper than what people can gain on a one-to-one basis, or in everyday conversation?

Wideman: No, it's just different, and has different goals. There are times when I'm reading in which I feel very close to the writer. I feel the spirit and a kind of understanding, an intimacy, that I seldom feel in an actual face-to-face conversation. On the other hand, talking to someone, that give-and-take process, is also extremely intense. It's just different. The fact is that when you're talking to somebody you're not limited to language—you're not limited to words. Now a good writer can suggest, with the word on the page, lots of other dimensions of communication. The language can have rhythm and the words can look a certain way. You can stimulate a person's oral imagination so that they hear what you're saying. You can create pictures in someone's mind. But all that is secondhand; it's a kind of trickery, whereas if you're actually sitting and talking to someone, the whole range of sensory apparatus comes into play directly. It's that kind of 360° in-the-round communication that good writing attempts, and that's the model the writer might be after. Writing comes from storytelling, and one of the essences of storytelling is that the audience is there so you can act it out. Writing is limited and it seeks that kind of immediacy.

Interviewer: Concerning your first novel, *A Glance Away*, Kurt Vonnegut wrote you a letter, which is quoted in an interview in *Pittsburgh Magazine*, that: "you have succeeded with time games and point-of-view games I wouldn't have the nerve or the brains to attempt." It seems to me that the techniques in the novel were not just decoration, or games, but had a specific purpose and function toward the meaning of the work.

Wideman: What's exciting to me about writing are the endless possibilities. I'm mostly trying to tell a story without playing with the language. Trying to express something about language doesn't interest me. When you begin to write you're less skillful than after you've written a lot, so probably in the earlier writing I would guess that some of the experiments don't work, that they get in the reader's way, and that they might be obvious. In my mind I wasn't parading or displaying these techniques for themselves, but I was trying to find a way to express the feelings that I had, and so stream-of-consciousness, switching narrators, using italics, and having people talking to each other without talking—having them exchange thoughts—all that seemed appropriate to what I was writing about. Vonnegut was speaking in that letter as a writer to another writer, and, sure, technique is artifice—it's an attempt to interest and fool people to get them believing and feeling what you feel.

Interviewer: Do you see yourself concerned more with reform in your writing, and being a "witness to the truth"?

Wideman: It would be nice to be a witness to the truth, but those two things aren't exactly separate. The truth will make us free—sometimes the truth makes you free, and sometimes the truth kills you—but I think it's something to shoot for. There is no THE truth, but if I can manage to get down on paper what I see and what I believe, and make a convincing case for it, I'm satisfied. And if it is a convincing case, maybe someone will look at my point of view and it will give them another picture of the world; one which they will have to modify and incorporate into what they see. So reform and witnessing the truth are more a *connecting of truths*. I have a perspective, and if I express it, then I've done the best I can.

Interview with John Edgar Wideman

Kay Bonetti / 1985

From *The Missouri Review* 9.2 (1986): 75–103. Used by permission.

Interviewer: Mr. Wideman, we know a lot about your biography from both the Homewood trilogy and *Brothers and Keepers*, in which you try to come to terms with your brother Robby's imprisonment for first-degree murder. But I wonder about your life as a writer. Can you tell us at what point you began to know that's what you wanted to do?

Wideman: I liked to get up and tell stories in grade school and I was pretty good at it. Most of my stories were bits and pieces of the reading I'd been doing, which would vary from the kids' fiction in the Carnegie Library to comic books. I loved comic books. I guess I began to identify myself as a writer even that early. Not as a writer with a capital W; I just liked to write and I had a lot of encouragement all the way through high school. But I don't think it was until probably senior year in college that I actually began to make life decisions based on the idea that maybe I wanted to write.

Interviewer: Were your parents supportive in that?

Wideman: My parents have always been enormously supportive. Anything I've wanted to do was okay. I was told do it well and work hard and make sure it's something you really like. That kind of support. But for my parents and really for the whole extended family I was a test case. Nobody else had gone all the way through school. Almost everybody in my parents' generation had a high school education, but nobody had gone on to college, so I was the flagship; I was out there doing things that no one else had done. My parents were smart not to try to monitor that, except by being supportive. The reasons that I went to college were basically mine. I thought I wanted to play pro basketball, and I knew in order to play pro basketball you had to play college basketball and to play college basketball you had to get a scholarship, so things sort of dovetailed and it was a lockstep kind of future that I had figured out for myself.

Interviewer: You were on an athletic scholarship at the University of Pennsylvania?

Wideman: Well not exactly, because the Ivy League schools claim that

42

they don't give athletic scholarships. That means that I had to qualify for an academic scholarship. In reality, if you were a good athlete they gave you a certain number of points so that if I were competing against some kid from Illinois who had the same grades and the same sort of test scores as I did, I would get the scholarship.

Interviewer: You went on to become a Rhodes Scholar. Were you the first black Rhodes Scholar?

Wideman: There had been one black Rhodes Scholar, Alain Locke, in 1905, I believe it was. And then the same year I was elected, 1963, another man, Stan Sanders, from the West coast was elected. So we were the first three. And Stan and I were the first two in about sixty years.

Interviewer: Do you have a political attitude toward the Rhodes Scholarship program? Do the origins of the money bother you?

Wideman: I'm not trying to hedge, but there's very little clean money. Whose money do you take these days if you look at it very hard? To tell the truth, when I won a Rhodes Scholarship, I didn't know a thing about South Africa, or Rhodes. I just knew it was a chance to go to England and study. So I went into it ignorant, and ignorance is bliss. I had a grand old time. Subsequently, I've been part of the Rhodes selection process, and I've served on the board of directors of the Rhodes Trust in America. Not very actively, I'll admit, but I've had an opportunity to try to change things from inside. That has its advantages. I've made it my business to look for qualified black applicants and also talked to other members of the committee in a political way. But for me it was not so much political as it was an attempt to explain why certain black applicants should be looked at very seriously. In any selection process, whether you're talking about Rhodes scholarships or Marshalls or Churchills, there's an old boys' network and it ain't all bad. Once you get blacks into that kind of process—blacks, women, anybody who hasn't been in that process before—then I think you can work to change the process and educate people within a particular system. In the past few years many large questions have come up before the Rhodes trustees, among them the admission of women, the question of whether to say no more scholarships to South Africa, the question of isn't it ironic that Rhodes' money came from Africa but there are only a handful of black African scholars. I've tried to vote and use my weight to move the trust in the directions I think are right.

Interviewer: When you went to Pennsylvania, what did you study?

Wideman: I started out as a psych major, found out that meant mostly counting the number of times a rat went down a particular tunnel and got tired of that pretty quickly. I wanted to learn about Freud and Jung and all that fancy stuff about the unconscious and be able to look in somebody's eyes and tell what they were going to do and who they were going to be. That wasn't what psychology meant at the University of Pennsylvania at that time, so I flirted with anthropology for about a half-semester and then I eventually became an English major. I took some creative writing classes there—one with a man named Christopher Davis, who is a very good novelist. Also I had a chance to meet Archibald MacLeish, who came in for a three-day stint at the University. He met with the writing class and looked at samples of writing from Penn students. I was very encouraged by having someone whose name I'd seen in the lights actually look at my writing, pat me on the back and say, "Son, you're doing pretty well and keep at it." The climate at Penn at that time was even freer than when I was a teacher at Penn in encouraging the arts and encouraging writers to come and spend time on the campus. All that helped me make up my mind.

Interviewer: Did you write while you were at Oxford?

Wideman: By the time I got to England I was fairly serious. I began to see myself as a writer and I saw the whole experience of getting out of the country as something that would forward a career in writing. I thought that was one way to get the kind of seriousness that I needed in my work. All of us grow up very confused and I thought writing was something that was connected with Europe. The matter of Europe. I didn't want to be a good American writer, let alone a good black writer. I wanted to be world class, man, and to be world class you had to be Thomas Mann and you had to be Marcel Proust and you had to walk along the Champs Elysées and you had to know about bullfights. Those were the things that were kind of stirring around in my head. I wanted to go where the action was. So going to Europe was a very conscious attempt to become part of that tradition.

Interviewer: Was James Baldwin much of a model for you when you were young?

Wideman: Not at all. I came through school with a standard Eng Lit education. I knew that there was a man named James Baldwin, because he made the newspapers, but he was not taught in my classes and I didn't know his work. I'm not sure whether or not I read any Ralph Ellison in college but if I did, it would have been probably the only piece of writing by a black writer.

Interviewer: Did you read Langston Hughes and Richard Wright in the public schools?

Wideman: They may have been in my high school anthology—"The Negro Speaks of Rivers" maybe for Hughes. But he certainly wouldn't have been picked out as a black writer and he probably was skipped because most teachers didn't know how to deal with it.

Interviewer: You went through mainly a white school system in Pittsburgh. In fact, didn't your parents move so you could go to a better school?

Wideman: Yes, but the race of the clientele didn't matter. Westinghouse High School at that time would have probably had 70% or 80% black kids.

Interviewer: And the teachers were white?

Wideman: There were schools that had predominantly black students, but the system was white. I remember in my senior year a black man came to teach and that was a real shock, a pleasant shock, but I didn't quite know how to deal with it.

Interviewer: Had you read Baldwin when you wrote *Hurry Home*?

Wideman: I had educated myself a little bit about black literature. I had taught Baldwin by that time, I believe, so I was much more familiar with black writers.

Interviewer: There are some similarities: the sensitive alienated black intellectual going to Europe, taking up with some kind of strange guilt-ridden white man, looking for a black son that he's never seen, who may or may not be real.

Wideman: When I wrote *Hurry Home* I was certainly trying to deal with that need to get out of the United States which Baldwin writes about quite explicitly. So sure, that was an influence and he was—as a black man wandering around in Europe trying to gain a purchase on his identity, trying to find out what he needed to write about—he was an archetype in the back of my mind, but by then I also knew about other people who had to go through the same kind of thing. Sculptors, actors, musicians. It was go to Europe, be appreciated, and then maybe they'll pay some attention back in the US of A.

Interviewer: You said that you had started educating yourself about black literature. What made you start doing that?

Wideman: One way I got involved was my own curiosity. I had begun to read a few things. The sixties brought that whole necessity to examine one's

own race and one's own background. I was part of that. By 1968 I was
teaching at the University of Pennsylvania, and a group of black students
asked me to start a course in Afro-American literature. I hemmed and hawed
because I didn't know anything and I had my own writing to worry about
and I didn't want to get involved in the work to put together a decent class
and I didn't want to do it in an off-hand manner either. So there they sat in
front of me and I suddenly heard myself giving them all the excuses, "That's
not my field, and I don't know it, and I have my own work." I sounded like
such a punk, I sounded like the very voice that had turned so many people
back that I stopped short in the middle of all my excuses and said, "Yes, I'll
do it, sure." It was the eye contact, it was the sense of myself sitting out there
listening to me, that did it. That was a very important moment and I think
my reading began to be quite serious at that point. I spent the next summer
in the Schomburg Library. I got a little research grant from the University of
Pennsylvania and some money from a publisher who wanted to do an anthology of black literature. They were shopping around for people to put that
together and asked me, which was really kind of a joke because I was a
neophyte, I didn't know anything, but I was kind of safe because I had an
Ivy League credential. I'm sure they were thinking about marketing. The
upshot is that I was given both the time and a little bit of money to put an
Afro-American lit class together. I worked for about a year and familiarized
myself, as much as I could, with a black tradition.

Interviewer: Had *A Glance Away* already been written?
Wideman: It was published, yes.

Interviewer: In *A Glance Away* you use different versions of the trio in
Sent For You Yesterday. Is there anything in *Sent For You Yesterday* that's an
attempt to go back and redo *A Glance Away*, or is it just that the threesome
has been ringing in your head all these years?
Wideman: Oh, it's probably a little of everything, except certainly no
conscious attempt to re-write *A Glance Away*. But on the other hand, as you
say, that trio may be reverberating in my imagination. The three main characters in *A Glance Away* and the characters in *Sent For You Yesterday* were
based on actual people, so in that sense a prolonged meditation on what they
meant to me and who they were would explain the similarities between the
two groups of characters. But I had to write a lot and think a lot and grow a
lot before I could visualize Tate and Lucy and Carl in *Sent For You Yesterday*.
In a simplistic sense I guess all the writing in between is a way of processing

that initial material, a way of learning to transform it. I frankly had not thought of matching the groups of characters in the way you have put it, but part of the correspondence is the simplest thing in the world—the actual, real-life models were the same.

Interviewer: I'm fascinated by the chronology in the beginning of *Homewood*, the story of Sybela Owens and her husband Charlie. Is all that true?

Wideman: Not exactly, which isn't going to help a lot, I know, but that's fine, because it shouldn't. For me any kind of writing is invention, selection. The more I write the more I'm sure that some generic discriminations we make don't really hold up. The most important matter is the author's intention and the degree to which the author shares that intention with the reader. The tables were simply to orient the reader. They are not accurate family trees. They're very close, but only somebody privy to our family history would be able to make the few little changes that actually would make them documentary.

Interviewer: Were the slave woman, Sybela, and her white husband, Charlie, based on real-life models?

Wideman: As real as the Bible, as real as most things. I heard those stories from ladies in my family who were seventy and eighty years old, and they had heard those stories from their mothers and aunts and grandmothers. They have the truth of oral history, which for me is a probably more reliable kind of truth than written history.

Interviewer: In the preface to the *Homewood Trilogy* you write, "By 1973 I'd published three critically acclaimed novels. It was hard to admit to myself that I'd just begun learning how to write, that whole regions of my experience, the core of the language and culture that nurtured me had been barely touched by my writing up to that point. If a writer's lucky, the learning process never stops, and writing continues to be a tool for discovery." What happened?

Wideman: Well, lots of things happened. To begin with, I was moving, I was learning about things, trying to understand things and I had a body of work to stand on. It brought me to a certain place. And then, what do you do next? A simple question. "What do you do?" Well, you can not write at all, you can write a book about basketball. While some of this was going on in my mind I moved out to Wyoming. We came out here for what seemed like good reasons at the time but it was another semi-conscious break. Unfortunately that first year out here two very important people died. My editor died, and then my grandmother died. I went back east both times, very upset and very emotional. The journeys took on a kind of archetypal shape because once more I was separated from the places and people that were familiar to me. I had to get on a plane and go back and become involved in the rituals that surround death and talk to people and share some things that all of us share at those junctions in our lives. The night after we buried my grandmother her house was full and my Aunt May was there drinking a lot of Wild Turkey—she's a little old lady and she sits in a chair and her feet don't touch the floor—and she began to tell stories. Everybody was telling stories but sooner or later she just took center stage and told the stories like the story of Sybela Owens and how our family came to Pittsburgh—and I listened.

Interviewer: Was it the first time you'd heard these stories?

Wideman: Probably not the first time I literally heard them, but the first time I paid the kind of attention which made them special. As I listened to the stories and heard about the past, it was a way of trying to capture some of the things that I believed were gone forever, because my grandmother was gone forever. I was hearing her life. That was what was done at these wakes. You talk about the person who died, you talk about their friends, you talk about the time you saw them with ice cream on their chin and the crazy situations that person had been in; it's almost like a voodoo ritual where you talk down a departed spirit. A communal, a collective will forces the spirit of the departed person to return, and you draw strength and direction from that spirit. And that's what was happening. As May talked about the old days I saw my grandmother as a little girl and courting and I saw John French coming to steal her away from Aunt and Aida and Uncle Bill. And I saw Uncle Bill sitting there with a shotgun waiting for John French. It was a way of recapturing some of my grandmother's spirit. It seems to me as I look back that was one of the first times that I was fully accepted as an adult—I must have been at least in my thirties—I was a full dues-paid member. I had my own children and now my grandmother was gone, so I had a place to fill. I came all the way back here to Laramie and I suddenly knew that I couldn't let all these things just wither away. Maybe I couldn't tell them the way the women in my family had told the stories, but maybe if I wrote them down. And this was part literary but also it was a way of healing. It was a way of dealing with my own sense of loss.

Interviewer: So it was one of those times in your life when things just start coming together?

Wideman: Yeah, I think it was, but there are always two movements. Things were coming apart, too. I had moved far away from Homewood, far away from Pittsburgh, far away from these people. I was an academic, I was out here teaching Eng Lit in Wyoming and people were dying back in Pittsburgh, people who were very important to me. So there was that sense of the world losing the shape that had been familiar and important to me.

Interviewer: In the preface to the *Homewood Trilogy*, you write, "It became clear to me on that night in Pittsburgh in 1973 that I needn't look any further than the place I was born and the people who'd loved me to find what was significant and lasting in literature. My university training had both thwarted and prepared me for this understanding." How do you think the university had prepared you?

Wideman: It kept me out of trouble for one thing, out of certain kinds of trouble. I had read lots of books and through reading these books and writing I was learning to take the language that I heard and give it a twist and get it down on paper. And through reading Joyce and reading Eliot I was learning the language, learning how to write, learning technique. I think that was the piece that had to go together with my own background.

Interviewer: How did the university thwart you?

Wideman: It gave me the crazy sense that I had to write about the same things that the writers I read in my English classes wrote about, that I had to go to school and learn their environment and learn their quirks and learn their social system and the religions that supported them.

Interviewer: This wasn't altogether easy for you was it? They even made you change the way you played basketball when you went to Penn.

Wideman: I learned to play kind of freelance, spontaneous, improvisational basketball. But for college basketball you had to learn systems, you had to put yourself within this kind of disciplined, coach-centered style. What I did was playground basketball and they erased that from the kids who came in.

Interviewer: That was funky.

Wideman: Yeah, that was bad. Not baad, but bad. So I learned to go along with that program and now, ten years later, the style of the game has changed and the very best ball being played is the style that originated on the playground. Of course, it's been renamed now; it's the passing game and coaches get the credit, but what in fact happened is that the players remade the game according to their skills and the coaches tried to catch up. As in most things in this country, if it comes from the street, if it comes from the underclass, it doesn't exist until it's given a name, until it's patented. Then the credit goes to somebody who's very late in the field.

Interviewer: You have written that you see your vocation as a writer to be that of authenticating your background, authenticating black life.

Wideman: Not so much a planned campaign but the inevitable direction that my writings turned. For me writing is more and more a tool of self-expression and as I understand better who I am, I understand more about the culture of which I'm part. That's what I'm trying to get into my writing. The possibility of individual growth, coupled with the idea that a given culture can help you select or select for you a framework in which it's most natural to work and from which you draw your range of choice. In any matter, whether it's playing basketball or dancing or speaking.

Interviewer: And in your case it's language. "Language is power," you say at one place. Beginning with the *Homewood Trilogy* it seems that you are trying to authenticate that language.

Wideman: It started even earlier than that; it just wasn't a central concern. I had to work my way through it. *Hurry Home* is all about mastering one's own culture and the kind of paranoia and craziness that comes when you can't make those decisions or when people keep making the decisions for you.

Interviewer: What do you value about the first three books?

Wideman: I don't look back that often. The work that's past is gone. Some of my books are going to be reprinted and I'll be curious to see what the reaction to them is. When the books were published they were always published in small editions and had readers who were very appreciative, but not many in number. Yet through it all I knew I was doing some things the other writers weren't doing and I knew that I was doing some things that might be valuable if somebody would listen, if somebody would pay attention.

Interviewer: Can you name any of those things?

Wideman: They're the same things we've been talking about. Experiments with language, experiments with form, bringing to the fore black cultural material, history, archetypes, myths, the language itself, the language that black people actually speak and trying to connect that with the so-called mainstream.

Interviewer: And yet you have said that what you felt like you were doing was translating one language into another language.

Wideman: I think I had my priorities a little bit mixed up. I felt that I had to prove something about black speech for instance, and about black culture, and that they needed to be imbedded within the larger literary frame. In other words, a quote from T. S. Eliot would authenticate a quote from my grandmother. Or the quote from my grandmother wasn't enough, I had to have a Joycean allusion to buttress it, to keep an awareness that "Hey, this is serious writing and this guy's not just a solitary black voice, but he knows the things that you know, he's part of the shared culture." I felt you had to leave a signpost to make that clear. Sometimes it works and sometimes it doesn't. But the urge to do that, the urge to make my work a blend of all the different cultures that have filtered through me is still there. It's tough, it's very tough because if you really do bridge two cultures it probably happens not because that's what you want to do but because you are so thoroughly part of both those worlds that what you do comes out being a true blend.

Interviewer: In our classes they teach us to distinguish between the local color writer and the genre writer and the regional writer. And in every case the local color writer is the outsider trying to write about something and his outsiderness both moves and somehow lessens the work.

Wideman: There's that and there's also simply the politics of writing in this country. And the politics of our national psyche which tends to see things in cartoons and tends to try to grab things without really touching them. We look for either/ors: things are either black or white, up or down, you're either rich or poor, you're a winner or a loser. Who knows where that fault in our imagination comes from: maybe it's because Americans have felt so alienated from the land, their past, that the notion of cleavage, the notion of either/or is fundamental. I personally think it comes from racial politics. In order to define yourself as an American you had to define yourself over and against something. And to define yourself over and against Europe actually meant always to put America in the derogatory light.

Interviewer: Toni Morrison has said that she is working for a black audience. She uses the analogy that if Dostoyevsky were writing *Crime and Punishment* for an American audience it would be a totally different book. I think she was getting at the universality that comes from focusing on the particular, focusing on one place from the inside. Do you think that in focusing on Homewood you have managed to move someplace that you didn't go in the first three books?

Wideman: The notion of being grounded is a very important notion in all traditional cultures. I'm using the word grounded metaphorically: the forefathers entered this land and it was dangerous and nobody ever lived here before. But they spoke to the spirits of this land and those spirits gave them information and knowledge that they needed to start a village. The village could grow and would be sustained because the people kept alive that knowledge of the original contract, a knowledge of the rootedness. Everything flows from that ancestral bargain. And I believe that in order for my art, anybody's art, to flourish it has to be rooted, it has to be grounded, in that sense. So, yes, particularity, yes, the very unique and real ground that you fought for and bled in and created as a people. In my case that's Homewood.

Interviewer: Does the epigraph to *Hiding Place*—"I went to the rock to hide my face, and the rock said, 'There is no hiding place.' "—represent a recurring theme in your work? Is the work that you've done since the *Homewood Trilogy* an acknowledgment that there is no hiding place?

Wideman: Oh, there is no hiding place, but that will not stop us from running like hell and trying to find it every chance we get. That's part of the irony.

Interviewer: And perhaps the guilt you felt about Robby—the sense that in your attempts to hide or to run, you were somehow bearing witness to the wrong priorities.

Wideman: Yeah, I think that was true. When you write a book you schematize things and you write for effect, so the whole motif of running was also rhetorical. There was never a stage in my life when I was not very worried about both the direction in which I was running and what I was running from. That was part of my culture, if you will: those warnings that you receive very early in life and those walls that you keep bumping into if you don't keep your eyes very alert. I was never simply somebody who bought the American dream, the Horatio Alger myth. I was always somebody who had ghosts, who had demons. The hellhound was on my trail. It was a question really of degree, and I'm sure that somebody who's smarter than I am, somebody who's standing on the outside, could point out at this very moment ways in which I'm going to the rock and hiding my face. The irony is, it's impossible to do that without endangering the very thing you're trying to protect. You put your head in the sand, your butt shows. You put your butt in the sand, your head shows. There's not enough sand to cover the whole thing.

Interviewer: It seems like that since the *Homewood Trilogy* you've been hurrying back home. How have you been received in Homewood?

Wideman: One of the most heartwarming experiences I've had in the last couple of years was just a few months ago when I went back to Pittsburgh to receive an award and speak at the 75th anniversary of the Carnegie Library in Homewood. They'd brought the kids from Peabody, my former high school, and our rival, Westinghouse. The privilege of being able to share with that group of young people the kinds of things that have been happening to me and at the same time have in the back of my mind, "Well, now this—my life, what I've written, what I've said, what I've felt—is now part of the record; it's accessible to them." I felt a great sense of completion in the same way I felt during the best moments with my brother as we were working on *Brothers and Keepers.* I'd been writing about Homewood and black people for a long time but Pittsburgh never paid any attention. But now if you live in Pittsburgh, you have to know about Homewood and you have to know that there's somebody who's talking about Homewood in a very special way. You have to take that into account and so yeah, that's important. On a different level there's my family and our story. I've gone public with lots of things but luckily, for the most part, people have been delighted. They've been delighted in the same way that they're delighted in hearing stories about themselves at a wake or a wedding or on a picnic. I'm very careful, I don't spill any beans or tell tales on folks. In fact I change names if there's any kind of intimidating thing. For instance, if it was really Ernie who drove to the ball park on the wrong day for the game, then I'll say it was Charles and everybody who reads it in my family will know who in fact did that and they'll all get a laugh out of it but Ernie won't be teased by guys at work. It's almost like "in" jokes. The information is coded, so that people close enough to know what it's about can have fun with it.

Interviewer: Do you have any feelings about the issue of the writer as a plunderer of other people's experience?

Wideman: I remember once in college reading a story by Henry Miller. It was a story about coming home from Europe and going back to a family gathering, and he used his own name and I assumed the names of the people

in his family. I was shocked. I was absolutely shocked by the candor and the
frankness and even the fact that he said his father had a wart, or his mother
was a crabby old bitch, that his father burped at the table, that somebody's
ears weren't clean. That seemed to be telling tales, seemed to be betraying
mother and father and home. I just couldn't believe that as a writer he would
trespass that way and reveal that kind of information, be that intimate. So I
started with a very conservative idea about what was okay to reveal and what
wasn't okay to reveal, combined with the very powerful cultural imperative
that you don't tell most of what you know. It would just get you in trouble.

Interviewer: Baldwin writes about that.

Wideman: It's crucial. You can find the same proverbs among the Russian
serfs.

Interviewer: It's the underclass, whatever that class is.

Wideman: Exactly. You can't speak what's on your mind, you can't be
frank with people because it will be used against you. Your language and
your customs, etc. revolve around the hard, cold facts of your servitude, of
the oppressed state that you live in. I couldn't ever see myself writing about
my family at all. So when I wrote my first novel, I didn't name the city, the
people were disguised very carefully, I didn't use things—I sort of made up
most of the book. I brought in major characters from my life as a student,
from my life in Europe, and put them into this sort of vaguely big city atmosphere. But it wasn't until the Homewood books that I actually began to try
to deal with that primal ground. It was a question of getting enough confidence in myself and knowing enough about my people so that I knew that I
wasn't embarrassing myself and I wasn't embarrassing them but that the truth
about them, if I could ever write the truth about them, would be powerful and
it would be beautiful and it would be true.

Interviewer: You have written, "One of the earliest lessons I learned as a
child was that if you looked away from something, it might not be there when
you look back. I feared loss, feared turning to speak to someone and finding
no one there. Being black and poor reinforced the wisdom of a tentative
purchase on experience. . . . If you let your eyes touch lightly, rely on an
impressionistic touch—then you may achieve the emotional economy of faint
gains, faint losses. Writing," and this is the remark that is so important,
"forces me to risk ignoring the logic of this lesson." Could you expand on
that a little bit?

Wideman: From the writer's point of view writing is a laying on of hands. I feel that if I'm going to write well, I have to take the risk, I have to take lots of risks, risks of finding out something about something I've done or something I haven't done and having that knowledge hurt me or hurt somebody else or disorient me. All those risks are involved if you want to write well. So I had to start taking some chances that go against the grain of that wisdom. I also learned that the people who loved me and whom I cared about most were people who flew in the face of that initial wisdom of touching lightly. The people I love most and who loved me most were folks who did expose themselves, who did make themselves vulnerable, went the whole nine yards, if you will. I reacted in a personal way to the examples of my mother, and my aunts and uncles, and my grandfather and the people who, as I wrote about and thought about and learned about them, came to be the most important people in my life again. I had kind of lost touch with them and lost touch with their importance. I was looking in other places for the nurturing and the wisdom and models. But coming back to them I found that they had taken the most dramatic kinds of chances. They had united their fate with mine. And as I looked around more carefully I found that that had occurred in no other arena of my life.

Interviewer: Then you would agree with Lucy's assessment of those people in the closing section of *Sent For You Yesterday*.

Wideman: Oh, yes. The people stood for things, they were their own people. The community was a projection of what was inside of them.

Interviewer: Do you agree with her assessment of Carl that he gave up too easily?

Wideman: Yeah, he should have taken some chances, there should have been some blood spilled, he should be marked by resistance. He should have taken his stand here and there and the other place.

Interviewer: Am I overreading when I say Brother is the central figure in that book? He's everyone's alter ego.

Wideman: In a funny way he's a mirror, but you can't see through him. He's not a glass. He's solid. But he has the qualities of a spirit, he's immaterial. He does have blood but everybody's afraid that when they look in there they'll see through his skin. And of course if they see through his skin what they'll see is their own mortality, their creaturehood, their own blood.

Interviewer: He's music, he's the force of art in this world.

Wideman: He does contain or express the kind of background music that

I sense is part of life. I do believe that music's there. When I'm going good, when I'm playing basketball I get attuned to some rhythm and become much more than myself. Two people are hanging on you and you're twenty feet from the basket and you go up in the air and as soon as the ball leaves your hand—you don't even see the basket, you may be falling down on the side of the court—but you know that the darn thing's going in. I wanted Brother to be somebody who had access to that in himself and could put people in touch with it, to be a vehicle for making that music real.

Interviewer: Is it correct to say that Brother is the muse, the embodiment of everything that becomes the tale and the telling of the tale?

Wideman: He's the quicksilver that the narrator's trying to catch in his net. But I don't want him to be an idea, I don't want him to be the Protestant God, I don't want him to be an African spirit who's transcendent, who's immortal. I want him to be flesh and blood, I want him to suffer, I want him to go through a lifetime, which in one sense is just the blink of an eye, but that's all any of us ever gets so it's also pretty important, pretty significant. If he had been some kind of transcendent supernatural being then the whole novel would have fallen apart because that has nothing to do with the lives of most human beings. We suffer, we bleed, we lose people, we grow, we decay, we're gone. But we take part in that sensual music and Brother embodies both what is transcendent and what is very earthbound. That's why he can be such a powerful personage to the people in Homewood. If he just walked all through it, through fire and earth and water and it didn't hurt him, didn't touch him, then what would he mean? But if he was really your brother, if you drank wine with him, if you saw him cry because he lost his son, if you were hurt because you learned that he died suddenly, then the music has a human scale.

Interviewer: The three central figures in *Sent For You Yesterday* seem to be displaced. Is that a theme in the novel?

Wideman: I hate to schematize, but you can see John French's generation as hardy pioneers. They came from the South and made a world. It was a world that was very tenuous, but they prevailed and had their children—the generation of my father and of Carl and of Lucy. They are the ones who were wiped out because they didn't have the pioneers' struggle to survive. They tried to move out from what the generation before had done, but society said no, there's no place for you to go, we don't want you here, you are no good, you are wasted. So that generation became sacrificial; they were just ground up. That's why the marriages didn't work, the children were stillborn. The animosity was so strong that as a generation they could not overcome it. Then my generation followed, and in looking back over this space, I think there is strength to be gathered from the experience of a Carl and a Lucy and a Brother but also from that other generation, the John French generation, and Brother is the bridge over the lost generation. That is the scheme of the novel that eventually came to me. Significantly Doot has children, so the future is open. The ones in the middle turn out to be not so stillborn because in a symbolic and a metaphorical sense they become brothers to Brother.

Interviewer: It's as though the interconnectedness of family is enhanced by the stripping away of literal blood ties. Lucy and Brother, who are in fact not brother and sister at all, have been raised by foster parents.

Wideman: Another way of looking at it is connected to statistics about broken homes, a definition of family codified in the Moynihan report. If you look at black culture, the black culture is deviant and delinquent because it does not have a family structure which reproduces the Moynihan model. But of course that is just a stipulative, narrow, and arbitrary definition of what a family might be. I think one of the powerful things that's happening, not only in black writing, but in contemporary writing, is a re-examination of bonding, male-female, older generation-younger generation. We're mixing it up and trying to see what it actually means. We're redefining what brotherhood and sisterhood mean.

Interviewer: There are people who think that writing being done in the black American tradition during the last generation is in many ways the very best writing that's being done, that being a member of an oppressed group in society gives you an insight that leads to the creation of novels that are beautiful and socially responsible at the same time, as Toni Morrison would say.

Wideman: I think that you might look at black writing and say that this is some of the best that the culture is producing and it's a splendid time for black writing. A judgment like that suggests that what's happening is new, that what's happening is rare, and that what's happening has no history; but there have always been powerful black voices. Ellison between 1940 and 1960, and before him Richard Wright and Zora Neale Hurston. They've been at the forefront of fiction; we just didn't know it, we just didn't know where or how to look. The other reason I don't like to endorse that kind of Golden Epoch of Black Literature notion is that the same conditions, economic and social, that made so many black writers invisible before could happen again.

A force of circumstances could quiet the black voice, but would that mean that there weren't any good black writers any more? That people could nostalgically look back at the 60s, 70s, and 80s and say, "Boy, there were some good black writers then, but there are none now." No. It would probably mean that publishing had decided that blacks are not in vogue this year, and so all those good black voices would just be quieted. Same thing as John Thompson winning the NCAA. Yeah, he's a talented man and a great coach, but the reason he's the first black coach is not because of his unique and individual talent; it's because he was allowed to be. He was allowed to be. We always have to keep that in mind when we look at firsts, and bests, among black people in any endeavor.

Interviewer: Many people point to Native American writing—work by Scott Momaday and James Welch and Leslie Silko—and argue that being in the underclass somehow gives you a better eye for creating these very beautiful and very big novels.

Wideman: When it works, yes.

Interviewer: But you don't think there's anything magic about it?

Wideman: It's hard work and it's discipline. The writers you're talking about are—first of all their art and genius should not be connected to the sociology of their lives because you could point to a hundred people who went through the same kinds of experiences and didn't write novels. So what's the difference. When you talk about cultures and styles even, you can't have it both ways: either you're ethnocentric or not. You're not ethnocentric if you believe that all cultures have values and you have to get inside and understand them and look at them in their own terms. You can't go around praising exotic people for being exotic, or outsiders for being outside. It's like lots of Americans will—I've noticed this, it's not original with me, but if there's an Indian woman, East Indian woman, at a party, inevitably someone will come and tell me, "Did you see that beautiful woman over there, isn't she beautiful?"—a white person will say that to me. That overcompensation is pigeonholing, is cataloguing, is talking about the otherness of the person, and I think we have to resist that.

Interviewer: James Baldwin felt that there was no way to tell the truth about the American culture without trying to get white culture to see its relationship to black culture.

Wideman: Well, that's not quite clear to me, I'm not exactly sure what he was getting at or what you're getting at. I think you have to be very cautious. I believe that I have a very definite advantage in being black in America. Both insider and outsider, that's the archetypal artistic stance. Whether or not that stance becomes a discipline, produces art, has to do with countless other factors. It may be a flying start, but there are a whole lot of winos and junkies who have been alienated from their society and stand on the outside—who have the perfect angle for writing novels—but they're killing themselves, not producing art.

Interviewer: You've said that the best stories are those written for a specific person to read.

Wideman: Yes, in a funny way I don't think a writer has a choice. How shall we write a universal story, how shall we write a story that's appealing to everyone? You might as well go to the Propp fairytale index and pick out one or two of those recurring myths and just put in characters and write them over and over again. No. You have to be aware of the particular. You have to be aware of the specific people, the specific words, the specific locales and then something grows out of that. It doesn't work the other way around. At least I've never seen it work the other way around.

Interviewer: Are the stories and the two novels in the *Homewood Trilogy* letters from home to your brother, Robby, as you say in the beginning?

Wideman: They didn't all start that way, but once I had enough of them done I did feel that was a fair way to describe them and some very consciously were that. What I look for when I write is a kind of register, an emotional weight, and I get that by thinking of particular people who would understand or at least care about what I'm talking about. It's best for me as a writer to think not of a group of people but of one person who serves as a funny sort of mirror. I create that person in the mirror. I mean I'm writing to Robby but as I write I'm also creating him as audience.

Interviewer: Is there a sense in which the work in the *Homewood Trilogy* is an attempt somehow to expiate—to somehow carry your brother Robby back to what had seemed to become lost in Homewood between your growing-up years and Robby's?

Wideman: I've thought about that a lot and find myself losing sharpness of response because I've gone beyond the simple answers, the answers that somebody could write down and figure—Yeah, now I understand what this guy's doing. So when you ask that question, yes, the answer is I love my brother and I was terribly hurt and frightened by what happened to him, and I feel a little bit responsible and guilty, as all of us should; therefore I want to do what I can with writing. But if it were only a question of somehow making this crazy instrument that could document the past in the way that videotape can document the present, I think writing would not have all that much interest for me. What's more important is the possibility of having an influence on my life now and on the lives of the people who are important to me. Writing is power. On one level I am wielding that power to the best of my ability to get my brother out of jail. If that happens then the effort is more than rewarded, and I'd be very happy. But I'm greedy; I'm hoping other things are also happening, I'm hoping I'm preparing a place for both my brother and me to live. I hope I'm growing, and I hope I'm connected with his growth.

Interviewer: Is there any chance that Robby can get a parole?

Wideman: There is hope and work is going on daily. I've dedicated myself to that; I'm determined, he is determined and we'll find a way.

Interviewer: Do you think the books have had a measurable impact?

Wideman: I hope so. Whatever public impact they've had, privately they've become a vehicle for us to get closer. The books have reconnected him to the world outside the prison walls. He has groupies, people who write him. People are aware that he's there. He draws strength and energy from those folks who are supportive of him.

Interviewer: And what about your community of readers?

Wideman: They're welcome to enter at any stage, whether it's learning something about a person like Robby or a person like me or even learning something about themselves. Writing is, after all, an enterprise of the imagination. If you look too hard for the way that it impacts our real world, then you either get phony answers or half-assed answers or maybe just confused. It's a very subjective and internal process and the rewards and benefits act themselves out in a realm that most people can't understand. What actually happens when you write fiction is still extremely mysterious.

Interviewer: In *Brothers and Keepers* you ask "Is what happened to Robby the price that had to be paid for my success?" Why do you feel that way?

Wideman: As I get older, it's become clear that there's the individual way of looking at things, the microscale, but on top of that there is the macroscale, which any individual behavior has to be balanced over and against. Those two worlds often contradict one another. It's perfectly understandable why I might buy a fancy new car for me and for my family, but it's not understandable when you look at it in terms of the fact that people are starving. I don't go around feeling guilty all the time for my good fortune and I don't cry all the time when I think about Ethiopia. But that inevitable clash is something that bothers me. I do believe that the idea of connecting oneself to a literal brother or to other people on the earth is probably about the only notion that's going to have any chance of saving us all. I've tried to do that with Robby. Working through a non-fiction book about him, a sort of made-up book about him, and a long story about him, I've been asking myself questions that have to do with how people are connected and what's at stake in these connections. And what, after all, do they mean? That's the meat of the fiction I've been writing. That's the meat of all of it.

Interview with John Edgar Wideman

James W. Coleman / 1988

From *Blackness and Modernism: The Literary Career of John Edgar Wideman.* Jackson and London: U Press of Mississippi, 1988: 145–62. Used by permission.

Coleman: In a 1982 interview, you say that in *Damballah,* published along with *Hiding Place* in 1981, you did not want to exclude the segment of your audience familiar with T. S. Eliot, James Joyce, and William Faulkner, the audience toward which, I believe, your first two books, *A Glance Away* and *Hurry Home,* were largely focused. But you made it clear that you were changing your focus in *Damballah* and writing a book with a broader scope that would be relevant to a black audience. You have not presented any extensive public statements about your fiction since *Sent for You Yesterday,* your next book after *Damballah,* but I see another change in your fiction, beginning with *Sent for You Yesterday* and even more clearly manifesting itself in *Reuben.* The emphasis is still on black community and culture, but it seems to me that Doot in *Sent for You Yesterday* and the character Reuben in *Reuben* take these books in somewhat different directions from *Hiding Place* and *Damballah* and also from your earlier work. Would you comment on this?

    Wideman: I guess the best comment would be "whatever book I'm working on now," because what you are talking about I believe is that endless process of backward and forward and overlap and self-echoing and recapitulation that is a career, that is an evolution of a way of seeing, eventually of a vision. I think in my own mind there is a sharp break, in some ways, between the first three books and the next two or three; but that's only sharp because I became conscious of it, I think, and began to talk about the break myself— that is, the movement towards other kinds of audience and the conscious attempt to include the audience members of my family represent. But even in the first three books, as I look back on them now, I was very much concerned with family and community and the people I grew up with, and I thought, in my own way, that I was addressing that audience quite directly. But then, on rereading the work and rethinking it—those earlier works—it seemed to me that I was missing the boat in some ways, that I had not done as well as I might possibly be able in inviting that audience, and I had done some things that probably worked against including that audience. But that was in retrospect. In all honesty, as I look back on the first three books, I was writing about who I was and what had happened to me and people that I knew, things that were important, but then I grew, and my sense of who I was and what constituted the important events in my past changed, and I hope it continues to change, and so the process is evolutionary, it's moving; and as writer, as artist, I'm like everybody else who experiences the books, both inside and outside, and so there is a process of the actual evolution of the work and then there is also my awareness of what's going on in the work, and my ability to stop it, change it, or give it direction, or to focus it. And so those are two things that are happening. A good critic, a certain kind of reader, may have more success, or may at an earlier stage figure out these changes, anticipate ways the work should go, ways that the work isn't going. So that's a long way of making the first distinction, that often—well, it has to come after the fact. There was no game plan at the beginning which was scuttled for another game plan somewhere in the middle. There is always back and forward and testing. I think the character of the crippled woman in my very first book, the grandmother. . .

Coleman: Martha?

Wideman: Yes, that is for me, in many ways, as much a picture of my grandmother as the one that occurs in *Sent for You Yesterday.*

Coleman: The thing about *A Glance Away,* particularly, is that many of the characters and many of the incidents are very similar, I would venture to say the same, to those we find in later books, that is, in *Hiding Place* and *Damballah* and other books. So it is obvious that you have been dealing with, it seems to me, the same family and very similar materials. What I see as a critic is how your approach has changed in the later books. It seems to me that you treat the materials somewhat differently in the books, particularly beginning with *Hiding Place* and *Damballah.* So there is a lot of consistency there as well as difference.

Wideman: It's kind of funny to look back, because I don't always maintain a very clear picture in my own head of the other books . . . in fact . . . in the sense that they all sort of blend together, and once a book is finished I never go back and read it again. So if you are writing a critique of my work you probably would be much more adept at calling out the names of characters and whatnot than I would be.

Coleman: You never read a book again?

Wideman: I have never read a book straight through after it's been published, because then it's out of my hands. I have read parts of some and I go

through them maybe if I'm going to give a reading or if I am going to give
an interview or something like that. I might review it just for informational
purposes, but it's the writing that's important. It's the writing that engages
me. So once the book is finished, there is no more. . . . It's not live any more.
I can't do anything else with it. Also it's a little intimidating, maybe nega-
tively intimidating. If there's something . . . , if I don't like the book, that
would be a problem because there it is—it's out there. Plus it's also just being
finished with something, really finished with it. You start with some small
idea, and it grows, and you work on it for a couple of years and then it
becomes a book and then it goes through the publication process, which
means reading drafts and reading version after version, having it copy edited
and you're just tired of it by that time. Maybe there will be a point in my life
where I will want to go back and look at some of these things, but at this
point it doesn't seem likely—I think I'd rather continue to move ahead.

Coleman: So critics and creative writers in a lot of ways have different
perspectives or maybe different jobs, different tasks, would you say? Because
critics, people like me, are trying to make sense of things and we just hope
that we don't impose too much on the writer, although I guess you can't help
doing that, can you?

Wideman: Well, you have an agenda, everybody has an agenda, and
everybody has a . . . critics particularly have sometimes hidden, sometimes
very exclusive motives for looking at any kind of literature, whether it's to
get tenure, or to prove that whites are superior to blacks, or to prove that one
culture is dominant to another, or to prove that one writer deserves all the
goodies and others should just shut up . . . , or to prove that you are smarter
than anybody else, that you know more about this. There are just as many
reasons for writing a critical book as there are for writing a novel, maybe
more. Because for a critical book you use your front brain a little more, so
you are thinking, and often a book of fiction or poems is written with the
back brain, so you haven't really thought out why you are doing it; the moti-
vation is unconscious. So in that sense there may be more reasons for writing
a critical book.

Coleman: Let me move on to another area here slightly different. You also
said in this same interview that I just alluded to, that between the publication
of *The Lynchers* in '73 and *Hiding Place* and *Damballah* in '81, you were
learning a different fictional voice and a different language to talk about the
experience in your fiction. Now, it is my perception that your fictional voice
grows and matures over time. That is one thing I try to talk about as a critic.

How does the voice . . . , how would you say the voice in *Hiding Place* and *Damballah* differs from the voice in *A Glance Away* and *Hurry Home,* the books before *Hiding Place?*

Wideman: One way they differ is simple enough, and that is I get older, and as I get older, maybe I become exposed to more. And I think also I grow. . . . I hope I am growing more independent. I hope I have stopped saying what I think people might want me to say and have gotten more confident about saying what I want to say, and in my own fashion. I think that's why old men can wear frazzled-collar shirts and young men wouldn't be caught dead in them, you know, because you're just paying too much attention to your audience when you're younger—in a bad way. So that's part of it—just a simple process of maturation.

Coleman: You think you were paying . . . in the earlier books in what sense were you paying attention to audience?

Wideman: What sense?

Coleman: Or to what audience?

Wideman: For me audience was something that I took for granted. My sense of audience came from my education up to that point, my sense of what the important works of Western literature were, my sense of the classics, my sense of the esthetics that govern those classics; and so I saw myself as writing for that tradition. The notion of a separate audience and the notion of another set of obligations that I might have as a writer, was very faint indeed. I thought that, yes, I would be bringing my own personal experience, therefore, a black experience, into this world of letters, but I didn't see myself as necessarily changing that world. So, I guess an analogy would be something like the early notions of integration. You go to the lunch counter and that's enough. Just so you get in and you're served there. And then later politically people figured out that that certainly wasn't enough, that the problem wasn't the lunch counter at all; the problem was the whole system that buttressed that kind of segregation. So that going to the lunch counter was an important first step, but then to really obtain some kind of freedom and some sort of autonomy and independence, it was necessary to penetrate the system—in a way deconstruct the system—and begin to own lunch counters, and begin to even say that the lunch counters are jive anyway, and that maybe what you want is to eat in a totally different place, and different food, and a different hour, et cetera, et cetera. I think in my writing I reflect some of this. As I look back it seems to me that I was too easily seduced into believing there was only one way to do things and that my job as a writer was to learn to jump through the hoops in the proper way.

Coleman: And a lot of that is along the tradition of the great—so-called—great white writers, i.e., Joyce, Faulkner, Eliot, people like that, that tradition?

Wideman: Exactly. The people who were on graduate exams thirty years ago, and still are, but there are distinctions that need to be made, because I still think those writers are powerful writers. I still use their models in some situations. The problem is to identify what I do and the changes that I have gone through along cultural lines rather than racial lines. Look at a writer like William Faulkner; he is saturated by elements of black southern culture. And so to say that what I needed to do was get rid of "white influences" doesn't really portray, doesn't really accurately reflect, what was going on. What I had to do was . . . what I think I have been able to do is look at these influences in terms other than race, so that I still am responsive to Faulkner's attempts to capture the oral cadences of southern speech—and often southern black speech—in those long flowing sentences, in that kind of crazy mix of vocabularies which comes from the King James Bible and from proverbs and illiteracies and all the rest. I still respect that. Joyce's improvisations and spontaneity, inventiveness with language are very, very important, still part and parcel of what I am doing. But I am doing it and using those models both because they are powerful examples and because I am responding to them, responding to techniques, to power in them that reflects my own cultural experience. I can draw from them in the way that, let's say, black religion drew from traditional African religions, the way that traditional African religious beliefs could find in Christian churches' familiar practices, concepts, eventually a home—things from baptism to all the other parallels. So I don't want to make it seem that I exchanged one set of masters for another, because I hope that what I am doing is internalizing many different influences and shuffling among those and picking and choosing. And that's the key. Early on, not having the sophistication and knowledge to be able to pick and choose, because I was only familiar with one tradition. And then there is one more trick—and this is a very long answer, I know, but there is one more trick—the black influences were never *not* there. Nobody had ever pointed out to me how they were there. A Faulkner and a Joyce are part of a world culture, and they have learned from Africa, they have learned things from the street, they have learned things from the process of urbanization. In other words, we share a common culture and it wasn't made clear to me, as I grew up and I was educated, that Faulkner was, for instance, dependent on black culture for many of the virtues of his writing.

Coleman: One thing I try to point out, one thing that I see in what I call the maturing of your voice, and this is what I was trying to get at earlier, is that you bring together these various influences from white writers, from black writers, but also from black people in general, from the oral tradition, from black ritual, and so forth. And particularly in the books after *The Lynchers,* starting with *Hiding Place,* that's what makes your literary voice there deep and mature, for me. So it's not so much that there really are new things there. As you said, the black influences were there from the beginning, and they are still there, but to me there is a different kind of blend, and there is a different kind of emphasis. And it seems to me it's that emphasis that creates the maturity in your voice. It seems to me that you draw on black resources much better, much more fully, than you did in the earlier works.

Wideman: Well, I hope so, and part of that is very conscious, because I went to school to those voices. They were always part of me, but I made an attempt to—by reading other black writers, by reading slave narratives, by immersing myself for a number of years in as many different aspects of black culture as I could, as was reasonable—I tried to learn and bring to my fingertips so it was second nature, but also have in my mind, exactly what those cultural resources were. So I studied them. I made that a study, the same way I had made *Ulysses* a study, the same way I studied Eliot: read about Eliot, learned where he grew up, read critics, analyzed his poems, wrote papers. I did the same thing for Afro-American culture, and I think that gave me much more access, and I could consciously use it. I had used black culture before in *The Lynchers.* I had also used black history before in a whole slew of incidents that began *The Lynchers,* and I was just at that time beginning to understand where those kinds of techniques were coming from, and why they might seem appropriate; but then in the later books also I began to understand how in using Afro-American folklore and language I didn't have to give up any of the goals that I was after when I was using more Europeanized and more traditional—literary traditional—devices and techniques. I didn't have to give up a thing. I could talk about the most complicated and sophisticated and intense moments and understandings and characters in the Afro-American idiom. That was a real breakthrough, but it was a breakthrough that didn't come accidentally. It was a result of study and concentration, and research in fact.

Coleman: In the book *Reuben,* the character there, it seems to me, is a servant of the black community. Reuben is very conscious of helping people in the black community, although on certain levels Reuben is a spirit—as I think you called him in some little thing I read about the book once—but it seems to me that in a lot of ways he is also a real person as well as being a spirit—if that is true—who is a servant of the black community. But Reuben says explicitly—and I think I see a connection here with Doot in *Sent for You Yesterday,* although it's not explicit in *Sent for You Yesterday.* But Reuben is always talking about creating fictions, fictions that will create positive illusions in the black community, as well as fictions that will undo, undercut, will subvert negative fictions perpetuated by the white community. Now, this is your first book at least where that kind of language has been explicit, certainly. Can you talk about that a little bit? What about Reuben as a servant of the community who lives in this nebulous world where he uses fictions and also deconstructs fictions and, it seems to me, that at some points in that book the narrative even deconstructs, briefly. Can you talk some about that— what's going on there? And it does seem to me that this has a lot to do with what I see as a development in your fiction, too.

Wideman: Well, it's one thing to be able to pick out items of folklore, items of black culture, and use them in a particular fiction. That's one process, but I think that process becomes much more powerful and deeper when one has an understanding of the meaning of those rituals and those items, that is, try to restore them to the integrity in which they exist within the culture. Call-and-response is not just a coincidence. It is an attempt by a community to come to some set of values, to work out right and wrong, to build themselves into a cohesive unit by this kind of, in one way, political device which is working out together what things mean, what is being said. Call-and-response. Okay, so that fits into the deep structure of culture, and I have been lucky because I've been able to . . . I have had the time to think about how these items of folklore fit into the larger picture and have begun to be able to capture—try to capture—some of their meaning within the fiction; so that I am writing—I would hope—from the inside out, rather than applying a sort of local color or pieces of exotica to a fiction which is related to those items only very tangentially. And that's my way of saying that Reuben has no choice but to be a servant of the people. He manifests a certain principle of magic. He manifests a principle of word magic that enables us to create our own institutions, our own identities, and he is a figure who will always be in the midst of trouble because the dominant culture resists any attempt to infringe on its power. And Reuben is a power figure. He is an

intermediary. He is in the battleground. It's his job to untangle people from
the negative effects of the dominant culture, to protect people from one another and also from these invidious forces that are all around them. That's a
ritualistic process. It is the same thing that a shaman or a priest does on a
traditional culture, and so he is a lawyer. But both plots and themes of the
fictions I write, and the fictions themselves, are an attempt to subvert one
notion of reality with others, to show that there is not simply one way of
seeing things but many ways of seeing things. And as a people and as individuals if we don't jump into the breach, if we don't fight the battle of defining
reality in our own terms, then somebody else will always come along and do
it for us. So that *The Lynchers* is another way of looking at the 60's. The
book *Reuben* is another way of looking at what's happened after the so-called
civil rights revolution, et cetera. And Reuben himself, the character within
the novel, is engaged in a struggle that I think I'm engaged in as writer
outside the novel, creating and sustaining a version of reality to compete with
those destructive versions which are tearing us apart.

Coleman: Is there a particular point or time when you become conscious
of doing this in your writing, precisely what you talked about there?

Wideman: Well, delusions of grandeur probably start pretty early, but
specifically it began very clearly in a kind of nascent form in *Hurry Home,*
and that's a book about cultural conflict. That's a book about somebody torn
between two worlds, Mallarmé and the Faun, that imagery—somebody's part
human, part something else—and the book is full of splits and double personalities and that kind of stress that comes there, but I think I had not learned
to, in a sense, lexify that struggle in indigenous Afro-American terms. I was
still reaching to other places for metaphors and symbols, and they are still
valid to a certain extent, but they don't have that local force and particularity
that are most appropriate for me in my works. So I had to shop around quite
a bit more. *The Lynchers* is an important book in this sense, because I knew
clearly in that book that something was wrong . . . , something . . . , and I
saw more in political and sociological. . . .

Coleman: Something was wrong with what you were saying?

Wideman: No, something was . . . the struggle for a kind of peace or a
kind of independence . . . got hotter and hotter. It wasn't a literary concept,
but it became a very personal concept. I felt threatened. I felt very threatened,
and the threat to me was not only personal, it was a threat to a whole people.
I saw as lots of us did, paranoid versions of—well, not so paranoid—versions
of a country that was just going to self-destruct because of its racism, and a

country which was at kind of a crossroads and had to make some really basic
choices. Was it going to move a little bit to accommodate new voices—young
peoples' voices, black peoples' voices, voices of change—or was it going to
puff up its chest and send out the immigrants to whip on the black people
again. And I felt that threat very personally and tried to talk about it in *The
Lynchers,* but I still didn't have the vocabulary, I still didn't have the tools I
required. I wasn't quite ready to set up a totally independent ground of reck-
oning. I didn't have the words yet. I didn't have the words yet to make the
stand that I wanted to make. So the novel *The Lynchers* is about things coming apart, things destructing. Then the next books are an attempt to reconstruct what came apart.

Coleman: It seems to me that in *The Lynchers*—and I distinctly remember
reading that; I must have read it in about '74, so not too long after it came
out—and it was, and still is, an extremely powerful book. One thing that is
very powerful about it is the language. There is a sense there that you know
so much about black culture, black ritual, black language, much more a sense
that you know about that than in the first two books. Now, of course, you
did, but it comes out so much more in *The Lynchers.* The thing about *The
Lynchers* though, as you say, is that things are so torn apart for black people,
things are so hopeless, in a sense, and it is not until you get to *Hiding Place*
and the books after that—*Hiding Place* and *Damballah,* particularly—where
I find you bringing together what you have in *The Lynchers* with other aspects
of black life, black culture, that create a kind of wholeness, a kind of broad
perspective. Now it's not sentimentalized or anything, what I am talking
about in *Hiding Place,* but it's there—what I'm calling wholeness at this
point, at least.

Wideman: It's clear to me—at least for the moment as we sit here and
talk—that there is in *The Lynchers* . . . thematically it's very similar to *Reuben* and the later books, because it's all about the attempt of a group of black
men to substitute, by use of myth and by use of a kind of a play—a kind of
a strange passion play, a lynching—to break through the hold of one illusion
of reality into a new day where there might be some room for change, and
that's what the book is about, about constructive change. But it's a very
negative myth and it's a myth that still . . . it's a borrowed myth, the myth of
the lynching, or the ritual of the lynching. So it's borrowed from the oppres-
sor. And it's negative. What happens in the later books I think is—if we want
to simplify it, I guess—the attempt to find positive rituals and myths that can
shore up, that can reconstruct, the sense of reality in the black community, in

its own terms, in terms that have been there all along, so there is that kind of distinction, I think. Now, where you put the book *Reuben* in all of this is another question, because *Reuben* has a lot of the pessimism of *The Lynchers,* but Reuben still goes at it from a positive point of view, as a traditional healer and magician.

Coleman: One thing is very clear in *Reuben,* and what pointed me to this was the acknowledgment of Robert Farris Thompson's book *Flash of the Spirit,* which I got and read. Part of what Reuben is using there, probably consciously, is aspects of Kongo cosmology and myth as part of his structure. Now, that's something that is a little bit, or maybe more than a little bit, different in your work, isn't it? I mean the specific use of African . . . well, maybe not—I'm about to say something that isn't true—because African and of course Afro-American are close and at a lot of points not separable, but still it seems to me that *Reuben* is, at least on a conscious level, doing something that your other characters haven't done, in terms of drawing on African motifs and myths.

Wideman: Again the process of self-education of the author and the ability to get some of that, some of what I learned, into the books, I think that's the simple way of explaining it or at least describing it. Explaining it is more complicated. It seems to me that what I am after, and what I would like to achieve, is not just the external changes that might enable a black guy or a black woman to walk into this two-hundred-thousand-dollar-a-year job in IBM, but to have that person—that black man or that black woman—earn a very good living and change IBM's act somehow. Or if that black man or that black woman had a chance to go into IBM, to make that person an agent for change, to make that person conscious of what's wrong with that step up as well as what the benefits are. To be able to critique it, to have choices, and to that extent, I'm working from the ground up. I want . . . the books have to reflect the deeper spiritual values that animate, for me, what's good and what should be preserved about Afro-American life. The rituals are a manifestation of some spirit force, which runs much deeper. That's why the outward shape or description of the culture can change. But it can maintain its integrity because of those forces that run underground. Those forces have always been there. And those are the ones I'm trying to touch upon. I might do something like try to show how Kongo cosmology might be relevant to what Reuben's doing—how it's tied up—the notion of doubles, the notion of two worlds. I want to show how that is as relevant as looking at the American. You can understand the American experience or the Afro-American experience in

Kongo terms as well as in terms of Calvinism and Protestantism and Roman Catholicism and Western humanism. Those are ways, those are containers— jails for the culture—which don't explain everything that needs to be explained, so I'm looking for other explanations.

Coleman: It seems to me that Doot in *Sent for You Yesterday* is creating a kind of myth or a story of Afro-American culture with black music and black musicians as symbols. I see that as one thing that's different about *Sent for You Yesterday.* The music and the musicians are certainly very important in *Hiding Place* and *Damballah* and also in the earlier books, too. But it appears to me that Doot is doing something—as an individual—is doing something different there. What is Doot doing in *Sent for You Yesterday?* And of course it's very complex because at points Doot is clearly the first-person narrator, I mean, he is the "I" narrator who is right there in the narrative. At points he seems to merge with an omniscient narrator, but it seems to me that he is deeply embedded in the whole structure. What's he doing?

Wideman: Well, he's learning to dance, and he's learning to dance to music that is not totally explicable in natural terms. That is, the music is magical. The music has a force that can't be explained in any satisfactory everyday way. The music seems to have an energy all its own that is rooted some place other than in individuals. And so in that sense the music is the pulse, the rhythm, the force, the expression of the entire culture; and by learning to dance Doot is learning to, like a fish, live in this medium.

Coleman: Music almost says something that language, that words, can't say?

Wideman: Well, it subsumes them, or language aspires to the condition of music. Music seems to me the medium that comprehends all others, because music can be silent. It can be Magic playing basketball, without a sound track, just his movements. Or it can be a woman dancing or it can be just somebody walking down the street . . . , so when you see people playing basketball, that music is there, even though it's not audible. It's the rhythm of the walk, it's the rhythm of the movement. So music seems to be just a medium of expression that subsumes the other. But where Doot comes into all this, he's a protagonist, and he's learning to dance in this medium, so that makes him the perfect exemplar of the writer. Because the book is about creating a useful past, creating a past that will sustain an identity and open doors towards the future, for the writer as well as the character. So the book is enacting in its composition that experience of letting the culture energize it and carry it along; in other words, the words are learning to dance, the words are learning to depend on their roots and their sources in Afro-American tradition. So that's what was happening to me as author. I was letting go, I was relaxing into that medium and that's what Doot is doing also, as a character within the story. And so there is naturally a great exchange between that Doot inside and the author outside, because they are all working toward dancing to the same music.

Coleman: Another thing that I'm very much interested in is the way that your main, primary characters who are academically trained, who are intellectuals, try to find their place in the black community in *Damballah* in particular. In several of the pieces here I see that process of the writer—and it sometimes is obviously, clearly a writer—that process of the writer-intellectual trying to find his voice, his place. "The Chinaman" is a good example of that. "The Watermelon Story," I think, is a good example, although it is a very perplexing story in a lot of ways. "Across the Wide Missouri" is another example and I think in some ways "The Beginning of Homewood" really brings the theme of the quest of the writer-intellectual together in a lot of ways—not that it necessarily reaches closure, but it does reach a kind of finish, at least for this particular volume. Would you talk about that process of what the writer and intellectual is doing there is in terms of finding his voice or his place in a black community and tradition?

Wideman: The novelist or the writer is a storyteller, and the process for me that is going to knit up the culture, knit up the fabric of the family, the collective family—all of us—one crucial part of that process is that we tell our own stories. That we learn to tell them and we tell them in our own words and that they embrace our values and that we keep on saying them, in spite of the madness, the chaos around us, and in spite of the pressure not to tell it. And so that storytelling activity is crucial to survival, individual survival, community survival. So the storyteller, the artist, is a crucial member of the community. He is also someone who perhaps by definition is outside the community—and should be and will always be—and so that yearning to be part of it may be one of the natural conditions of being a storyteller. Storytellers are always inside and outside the story by definition. Sometimes in Afro-American culture there are these little doors, there are these wonderful windows by which the storyteller gets pulled back, so he doesn't feel too lonely, doesn't feel left out. The call-and-response business, everybody sitting around on a mat sharing a story, the redaction of older stories, the retelling them. So our tradition seems to have a way that, yes, you can come back home again. If you tell your stories in a certain fashion, we'll help you tell them, they'll be ours, we'll reclaim them. And so I think my writer figure is the taleteller who is in that inevitably divided position. He has a voice, he's using it in a constructive way, but he also wants to blend, to merge. That voice to achieve its fullest resonance needs the voices of the rest of the community. And so, in all the stories that theme and that figure occur. The writer off, thrusting himself above the action to check it out and then trying to reengage, trying to be part of the very story he's telling.

Coleman: The process of reengagement is very clear throughout *Damballah,* as I said, but particularly in that last piece, "The Beginning of Homewood," where the writer draws upon the voices of community and family people, particularly Aunt May, to tell the story, but finally by the end he still has to rely on his own voice, which has incorporated or perhaps subsumed those other voices. It seems to me that in later books, particularly *Reuben,* for example, you have a figure who is set above and away from the community. So, I guess that tension remains, that whole process of moving toward reengagement and I suppose moving away, but the distance, or some distance, is probably always there.

Wideman: Yes, and it's not always pleasant, but it's the condition for creativity. The wound comes first and then the healing and then the growth.

Coleman: Wally in *Reuben* is an educated character. He is different from Reuben, in a sense, but he has got the University of Pennsylvania background, the formal education. In fact he has a formal education that Reuben does not have, but the more important point is that he seems to represent the destructive, and Reuben seems to represent the constructive. Is this true? What does Wally represent for you?

Wideman: Wally is out there. He has been kicked in the behind an awful lot and the worst kinds of kicks, because often they were disguised as bones. You know, he bent over to get the bone and found a foot in his ass, and that happened to him a lot. And even the bones he picks up and chews on he finds out very often they have been laced with arsenic or that they are not bones at all, that they are fake; they are pieces of wood or pieces of stone. So that's been the kind of experience he's had. It doesn't necessarily make a very pleasant personality, and so he is out there in a sense of, "Well, I get done in, and somebody seems to be making a living off doing me in so I'll return the favor in kind. It's war. I'm out here all on my own and I'll do the best I can and not look back." That's his attitude, and it's a very common attitude. In an educated person it shocks the at-large society more because they say, look, he had all the advantages, he had all those privileges, he could be an

honorary white guy if he only played his cards right. And also, he's a dangerous and threatening person because he did get some of the goodies. He did
follow . . . he looked at the carrot and followed it, and so the notion that you
can control a subject people by letting a few of them off the hook becomes
threatened by Wally, because he is one of your honorary white men and he's
turned against you. So I think for me Wally embodies a lot of that, that kind
of stuff—the rage, the anger that is inchoate but is always possibly there to
burst out. And for me, a guy like Wally, what he doesn't do or does do is less
important than that edge, that violent edge that he's forced to live on. Because
that's destructive of his personal integrity; whether or not he strikes out and
hurts someone else, he is already a victim, he has already lost. But he's not
totally lost, because he's tough and he does have a friend that he cares about,
he cares about this Reuben, and he's smart enough to know that he's missing
something. He's smart enough to know that, if he lets himself become a kind
of an educated Bigger Thomas, that he's sort of cooperating in the final act
of his own destruction, and so there is part of him that is resisting that. He
doesn't want to give his enemy that satisfaction. Those are some things I
think about him. Reuben sees possibility in him; in fact, Reuben likes him,
has a kind of affection for him, and in fact he turns to Wally when he's in
trouble.

Coleman: And Wally does come to his assistance. This relates, I think, to
something that I was talking about earlier and maybe the answer to this is
obvious. I'm not sure. The writers in *Hiding Place* and *Damballah,* the characters who are writers, and there's a number in *Damballah,* often have your
first name, John, and are part of a fictional family that is, I think, derived
from your own family. Is there a particular significance to that, or is the
answer to that obvious?

Wideman: Well, it's a kind of personal game that I play—sometimes. I
use actual names of people, but they are not based on people who hold those
names. And I thought it's kind of fun for people to see their names in print.
And also, you know we've had a lot of problems with names in this country
and being noticed as people, as individuals, and being on the record, and
being part of history, being part of what counts. And so John French's name
now is out there. He's on the record. Sometimes John French is like my
grandfather, sometimes not like my grandfather, but either way he's on the
record, and Harry Wideman is on the record. I'm on the record. But anybody
who would try to make one-to-one correspondences, or think that the stories
reflect the biographies of the people who hold the names would just get in a

mire, and that's also kind of delightful to me. Because it's like a minefield, it's like a trap, because the further you go to try to connect the names to actual people, the more confusing it will be. Eventually you just come right back in a circle. But you see the family—my intimate, my personal family—could look at the names and play games and could identify to a certain degree. So there is a kind of a key, but even the key is not consistent. That is, they will see in Aunt May some things about the actual Aunt May. But then in the next paragraph there will be something that is really about Aunt Rachel, or Becky, or somebody else. So somebody in the family can have fun with it, because they can say, "Oh, yeah, I remember when May did that," but the whole character is not May.

Coleman: So you have to be careful in going too far and making too much out of one-to-one correspondences.

Wideman: Right. Even among books. You know I never sat down, for instance, and tried to figure out if Brother Small and Brother Tate, if I really wanted them to be the same person—you know, if the dates worked out and every other thing worked out—yes and no. It's a kind of shifting spirit . . . , so you couldn't take these books and find an orderly scheme of relationships and dates and time and correspondences, I don't think. I'm sure you couldn't.

Coleman: It seems to me that there is similarity and consistency, but if you try to structure it too tightly, then it will get out of hand. You really can't do that.

Wideman: Well, they are stories, and as the Igbos say, all stories are true. And my own sense of identity, or the sense of identity which I am evolving as I write books, has a lot to do with the . . . what is fragmentary, what is discontinuous, more and more so. So that my whole way of looking at human beings and lives is changing all the time. I probably believe more than most people that the notion of a stable, underpinning personality is itself a fiction. That people have different stages and go through different personas and they are really drastically, drastically different in the sense that you could talk about one person's life as many lives.

Coleman: In *Reuben* your setting is still Homewood, but you mention only a few of the Homewood characters you dealt with in previous books. Are you getting ready to move away from the Homewood material to deal with different material?

Wideman: Well, the next book is about Philadelphia, but you can get the boy out of the country, but you can't get the country out of the boy. No matter what I write about it will be through the eyes of someone who grew up in a place like Homewood, and so there will always be connections.

Coleman: You once said that improvisation, what you called "writing on the edge," was very important to you. It seems to me that you have taken this kind of writing to new heights in *Reuben*. Would you say that's true?

Wideman: I don't think that you can write a very meaningful book about a culture that's in flux, a culture that is changing all the time, and a culture which is infused with minority points of view which haven't been fully represented before—you can't write about a culture meaningfully and use the conventions and traditions of narrative fiction which have existed and grew out of attempts to describe that culture in other times and places. So that the connection between form and meaning is organic and in a book like *Reuben* if I want to tell the truth I have to invent ways of capturing. . . . I have to invent new nets for it, the old nets don't work. And so each book has to be an adventure in that sense. Each book is a redefinition of what counts and how it counts and how you can capture it.

Coleman: How would you describe the development of formal, stylistic qualities in your writing during your career? Is there a development there that you can talk about? You know critics, like me, always want to talk about development.

Wideman: I like to take chances, and one chance that I have been taking lately, and continue to take, is a chance with the texture of the narrative— letters, hymns, poems, song lyrics, thoughts, speech, time present, time past, future time, philosophic discourse, scatting, etc., etc. . . . a kind of collage . . . you find in somebody like an Eliot, but that you also find in traditional African art. In masks or dance, you have that eclectic combination. So that's one thing, that's one way I take chances. Another way is I try to invite the reader into the process of writing, into the mysteries, into the intricacies of how things are made and so, therefore, I foreground the self-consciousness of the act of writing. And try to get the reader to experience that, so that the reader is participating in the creation of the fiction. In fact I demand that and in fact scare lots of readers away, because that's not light stuff. But for me that's a funny version of call and response, my particular version of a communal work being made.

Coleman: Part of what you try to do in *Brothers and Keepers* is help your brother, Robby, but the book is also about your attempt to face yourself, your own life. Is that true?

Wideman: Well, the book had a very instrumental purpose. It was to help

Robby, help him legally, help him spiritually; but at the same time it was an attempt to help myself, because I was in a state of despair because of his situation. I . . . felt helpless and needed to try to do something about it. I also learned that a lot of space and a lot of time had come between my brother and myself, and I didn't know who he was. And of course I felt somewhat guilty about that and I thought well, hell, was there some way I might have been able to help, was there something I could have done to prevent this. Now, I still don't know the answers, but I do know now that everybody has their own life. You do the best you can. But the point of the book and the point of trying to rediscover who my brother was and have a relationship with him, all that reflected things that were going on, that were less personal. Questions I was sorting out, okay? I had separated myself in lots of ways from my family, because of my job, because of what I do. I had separated myself in lots of ways, physically and emotionally, from the larger black community, the majority of black people. And here was a situation in which my own brother was beckoning me, demanding that I pay attention, that I make some sense of that enormous gap between us. And so the book was an occasion for me to try to make sense of that, the enormous gap between myself and the place where I was born, the place where I grew up.

Coleman: Family, community . . .

Wideman: Family, community . . . I was still in touch in many ways with family and community. Important, sustaining, natural ways. Yet I had lost touch also. I don't know exactly how to say it. I tried to say it in my book, but . . . There is a whole issue of what happens when anybody, any black person in this country, gains a skill, gains an education, gains some sort of power, whether it's a doctor, lawyer, businessman. How does that individual success relate to the fact that most people are far from successful in those economic terms, and how does success perpetuate the system that is in fact oppressing so many black people? And that issue is a vexed one and needs to be looked at and so *Brothers and Keepers* is an attempt to look at that as well. Systemically what does it mean that there can be one or two of us who are allowed to filter into professions, become college teachers, become writers? What is our responsibility, to ourselves, to the ones we left behind? Do we have to leave them behind? Are there ways that we can be successful without perpetuating the class and the racial hierarchy that produced this?

Coleman: Do you have any other comments about your work?

Wideman: The trouble with talking about my work is that I become more and more self-conscious. What's involved is a process of simultaneous self-translation. A double-voiced voice. Writing is a unique act, a unique kind of process, and talk about it doesn't necessarily capture what the process is. In fact it distorts, and as much is lost as is gained. I hear what's being lost even as I speak. It's like digging myself deeper and deeper into a hole.

Coleman: I'm glad you're saying that because to some extent that lets critics off the hook. No, I'm joking; not really.

Wideman: Talking about one's work can be an interesting activity and maybe some might even say it's necessary. I certainly know that readers are interested in deciphering the magic, but in fact it's the magic that draws them. That is, you can put together all the information possible about a writer or about a book and it still won't equal the book. And the writer can talk about it forever, and it won't produce the book, nor will he or she get close to reproducing the effects that the book produced in me, in the reader. So it's almost a kind of futile effort. And then there's my personal distaste for too much talk about what I'm writing. I believe it's dangerous to think of oneself as having a career, to allow oneself to become the object of prurient or even well-intentioned curiosity. Writers shouldn't be commodities. At best, talking about one's work is a strange, uncomfortable position to be in. To trot out one's interviewing head and interviewing face becomes a kind of comic process. There is a certain level at which I am constantly suppressing laughter. Anyway, why should we try to talk art into being any less of a mystery.

Coleman: What good are critics?

Wideman: The good ones are very good. Criticism in this country, since it's such an established institution, reflects some of the worst things about the country. It tends toward *People Magazine* profiling, and it promotes an interest in the artist rather than an interest in the work. The work, if it's good, is doing serious business. Artists in their private lives often do pretty junky, tacky, trifling business. What I do or who I do it to and how I do it—these personal matters are just gossip. There's often a confusion between the person I am and what I do in my work. If the work is serious it should stand on its own. It shouldn't need the prop of a personality behind it. Another side of this cult of personality is that it perpetuates our confusion about race. The author's race or sex determines the kind of critical commentary that appears about his or her work. This stupidity is institutionalized in traditional literary studies. If we didn't have pictures of writers, would critics discuss books on the basis of what's in them? Furthermore, there is a tie between criticism and the academy that is somewhat unhealthy or very unhealthy at times. Academic critics sponsor reputations and the more information there is, then the more attractive you are to a certain kind of unimaginative, fact-collecting critic. Then more begets more. Gossip mongering, personality contests trivialize art, and it will inevitably go that way if critics pander to the publishing industry's tendency to promote superstars and ignore art. . . . One reason I am sitting and talking with you the way I am is because writing by Afro-Americans remains a stepchild, and Afro-American critics, if given a chance, may be able to do things that their fellow critics don't do. Maybe the stake that you have in literature might be a little different, and if given a chance, you may be able to express what it is. There is at least one service you can perform. You can be a link between Afro-American writing and an Afro-American readership. That's my kind of not-so-hidden agenda when I give interviews like this. Ideally, the good critics will get the writer to audiences that are looking for him or waiting for him and his work.

John Edgar Wideman
Judith Rosen / 1989

From *Publishers Weekly* (17 November 1989): 37–38. Used by permission.

John Edgar Wideman is a man who disdains labels, who refuses to allow either his life or art to be boxed in or dismissed by descriptive terms like "black writer." The problem, he says, "is that it can be a kind of backhanded compliment. Are you being ghettoized at the same time as you are being praised?"

His writing, too, refuses to be pigeonholed. He has written one work of nonfiction, *Brothers and Keepers,* which was nominated for the National Book Award; five novels, including the PEN/Faulkner Award-winning *Sent for You Yesterday;* and two collections of stories. In addition, he is a professor of English at the University of Massachusetts, Amherst, where he has taught for the past three years.

But Wideman the writer/professor is inextricable from Wideman the man dogged by a tragic past, which is ever present in his work. In *Brothers and Keepers, Hiding Place* and *Damballah* especially, he has tried to better understand the twists of fate that have made him what he is, while his brother, Robby, is serving a lifetime prison sentence.

On this beautiful fall afternoon, we have come to Wideman's newly built house on the outskirts of Amherst not to dwell on the "time capsules of his past" but to speak of his life as a writer and the publication of his newest book, *Fever,* out from Holt this month, a breathtaking collection of 12 stories written primarily over the past few years.

A tall, handsome man in his late 40s, Wideman retains the physique of the basketball star he once was. (During his undergraduate days at the University of Pennsylvania, he not only played all-Ivy basketball but also ran track.) The basketball hoop is still very much with him; materially, at the edge of the driveway of his home in western Massachusetts; metaphysically, in his stories, which frequently feature a hoop and the male camaraderie associated with team sports.

We sit in Wideman's book-lined study overlooking the woods as he talks about *Fever,* which he regards as "his first collection per se." For him, the earlier *Damballah*—reissued by Vintage last fall along with the other two volumes in the Homewood trilogy, *Sent for You Yesterday* and *Hiding Place*—is closer to a novel with its discernible beginning, middle and end.

"These stories are more miscellaneous," he explains. "The key story, the pivotal story, is 'Fever.' I see the others as refractions of the material gathered there. All the stories are about a kind of illness or trouble in the air. People aren't talking to one another or are having a difficult time talking to one another. There's misunderstanding, not only on an individual level but on a cultural level. These stories are also about ways of combating that malaise through love, through talk, through rituals that families create."

The malaise of which Wideman speaks cuts backwards and forwards into the past, into the present, because of the very ambiguity of time, of history, of fact. ("I never know if I'm writing fiction or nonfiction," he remarks several times throughout the interview when speaking of his stories and books.) And that very ambiguity accounts for much of the bite in "Fever," which serves as a bridge to his forthcoming novel, *Philadelphia Fire,* due out from Holt in the fall of 1990.

On the one hand the plague described in "Fever" is a historical fact of colonial Philadelphia; on the other hand it provides a powerful fictional prelude to the MOVE bombing that destroyed an entire city block in 1985.

That the story should float so freely from one period to another is, for Wideman, what makes it work: "It shouldn't be tied to any historical period, because it starts in this very room. I was looking out there, out this window, when I saw the snow, and that's where the story starts."

It is no coincidence, then, that this and other stories in the collection achieve a certain timelessness. "Stories are a way of keeping people alive," says the author, "not only the ones who tell the story, but the ones who lived before. You talk about authors being immortal, but there's not only the story, there are the people inside the story who are kept alive."

Wideman thrives on the potential for experimentation in storytelling. "How does one person tell a story that is quite meaningful to that person but is really someone else's story? What does it mean for people to carry around stories in their heads, little time capsules from the past? Yet if I'm telling it to you, it's present."

Elsewhere, in *Brothers and Keepers,* he writes about the pointlessness of telling stories in strict chronological sequence, as "one thing happening first and opening the way for another and another. . . . You never know exactly when something begins. The more you delve and backtrack and think, the clearer it becomes that nothing has a discrete, independent history; people and events take shape not in orderly, chronological sequence but in relation to other forces and events, tangled skeins of necessity and interdependence and chance that after all could have produced only one result: what is."

As the interview goes on it becomes obvious that time, like race, is one of the many barriers that Wideman seeks to overcome with his art. "Stories break down our ordinary ways of conceptualizing reality. Because when we talk about what's alive and what's dead, what's past and what's future, male/female, all these dichotomies that we need in order to talk, they're not really very accurate or descriptive.

"On one level of language we do that kind of crude conceptualizing, labeling, and it's necessary. But language can break down these categories, free us. So that we suddenly realize that past and future are not different. That living and dead are kind of arbitrary categories." Switching gears, he adds with a smile, "Why can't a blind man play basketball?" referring to the central image of "Doc's Story," the first offering in *Fever*.

With this deceptively simple query, he opens a Pandora's box of questions about some of our most basic assumptions about what people can and cannot be, do or say. Wideman himself has consciously attempted to break stereotypes. "If somebody told me I couldn't do something, that was often a good reason to go ahead and try to do it. And I got satisfaction out of that. On the other hand, as I get older I think I do things less because I'm oriented toward the outside, toward what somebody's thinking, than because I have some inner drive. But it often works out to the same kind of iconoclasm. Because if my goals are unusual and I accomplish them, then they'll be noticeable and will have the same effect as consciously trying to break a mold."

It's only natural that Wideman challenges the boundaries of writing. In "Fever" the narration passes back and forth from white to black, male to female, young to old. The rhythms beneath the prose also evoke a sense of flexibility, infused with lyrical sounds ranging from gospel singing to Rachmaninoff.

His home is filled with music as well as books. For him, "music breaks down the racial criteria by which we judge so much that goes on in our culture."

Wideman's prose seems to sing with cadences, too, especially those more typically found in oral storytelling traditions, a fact that he explains by describing his writing process. First come the many hours of thinking. ("I give myself space to imagine. I work really hard to get childlike, to get innocent.")

Next he writes everything out longhand with his trusty Bic pen, then reads it aloud to Judy, his wife of 24 years, who not only types his work (the computer is kept in her study upstairs) but acts as his editor. "There's almost an umbilical relationship between Judy and me. She's always typed what I write and put it in an objective form. I'm very dependent on her willingness to go through that process with me. It's a real luxury to have that kind of closeness."

But a literary confidante is not his only luxury. Some would say that his career has been charmed. Unlike most would-be authors, he earned the attention of a distinguished editor, Hiram Haydn, before he even penned the first word of his first book. This happened in 1963 when he and another college graduate on the West Coast became the first blacks in 60 years to be awarded Rhodes scholarships. In newspaper interviews, Wideman was asked what he wanted to do with his life and responded: to be a writer.

Haydn's son spotted one of those news stories and said to his father, who was then editor of the *American Scholar* and an editor at Random House, " 'You always say that you want to help young writers. Why don't you help him?' So he sent me a letter." Wideman recalls, "The first time I had 30 pages, I sent something off to him." From those pages came Wideman's first book, *A Glance Away,* which was published in 1967 when he was just 26 years old. *Hurry Home* and *The Lynchers* followed soon afterward.

Wideman believes that such fortune is unlikely to strike today. "Now it's real tough to get published and to publish well. We're in a superstar syndrome just like in the movies. A book is either a big book or no book at all."

In Wideman's case it took an eight-year hiatus and the release of *Brothers and Keepers* (his first book with Holt) for him to achieve the type of media attention that sells books in a big way. Although that book was featured on *60 Minutes,* the three novels that he wrote in the early 1980s following Robby's arrest, and which later became the Homewood trilogy, were published to little fanfare. To some extent, the disappointing reception might be attributed, he believes, to the tendency of non-fiction to outsell fiction. More importantly, however, Wideman attempted to put some publishing stereotypes to rest by insisting that Avon issue the three novels as paperback originals.

"I realized that they were set in Homewood [a black ghetto of Pittsburgh, which remains his spiritual home] and that they are about black families— books nobody I knew could afford to buy. So I thought, why not go paperback? Paperback because it's cheaper, and because I had experienced the pointlessness of doing hardback novels without huge advances and just a few small printings in the beginning. Those just disappear."

Looking back, Wideman acknowledges his naïveté, yet he is also proud that those books were among the first, possibly *the* first, paperback fiction originals to be reviewed extensively in the *New York Times*. The author has nothing but praise for his agent, Andrew Wylie, who numbers Beckett and Rushdie among his clients, and who has helped steer Wideman's career over the past 10 years. Wideman considers him an editor in the Maxwell Perkins tradition, and applauds his determination to get "decent money for good writing . . . not just a polite smile."

Nonetheless, as a writer, Wideman is not content with what he perceives as business as usual. "Each book is treated as a commodity. This is particularly a problem for minority writers." He would like to see a new approach to book marketing that would look at who in the black community buys books, rather than ignoring that audience because conventional wisdom dictates that black people don't buy books.

But despite the statistics and the odds against minority writers—or perhaps because of them—Wideman, a man who likes to compete, has managed to make his writing stand out by turning the tragic and joyful sides of life into enduring works of art.

An Interview with John Edgar Wideman

Charles H. Rowell / 1989

Reprinted by permission. Charles H. Rowell. "An Interview with John Edgar Wideman." *Callaloo* 13.1: 47–61. Copyright © 1990. The Johns Hopkins University Press.

This interview was conducted by telephone between Charlottesville, Virginia, and Amherst, Massachusetts, during the morning of Tuesday, October 17, 1989.

Rowell: John, what brought you to writing and publishing creative texts? When you were a student at the University of Pennsylvania, you were captain of the basketball team. Then later you became a Rhodes Scholar at Oxford University. How did you resist becoming a professional basketball player? In other words, what made you take the risk of becoming a creative writer?

Wideman: Well, for me, I guess, it wasn't really a risk. Writing was something I had done as long as I could remember—and I simply wanted to try it seriously, full-time. I was very obviously young and ignorant, and I thought if you wanted to do things and if they were important to you that you could do them. And so I had that kind of optimism and, I guess, in a way arrogance. But storytelling and writing have been a part of my life forever, and I have enjoyed them for a long time.

This goes back, Charles, to when I was in grade school in Homewood in Pittsburgh. There was no auditorium in the grade school that I went to, which, by the way, was the same one that my mother attended in the 1920s—the same building, same location, obviously, and probably the same pencils and paper, I think. But this school had no auditorium, and so any time there was an assembly people simply sat on the steps in the center hallway, and I found myself, on more than one occasion, being called out by teachers to talk to the entire school when we had an assembly, when we had a program. Also, during homeroom I would get a chance to get up and tell stories, and that was my thing. I guess I was pretty good at it, because I could hold people's attention. I was fascinated by that. Even as a kid I recognized this as power and attention—the attention that I could get, the sense of control that I could have for a few moments, and just the whole fun of spinning out a story and making something up and, as I was making it up, engaging other people. So storytelling was a very satisfactory, personal kind of experience for me, going way back.

And then there were great storytellers in my family, and family gatherings—picnics and weddings, church socials, funerals, wakes—were occasions for other people to exercise their storytelling abilities and talents. So I had around me a kind of world, a creative world, an imaginative world, which I could draw from and which I very much wanted to participate in.

Let me bring it a little closer to the time we're talking about. By the time I had graduated from college and had gone to graduate school, I was thoroughly interested in the romantic notion of being a writer. What power the writer could have—and now I'm talking about the literate tradition—the sense of the writer as adventurer, the writer as explorer. That part of it was something that appealed to me greatly.

Rowell: Well, how do you move from the orality of the past—that is to say, storytelling—to the writing of stories? How does one make that transition? What in your studies at the University of Pennsylvania or Oxford University, or in your private reading, helped you to make the transition from the oral to the written?

Wideman: The written had been there from the beginning. I was very lucky in school. I went to school at a time when there were teachers who encouraged writing. We were required to write, and our writing was corrected, critiqued. So writing was very natural for me. I learned to do it early and, again, I enjoyed it. I also had little stories and poems published at an early age, and this wasn't because I was particularly precocious or had any sort of unusual ability, but because I did it, I worked at it, and I was in a circumstance where people responded and reinforced that kind of activity. In that sense I was quite lucky. The reading part is again something I came to early. I loved to read. I read all the books I could get my hands on. That was a way I spent an awful lot of my time.

I was very active; I played sports. But then there were times when the sports weren't available to me. When I was about 12 years old, we moved from Homewood, which was essentially a black community in Pittsburgh, to another community that was predominantly white, middle class and upper-middle class. That meant that the very lively world of the playground, which was part of my life in Homewood, had really more or less dried up. So I had a lot of time on my hands, and I couldn't always find games. And reading became something I really enjoyed. That literate world was there from adolescence and continued to be there.

Now I think that the kind of experience, the kind of movement into writing that you asked me about, I can identify clearly the moment that it happened. It was after reading, reading, reading lots of books. I guess I was about 16, 17, 18 years old, somewhere in there, the end of high school, early college. I began to feel that this book writing wasn't that complicated, and I had that feeling because a lot of what I read was trash. I mean I read Westerns, I read adolescence fantasy stories, I read the Tarzan and sci-fi stories of Edgar Rice Burroughs, things that were heavy on adventure and unusual characters. I began to see the formulas, I began to see how these things worked, what the parts were. And it was pretty easy for me to think at that time, "Well, hell, I can do that too." So I guess I learned to read between the lines and began to become fascinated with how things were made. And I thought I could do it. From that point on, I guess I wrote more and more, but certainly not on the scale of a novel. Yet I had just had a feeling that I possessed the requisite abilities to write a book.

Rowell: What do you describe as your first significant text—that is, the first following your early practice as a beginning writer? Did one of your high school teachers or college professors tell you, "Well, maybe you ought to try to get this published"? Had you been discouraged you might have gone another route. You might have been a basketball coach for the Philadelphia 76ers or the Boston Celtics. [*Laughter.*]

Wideman: Well, I guess the reinforcement occurred at the beginning. I took writing classes at the University of Pennsylvania, and I had a teacher named Christopher Davis who was very encouraging. Also, visiting creative writing teachers came to Penn. I remember Richard Eberhart. I remember Archibald MacLeish. They, to me, were people from a distant and very dreamlike world, big names—poets with a capital P, writers with a capital W. And they dropped in for their usual kind of seminars and readings. Both of these people looked at some early writing of mine and were quite encouraging. I sat down with them, and they said this is good, and this makes sense; you seem to have a talent, and you're a smart young man. That kind of symbolic pat on the back and recognition, both from the writing teacher and these visiting dignitaries, was quite important. And then my peers, people I would share the writing with . . . that always helped. When you are a young

writer, what you're looking for is the same thing everybody is looking for—
that is, approval, people to like you. You are looking for some sort of acceptance. You wear this writing as a kind of a badge or a way of introducing
yourself or a way of trying to share with people what's important and who
you are, and if folks respond positively to that, the writing becomes part of
your persona, part of who you are, what you are. And I think that happened
pretty early for me.

Rowell: You entered the literary scene in 1967 with the publication of *A
Glance Away,* your first novel. That was during the height of the Black Arts
Movement. One critic (I think it was Addison Gayle) has described the Movement as "a Northern urban phenomenon." You are Northern and urban. In
fact, you spent a great deal of your life in Pittsburgh, but you were born in
Washington, D.C. Why were you never part of the Black Arts Movement?
Hurry Home, The Lynchers, and your first novel suggest that you did not at
all subscribe to the tenets of the Black Arts Movement. Without provoking
any people out there in our age group who were the architects and the advo-
cates of the Movement, will you comment on why you and many Southern
writers like Albert Murray, or the younger Ernest Gaines, or the even younger
Alice Walker, were not really part of the Black Arts Movement? Then, too,
there were also the non-Southern Black writers like Michael Harper and Jay
Wright who were never part of the Black Arts Movement.

Wideman: Well, this is an enormously complex issue and also, at some
level, pretty simple. For one thing, I was out of the country. I was away in
another country, England. That was between 1963 and 1967, and so at a time
when I might have become intimately, physically, literally involved with the
Movement I couldn't. I read about it in the newspaper; I was a distant sort of
witness. That's part of it. The second part of it might be that I've always
been sort of a loner, and very suspicious of groups and organizations and
movements, and suspicious and not really at ease in that kind of situation.
Maybe because of an ego that's too large or maybe because of some healthy
skepticism or whatever. I won't try to figure that out. But, personally, my
sense was that I didn't—I still don't have—an affinity for groups. If something is important to me, maybe I'll talk about it to one person, or maybe I'll
talk about it to no one. I try to resolve things on a personal level, and I realize
that there're some problems there, but I'm just trying to get at, maybe, why
I was not attracted to the Black Arts Movement.

But there are many more general issues also that need to be touched on when someone asks why a person is part of the Black Arts Movement and why they're not. First of all, Alice Walker and myself . . . Albert Murray is really a generation ahead of us . . . if you look back now and ask what was produced, what came out of the sixties that remains of some significance to Afro-American literature, then I would hope that people would say that we were part of it, the Black Arts Movement. (As long as you don't put capital letters on "black arts movement.") In other words, there were many, many things happening. It was a multifaceted cultural event, this growth, this consciousness that was arising in the sixties, and the artwork that was being produced in the sixties. During the sixties, some of the activity was recognized and anointed—that is, got the publicity, got the attention—and a lot was missed. Just as the writers who are "significant" at this present moment are significant for a lot of reasons, but not necessarily because they're the best writers. So when we look back at the sixties, with the advantage of hindsight, we see a different configuration than we did then. When we're in the middle of something we always see as through a glass darkly. We mistook, during the sixties, a lot of attitudinizing and posturing for the real thing, for the leading edge. We confused dogma with innovation, adopted ideas that really weren't all that significant or that were only of secondary significance. And so, as we've tried with the Harlem Renaissance, we're reevaluating the sixties. That period is 20 years away from us now. We have a different picture of what went on, because we've seen what has lasted. Black Arts theorists— and we must remember there were many points of view—should not be dismissed. They deserve study and reconsideration. What was actually happening was complex, irreducible as life always is. It comes down to the individual, the individual artist, who for one reason or another has that strange combination of gifts and luck and perseverance that has made his/her work endure. The current events, ideological and aesthetic preoccupations of a given time, of the sixties for instance, are always the surface below which the significant activity occurs. Very few people understand at the time where the real action is.

It's not a simple question of repudiating certain figures and certain attitudes of the sixties. For instance, the notion that black people had to tell their own stories, that black people needed to investigate the language, that black people are on the edge of a kind of precipice and that, as a people, we might very well disappear if we didn't start to, number one, demand equality in the political sense, if we didn't begin to investigate our past, if we didn't begin to see ourselves as part of a world, a Third World—all these ideological and philosophical breakthroughs were crucial to reorienting us, and they still provide a basis for much of the thinking and the writing that is significant today. But it's one thing to make lists and programs and then write stories or paint pictures that very baldly reproduce ideas. It's another thing to struggle and refine a medium to embody ideas in an artistic way that will last. And so those of us who are still writing now, I hope, really are beneficiaries of what was going on at all levels in the sixties. I hope we've carried forward the ideas that are most significant, profound, important. I see continuities, rather than simply a break with or repudiation of the Black Arts Movement of the sixties.

Rowell: In spite of what you say in this interview, some of your readers who know you will probably say, "But John Wideman was a professor at the University of Pennsylvania. He participated in the instituting of the Black Studies programs in the University during the same period." How do you respond to that? I have been told that you had a great hand in the origination of Black Studies at the University of Pennsylvania.

Wideman: Sure, I was involved. When I came back to the United States, I was stunned in lots of ways, and swept up in the currents of the time, and needed to reorient myself. I understood very quickly that I was in a unique position. For one thing, I could get a job at any Ivy League university. How many black people were in that position at that time? Given that unique opportunity, I felt the responsibility to try to do something with it.

At that time also I began to sabotage my "classical" education (you can substitute "European" for "classical"). I began to broaden the base of my knowledge and understanding and read black writers, and Third World writers, and became aware of the Caribbean and aware of Africa and aware that there were entirely new ways to look at the history of the West. Reinterpretations of world history and culture provided terms I needed to reinterpret my own individual, personal Afro-American past. And in the midst of all this there were the day-to-day responsibilities of being at a school like the University of Pennsylvania. Of course I felt privileged to have a job there and lucky to be in a position to partake of the bounty, but then again a destructive kind of guilt came along with the goodies. I was a black face in a white sea, so I wanted to help transform the University; I wanted to help try to raise its consciousness as I was raising my own.

To some degree I had success starting Afro-American studies at Penn. I learned that W. E. B. DuBois had attempted the same thing about 60 years earlier, and that was an inspiration. I worked in all areas, from recruitment of black students, graduate and undergraduate, to setting up an Afro-American studies curriculum and recruiting Afro-American faculty. It was a busy time. In fact, it was so busy, demanding, and frustrating that one of the reasons I left Philadelphia and left the University of Pennsylvania was because it became clear to me that there was so much work to be done and I could spend all my time doing it, and it would be very satisfying and possibly significant, but I also knew that I had a need and desire to write and there just was not time for everything. So I very consciously made a choice that I would have to withdraw at some point from the front-line work, and try to pursue what I thought might be another way of contributing to the cause with whatever talent I had for writing.

Rowell: Did any of the activity you engaged in prepare you for, assist you in, your second stage (or could one call it your new stage?) of writing after you moved to Wyoming?

Wideman: Oh absolutely, there are scenes in novels, scenes in stories, that are drawn directly from that experience. What I was doing on one level, Charles, was reorienting myself to my life up to that moment. Rethinking, reseeing things, becoming conscious, becoming aware how the person I was, partly and maybe in too large a degree, had been molded and structured by the college education I had received. How I had been changed, what price I had paid to become a college professor in an Ivy League institution. I wanted to stand back and measure what all that had meant, what that had cost me, what it meant in terms of this new consciousness of blackness. So therefore I stood back, took the luxury of leaving Penn and going to a totally different place, a quieter place, a place where I could get some perspective. The time at Wyoming was spent going over and over and over my life before and after the University and trying to put those two pieces back together again—the life of the black kid growing up in a predominantly black neighborhood in Pittsburgh, the life of a middle-class academic in a white world. I was trying to make sense of the conflicts, contradictions and possible resolutions.

Rowell: My next question relates, in part, to the previous one on the Black Arts Movement, but its focus is what I continue to witness as the audience's demand of or prescription for black writers in the United States. How do you respond—or do you respond at all—to readers, especially black readers in the United States, frequently demanding "critical realism" from black writers? That is to say, readers so frequently desire to have the black writer

engage, socially and politically, his or her own fiction. How do you respond
to such a demand?

Wideman: I don't respond well to anybody who tells me what to do.
Whether it's in sports or dress, and certainly not in something as personal
and intimate as literature. I listen and I try to make sense of criticism, but I
listen much better when I'm not commanded to do something, when I don't
feel pushed and shoved. So the bullyish tone and one-dimensional demands
that characterized certain critics during the sixties, if anything, made me
more sure that as a writer I was responsible to something other than somebody else's ideas of what I should write and how I should write. Especially
since I was working very hard to escape the strictures, to break out of the
mould imposed by my "classic," Europeanized education. I didn't want to
be J. Alfred Prufrock, I didn't want to be Hemingway anymore; I wanted to
strike out on my own. And so I wasn't looking for anybody to give me
another set of parameters or another path that I had to follow or another load
or burden or harness on my back. It was important that I exercise independence and find my own voice, my own prerogative, at this time.

Rowell: I'm fascinated by your expression "intimate as literature." Will
you talk about that? How is literature "intimate"? I love that phrase, "intimate as literature."

Wideman: Writing for me is an expressive activity, so it's as intimate as
my handwriting, or the way I dance, or the way I play basketball. And when
I do those things they're not simply instrumental; that is, when I write I'm
not only writing to give a message; when I play basketball I'm not doing it
simply to score points or to win. But in all those activities—and I think this
is true of Afro-American art in general—there are ways of being who I am,
and so I need to find the space to express what I am, who I am. Writing for
me is a way of opening up, a way of sharing, a way of making sense of the
world, and writing's very appeal is that it gives me a kind of hands-on way
of coping with the very difficult business of living a life. What could be more
intimate than that, what has more significance than that? Writing is like
breathing, it's like singing, it takes the whole body and mind and experience.
It's also anarchistic. I like to write because it allows me to do things my way,
to say them my way. So what if everybody else's way is different.

Rowell: I want to go back to a question I asked earlier about critics' and
general readers' demands on black writers. The case of Irving Howe on Richard Wright is one we all know about. Ralph Ellison and James Baldwin re-

sponded—each in his own way—to Howe. Some years later Albert Murray responded to James Baldwin in *The Omni-Americans*. Do you think this dialogue, or this discourse, is unfinished? Is the black writer now free to proceed to write? I admit, of course, the way I raise the question loads the case. You can tell where I come from aesthetically.

Wideman: Number one, Charles, I'm having a hard time hearing you, but for me one of the most important functions for writing—Afro-American writing, Eskimo writing, whatever—is identical with one of the most important functions of any art, and that is to be a medium of expression, a free medium of expression, a way that people can say what they want to say, do what they want to do, play in a way that they want to play. Art should be something that in many senses goes against the grain of the culture. That's one of its values, disruptive as well as integrative. It's the place where there's craziness, where there's unpredictability, where there is freedom of expression. Art should always be something that to some degree shocks and changes people and worries people and contradicts what the king says. Achebe makes the point that the writer or the artist is always the enemy of the king. Writing, art, is subversion, it turns the world on its head, it makes up things. That's its power, that's its joy. Play, illusion. Any constraints on that, any kind of rules or any allegiances that are externally imposed, have to be looked at by the artist with a lot of suspicion, a lot of skepticism. And that's the point of view where I come from. Which is not to say that an artist cannot be socially responsible, but I think the issue here is that the notion of social responsibility is really quite a wide one. The policing of that responsibility will be done or should be done by the audience. If you are on an ego trip, if you are too deeply involved in some kind of idiosyncratic masturbatory activity, well, people will eventually peek your whole card and not care about what you do. Or critics will come down on your case, etc., etc., but we can't police the activity before things are done, we can't direct art, we can't tell people what to write about, we can't ask people to follow rules. Rules are the anathema as well as the bones of art.

Rowell: Am I correct in assuming that what you have just said is part of what one might describe as your theory of art? And I don't mean to make it so tight as to say that you have given a manifesto for art. That is, are these some of the aesthetic imperatives you have set for yourself as a fiction writer?

Wideman: Right. In a casual way, I guess I have come to a very distinct set of ideas about writing at this point. But I think I have different ideas at different times in my life, and if you look at one of my books it probably contains an implicit theory of art, a theory of composition. As I grow older and look at the world, I see art as a gift to people, certainly a gift to the artist, though sometimes it's also a curse. Art is an area where the human personality gets to fulfill itself in a way that it doesn't in most other activities. This is not to make the artist a cult hero, or a priest, or anything like that, but simply to say that all human beings have the capacity for wonder, for play, for imagination, and that's the capacity, the faculty that modern civilization, mass civilization, is eroding, crushing, and so the artist has a crucial role. I like to think of everybody, of anybody with a healthy life, as an artist to some extent. What my grandmother did, what my aunts do, what my brothers do when they tell stories, is a form of artistic expression, a form of salvation. Life is tough, and we need the ability to dream, to make things, and that ability is epitomized by the artist. It doesn't mean that artist is sanctified, but the artist is someone with whom we can identify, who causes us to remember that there are sides to the human personality—creative, imaginative sides— that allow us to escape, transcend, remake, transform a life that is too often pretty brutal, nasty and short.

Rowell: You mention that there might be a shift if you looked back on your texts, specifically *Hurry Home* and *The Lynchers*. Do you see a shift between those texts and *Damballah* and *Sent for You Yesterday,* for example?

Wideman: Oh, I hope there are many shifts and changes, because as a writer I want to grow. But I see both continuities and shifts. All my books are about family, family relationships, and reordering and transformation of family. Also I think in all of them, one of the major subjects is writing and imagination. As I grew as a writer, I very consciously decided to change some of what I was trying to do stylistically in the earlier books. What I mean by *stylistically* is how I connected my books to what I assumed was the Great Tradition, the writers who came before. In my first three books, the ways I tried to assert continuity with tradition and my sense of tradition were quite different than my understanding of these matters in *Damballah, Hiding Place, Sent for You Yesterday.* It became clearer and clearer to me as I wrote that the tradition in which I wanted to place myself was much richer than I had first imagined. That is, for my first books, the tradition was mainly European, mainly literate. Because I was a black man and had grown up in a black community I sort of divided my books. Blackness provided the local habitation and names; the scenes, people, conversations, were largely drawn from my early experience, because that's what I knew best. But I was trying to hook that world into what I thought was something that would give those situations and people a kind of literary resonance, legitimize that world by infusing echoes of T. S. Eliot, Henry James, Faulkner, English and Continental masters. I was attempting through the use of metaphors, images and allusion, through structural parallels, to connect with what I thought of as the Great Tradition. For me, at the time, that strategy was valid, and I think some of what works in my early books validates that approach. But as I grew and learned more about writing, I found, or rediscovered I guess, that what Bessie Smith did when she sang, what Clyde McFater did, what John Coltrane did, what Ralph Ellison did, what Richard Wright did, what the anonymous slave composer and the people who spoke in the slave narratives did, what they were doing was drawing from a realm of experience, a common human inheritance, that T. S. Eliot, Faulkner, Tolstoi, and Austen were also drawing from. As a writer I didn't need to go by way of European tradition to get to what really counted, the common, shared universal core. I could take a direct route and get back to that essential mother lode of pain, love, grief, wonder, the basic human emotions that are the stuff of literature. I could get back to that mother lode through my very own mother's voice. Some people might argue, and I'd partly agree, that understanding and reading *The Waste Land,* being totally blown away by that poem as a kid, taught me how to get back to my own mother's voice. Nothing's easy, you can't skip stages. My writing is what it is because it did follow a particular circuitous path. I blundered into dead ends, made mistakes, had infatuations at one point or another, models that I imitated without really understanding what I was imitating. But that kind of trial and error and back and forth is what learning to write is all about, and that's how I visualize progress in art, not linear but circular, mysteriously wrapped up in time's mysterious unfolding. Circles. Layers. What seemed complex becomes simple, and what seems simple becomes complex.

Rowell: There is, in *Damballah,* a "letter from home." Does this phrase have anything to do with what you've just talked about?

Wideman: Well, I think very much so. "Letter from home" is a phrase from Homewood. I first heard my Aunt Geral use it, and she used it in a humorous way to refer to a watermelon. When you examine that little idiomatic phrase, it's enormously complex. It has a kind of immediate, concrete substantiality, but then it goes off in many different directions and works on many levels, and that's not even counting the levels that you can't get into writing very well, the tonal qualities produced by the speaking voice. So much is comprised in that phrase, a sense of history, a sense of play, a metaphorical conceit—you take something written, words, and change them into food, into substance. The phrase depends on in-group knowledge and understanding, it turns on its head a stereotype of black people as watermelon eaters; it asserts that even though my aunt and most of my family were born and raised in urban North, "home" was understood as the South. Then along comes a writer who picks that phrase up and puts it into a book about storytelling and letters, in a story which points out the importance of trying to connect, needing to connect through writing and any means possible to members of the family. That's just stuff that comes off the top of my head right now as giving the phrase resonance. I learned that phrases from the oral tradition could accomplish the same kinds of work as the metaphors, symbols, and allusions of twentieth-century written poetry.

Rowell: I was going to ask you a question about the use of one's private life in one's own creative writing. I know that one's private life is often important to contemporary poetry. Is it important to the contemporary fiction writer? More specifically, is your private life, your family history, important to you as a fiction writer? How does the fiction writer transform that private life in his or her texts?

Wideman: Well, my work itself is the answer to the question because I write out of who I am, and my identity and my writing identity, my life as transposed into the art that I practice, are becoming more and more of a piece. I don't make distinctions, I think that's one satisfying development; I don't make distinctions in a way that I once did. I don't think of myself as writer only when I'm sitting down in the morning at my desk in my study, scratching on a piece of paper. I use my imagination, I use what I do when I write all the time, and I feel that anything that happens to me is fair game. And more and more the subjects of the fiction are this strange interpenetration of the imagined life and the actual life and the inextricability of the two. That's what my career, if such a word is appropriate, is all about. Finding a means to live in a world and finding that art is a crucial tool for negotiating that life. This cuts in a lot of different directions; I write about the most intimate, the most personal events in my life, but the fun or the privilege of the artist is that through transformation, through the use of a medium, like language, everything becomes coded, and the reader no matter how astute or how familiar with the writer or the writer's life, can't really decode the real life from the fictional life. So that although I tell all, I can tell it the way I want to tell it. Which doesn't exactly make the private public, because I am the one who's filtering it, I am the one controlling what goes forth. I may have a problem about something, about sleep for instance, but I can transform it into something else, a story about waking, a problem about being awake, and no one would ever know what I was dealing with. Fiction/facts are what the artist creates. Good writing is always about things that are important to you, things that are scary to you, things that eat you up. But the writing is a way of not allowing those things to destroy you.

Rowell: Twice in this interview, you used the expression "a sense of play," in reference to the writing of fiction. What do you mean by "a sense of play"? There is "a sense of play" in Albert Murray's *South to a Very Old Place* and *Train Whistle Guitar.* There is "a sense of play" in Melvin Tolson's *Harlem Gallery.* What does "a sense of play" mean to you in reference to writing?

Wideman: Well, it means mostly freedom. It means freedom and it means an outlet for imagination. Maybe a metaphor, maybe a parallel. When I play basketball, it's important to win and score points, but how I score, the personal expression that I can accomplish while scoring the points or while winning the game are, in a way, just as important. No matter what job I'm attempting to accomplish, I need that playful perspective which lets me know that, okay, it's a job, and I'm trying to do it, but hell, who is going to know about this job in a 100 years, and if I get my nose too close to the grindstone doing the job then what's the point of it? It's all pretty arbitrary. Job or no job. I mean from someone else's point of view it may not even be a job, so don't get totally absorbed, don't get totally task-oriented, don't become the task in a sense that it buries your personality, buries your individuality; let something shine forth, let something come through. That side, that playful side, the side that says yes, I'm doing this but I'm also a little boy, maybe I'd rather be someplace else and yes I have to cross the *t*'s and dot the *i*'s but maybe every now and again I'll dot a *t* and cross an *i* and when I talk to you in the writing I want to remind you that this is not some sort of sacred act, it's also a silly act; if it's sacred, it's also very profane. I'm doing something for you, I'm also trying to take something away from you. Multiple consciousness and energy, the fluid situation of freedom that multiple consciousness creates, that's what I mean by play.

Rowell: You've commented on your use of private history in the writing of *Fever* (1989), a collection of stories. In the title story of that collection and in your forthcoming novel (1990) *Philadelphia Fire*, you introduce us to "public history" as one of your sources. What does this mean for you as a writer? Is this another shift or stage in your writing career?

Wideman: It's not exactly new because I took a lynching and made a story about that. And it wasn't based on a specific lynching, but at the beginning of the book there is a litany of actual lynchings and atrocities committed against black people. But there is a difference. I think that certain public events occur and they have lots of significance, they are very important, they define powerful currents, they are events we shouldn't ignore, that we shouldn't forget, that we should try to make sense of. But at the same time because of the speed of the media and because of the activity that goes around us all the time, the accelerated push of contemporary life, we miss these events. Then there is also the very conscious censorship and infantilization and lying and distortion the media perpetrates. And there's the political reality of the social environment that we live in, where an individual life counts for less and less. We are being pushed into a communal anthill, living willy-nilly whether we like it or not. Blackness is being attacked not simply in the old ways because of difference, difference *vis-à-vis* whiteness, but just because it's different. There's no time for somebody who asks too many questions. No time for people who want to bring up the past, and reconsider the past. There's no time for people whose lives present a different agenda than the agenda that is central—the majority agenda. And so I'm looking at this kind of situation and I see things happening and I see them getting buried. *Fever* was based on an actual occurrence of yellow fever in Philadelphia, Pennsylvania in the 1790s. Like Antonin Artaud, I think that societies, in some metaphysical sense, create the diseases they need and that those diseases are metaphors for the basic problems of those societies. It's no coincidence that the yellow fever epidemic, described by many at the time as the end of the world, was allegedly brought to the Americas by slaves from the West Indies. We need to stop the wheel and look at things again, try to understand what they mean.

The events in Philadelphia in 1985, the MOVE massacre, really began in 1978 when a bunch of MOVE people were arrested and put in jail forever for allegedly killing a policeman. The concerted, ruthless campaign of a city government—ironically, a city government under the control of a black mayor—to destroy difference is one of the most important public events that

I've observed. It was particularly important because it was buried. A whole city is afflicted by amnesia. In the press it got a little play for awhile, but then it was forgotten. And I think that, maybe in the same sense that you can see the universe in a blade of grass, if we look at certain events long enough and hard enough through the lens of fiction, maybe we can learn more of what we need to know. If we don't try, if we don't fight for the little light there is, then we're going to suffer. In "Fever" and the stories that go with it, and in *Philadelphia Fire,* I'm trying to make myself stop, look, listen, and think about what's happening to us.

Rowell: You have referred to *Damballah* as a novel. I've always thought of it as a coherent collection of interrelated short stories. *Fever,* of course, is a collection of short stories in the traditional sense of a collection. Is that correct?

Wideman: I sort of thought that too, Charles, but I'm not so sure now. Because a lot of the stories were reworked and reorganized for the volume, and over half were new. And it doesn't have the kind of organic unity that *Damballah* had. But I'd like to think that the stories have unity in this sense. There's something really rotten in the state of Denmark. Something's really screwed. And the stories are ways of coping with the malaise which is in the air. "Fever," which is the final story in the book, attempts to render that essence, that unnameable uneasiness, that quality of decay or threat or collective anguish that permeates many of the other stories. Many of the other stories are about trouble, either people who are in trouble or who've fallen, and people who are working very hard to keep themselves from falling. And so the idea of the book, of the collection, is that this fever is amongst us still. This fever is something that we are subject to. Its ravages are still among us. So watch out folks. The final story in the book attempts to bridge, to synthesize past, present, and future sources of this fever, which to me clearly is the unresolved question of slavery, the unresolved question of racism, the unresolved question of majority rule that leads to majority domination and oppression.

Rowell: You are not only a fiction writer and an essayist. You are also an excellent literary critic. Do you see the literary critic or literary theorist as having specific functions or roles? If so, is that reflected in your own writing of criticism?

Wideman: I still think in the old-fashioned sense that the best criticism is a kind of handmaiden to the arts. Good critics through precept and example remind people that writing is fun, that writing is enjoyable, that writing has a serious side, a constructive side, that if you put work into it, it rewards that work. I think of critics also as a sort of conscience, as well as tour guides. Criticism can be a creative activity in which the critic dreams, the critic plays, the critic experiences a work of art and comes back changed or thoughtful or angry. Those emotions are a kind of evidence or witness to the power of fiction. And I think the best criticism makes us remember what it's like to have a powerful experience with this made-up stuff, this imaginary stuff. And so there's an organic relationship between good writing and good criticism. Too often that meeting doesn't occur. So we keep trying. We should keep trying.

Rowell: I shall never forget seeing a photograph of you in an issue of *Sports Illustrated,* where you were standing before a chalkboard. On that board, you had written statements about Albert Murray. You've also written literary criticism about his work. You've also written about Zora Neale Hurston, about Charles Chesnutt, and about Gayle Jones. These writers are Southerners. Do you find something in them, artistically, in a positive way, that you don't find in other African-American writers? I'm thinking now about your interest in voice, in an article you wrote for the *American Poetry Review.* Voice, of course, is of primary importance in the elegant writing in *Damballah,* and in the texts which follow it.

Wideman: I think there is such a thing as a core to Afro-American culture. There is a core culture. And part of it can be identified. And you can have fun talking about what you think the core is, but there is definitely one there. We'll never be able to define it once and for all, because then we'll probably start slipping into ideology rather than description. But there is a core and it has to do with the South. It has to do with the locus of that "letter from home" phrase you mentioned before. There was an understanding in me of Southern culture although I never ventured further south than Ohio until I was about 20 years old. As a kid I didn't know I was a carrier of Southern culture in Pittsburgh. My parents were not born in the South. You would have to go all the way back to my grandfathers, both of whom were born in the South. But indirect exposure to that core culture generated by the African background is enough to stamp us. It's what we all share. Knowing the deep structures of African-American culture can tell you more about people than knowing the part of the country that they come from.

Rowell: Your work obviously indicates that you have studied different literary traditions. In fact, you talked about those traditions earlier in this interview. In terms of what you have set for yourself as a writer, as an artist. How do you view yourself in relation to other American writers, specifically African-American and European-American writers?

Wideman: I like the idea of a writing community. And I'd like to feel myself a part of one. I'd like to feel that we are all in the same ballgame. I like that sense of respect, mutual respect, that you get when you go to the playground. When you go to the playground to play basketball there are no referees. And the game can't be played unless there is a certain degree of mutual respect and understanding about the rules. And I think it would be wonderful if we had that kind of community and that kind of mutual respect and understanding in this country, rather than cutthroat, commercialized competition and competitiveness. If the rewards were more evenly distributed, if we weren't all fighting the blockbuster syndrome, in which a piece of writing either goes to the top or gets no attention at all. If we had more good bookstores. If the literary establishment had a wider sense of what's valuable. If there weren't so many goddamned unexamined assumptions about what's good. If we taught writing and language more rationally, more humanely in schools, maybe this ideal sense of a literary heritage and a literary community would be a reality. Of course it isn't, and I guess I'm simply describing what it might be at its best and what I'd like to relate to and feel myself part of.

Rowell: Obviously European-American musicians have learned a whole lot from African-American music. You can say that they've been to school in African-American musical traditions. Do you find anything in African-American literary tradition that European-American writers can benefit from? Have you seen evidence of their using the tradition? If I wanted to load the case, I would say that, obviously, Mark Twain learned something from the slave narrative. It is obvious too that Tennessee Williams and William Faulkner were aware of the poetic beauty of African-American speech. Faulkner apparently knew the African-American folk-sermon.

Wideman: I think your examples are well-chosen. You can't really separate the strands out very easily. And what's incumbent upon critics and writers and all of us is to understand the interpenetration that's always existed from the very beginning. The tension that existed between the literate and the oral traditions is epitomized always in the black tradition. And all writers learned from that. It is no coincidence that some of the earliest appearances of Afro-American dialect or vernacular occurred in eighteenth-century American drama, that from the very beginning our fellow Americans, European-Americans, were listening to what we said and how we said it, and it entered into their artistic creations at the very moment those artistic creations began. And that's just a kind of a simplified identifiable influence. You begin there and it just proliferates. You can't scratch very deeply below the surface before you discover evidence of cross-cultural borrowing, revision, etc. All American art has these kinds of multicultural strands, these layered influences that you can identify and point to, and then if you want to go further than that, the unconscious life of the arts which of course is very important, the unconscious life any American has as part of its armature, as part of its furniture, the sense of a captive population, of oppression, of invisible people and people who were forced into a certain caste. The American imagination, in its subconscious and unconscious, is permeated by the facts of our history, the facts of our lives. So you can't talk about Americans and not talk about Afro-Americans.

Rowell: We—the *Callaloo* staff and I—are about to sponsor a symposium (November 8–11, 1989) which I'm calling "Economic Censorship and Canon Formation." In that title I'm referring to poverty and, hence, black Americans' lack of autonomy. Will you talk about the implications of this problem for black writers in the United States, and about how economic censorship has played a major role in canon formation in and outside African-American literature?

Wideman: You will have a lot to talk about in your seminar. And the problem breaks down into many, many different aspects. For instance, in my experience, as a kid, the people around me, the black people, were of crucial importance to my life. These were my folks, these were the people from whom I'd learned to walk, talk, dance, and love, and that was my world. So of course these people weren't marginal in any sense of the word. Nor were they a minority, because they were mostly the majority of people I saw. But from somebody else's point of view they were marginal, and we were a minority. And as I grew up that message was passed along to me: that my people were marginal and that I was a minority, and that we really didn't count for much. Part of the reason why that message penetrated my consciousness was because of economic conditions. It was clear that we didn't have power, we didn't have big houses, we didn't have fancy cars, and those that did were sort of criminal people, sort of outlaws, so this economic marginality reinforced my sense of the fact that we were outside the mainstream,

and for the longest time to me that meant that maybe my life was not that
important. And that maybe if you wanted to write about something important,
surely you wouldn't pick these people off here in this little quadrant, in this
little camp over here. You want to write about the big life, Europe, Sartre and
all that shit. So at the very beginning there's an invidious effect, a drastic
loss of self-worth caused by economic marginalization and class consciousness and all that. That's one answer.

And maybe at the other end is the materialism of this particular American
experiment in civilization. It's a society in which, black or white, what you
possess, what you can show, what you can pile up, is an index to how important you are and how successful you are, and that materialism pervades every
institution and every value, and it's a hell of a rock to get past, it's a hell of
a hard nut to crack. It's almost impossible for a writer, and getting more and
more difficult for any artist, to have a decent career in this country. And by
decent career I mean not making a mint, but being able to support yourself
with writing of quality. Once that impossibility happens—and it has happened, it's true today—then art begins to occupy less and less of a significant
place in the society. And for the minority writer, the effects of that kind of
economic exclusion are exacerbated because if only a few are going to be
chosen, you know damn well we are going to be a very few of those few, if
any. And if the literary society or the literary culture is going to be made up
of people who are featured in *Time* magazine and featured in *USA Today* and
who are profiled in *People* and stuff like that, then the chances for us to
penetrate these upper levels are very, very small indeed. You get the sense
among younger writers that if they don't get up to that level then they've
failed, that their ticket to the lottery didn't come up. What's lost is the notion
that art has something to do with honesty. It has something to do with self-
expression, self-respect and inner satisfaction, it has something to do with
fighting for a voice and achieving that voice and sharing it with a group of
readers who care about what you do. Those values get lost in the shuffle.

John Edgar Wideman

Rebekah Presson / 1991

The interview printed here has been prepared for publication from an unedited transcript. John Wideman was interviewed by Rebekah Presson for the weekly radio program *New Letters on the Air* which originally aired February 1991 over National Public Radio. It is published here with the permission of *New Letters* and the Curators of the University of Missouri-Kansas City.

RP: Let me ask you first about *Breaking Ice.* This is for the NPR news program called "Crossroads." Have you heard of it? It's a weekly program— it's just minority news—and they want to do a piece on this anthology that Terry McMillan edited and that you're included in, and I just wanted to ask you with reference to *Breaking Ice* how necessary you think a book like this was?

JW: It certainly was time, and it was necessary. What shows that it's necessary and demonstrates that it was necessary is the fact that nothing else like it exists. The last anthology of African American fiction is at least ten, maybe fifteen years old, and many of the voices represented in this anthology do not appear in the magazines and journals that most people interested in literature would be reading in America. The voices, to that extent, are new to the reading public. So that shows a couple of things: It shows not only the necessity of the book, but it shows the lack of responsiveness of the magazine journal community to African American voices.

RP: And in a perfect world the African American would simply be included in the regular anthologies, but they aren't—is that the way it works?

JW: I get worried about these presumptions of perfect worlds. I don't know what a perfect world would be. I think it's just politics when people talk about perfect worlds. I'd like to see an anthology that would have the best stories in America in it. That would be my criteria, and that book would come out every few years. But, how to separate best from opinion, from politics, from ideology—that one I don't know. Until we figure out that and make that kind of perfect world we have to consider that the literary community is beset by politics and beset by the same kinds of negative forces like racism that beset other institutions in the culture.

RP: This is slightly off the subject, but maybe not too far. Do you consider, then, the recent finalists for the National Book Awards to be a step in the right direction?

JW: I don't have anything to say about the National Book Awards because I'm not privy to the situation. I don't know all the books, so I don't know whether they're representative of the best that's been written in the communities they tend to represent or even if they're among the best books that were written, period. I just don't know.

RP: Well, your contribution to the *Breaking Ice* anthology is the title story from your book of stories, *Fever.* Did you choose that story, or did Ms. McMillan choose it?

JW: I chose the story. I suggested the story, but Terry certainly had the last word on that.

RP: Can you tell me why you thought that work would best represent your writing?

JW: It was a recent story, one which had come out in the past year or so and which I had written probably about two years ago. So the last work, the latest work for me is always the most fun and the most interesting. Also, it's an ambitious story. It's a story that takes lots of chances and I think an anthology—if it's going to be useful—should have stories from the edge— from the edge of a writer's career and style and pot of ideas, as well as stories and writers that people wouldn't necessarily come in contact with.

RP: That sort of anticipates what I want to ask you next. That's a pretty experimental story and you seem to continue the experimental style with *Philadelphia Fire.* Is this something you're working towards? What are you trying to do with this new experimentalism?

JW: For me, writing's always been a matter of taking chances and pushing a form, as well as pushing my own development within the form. I think that's part of the fun of writing, part of the excitement: taking chances, playing games. The other side of that is that this kind of technical and stylistic elaboration and chance taking should be wed to some vision, and that's the key. That's what separates experimental writing that is simply fun and experimental writing that's going to take the form and the medium in the society somewhere.

RP: Can you give me some idea without just saying, "Well, read the books," what your vision is?

JW: What my vision is? Twenty-five words or less? I worry about a lot of things, and I worry about them in my own peculiar voice. I think that we have a very good country—a country that's unique. But, I think we're falling, we're moving backwards in lots of ways. There's been a kind of pall on the land and, as a writer, I feel I want to describe those things that aren't working. I want to develop a voice that can talk about those matters that concern me, a voice that other people will understand and respond to.

RP: That sort of leads to a discussion of *Philadelphia Fire*. This novel is ostensibly about a man who's trying to find a boy who survived the bombing of the MOVE house, and yet it's really a story about the state of black males in America—at least that's what most people think. Is that what you think?

JW: Yes and no. I try very consciously in the book to get different points of view. To find a character who is interesting who lived at the bottom of society—somebody who actually was a street person and had to live out of garbage cans, etc. I wanted young people, old people. I wanted people who were up near the top who were involved in city politics and rode around in limousines and traveled internationally. I wanted a college person, a college teacher to be represented and, in that sense, it's a potpourri of personality types and social types. So if the reader's paying attention, the reader will get at least my idea of how these types interact and interrelate. But there's no attempt to be exhaustive. Each character was also chosen because he or she has a role in the particular story I'm telling—the story of the fire.

RP: Most of them, I guess like most fiction, show a side of the author—of John Edgar Wideman—as well. Do they not?

JW: Sure, that's always the case. The men, the women, the old ones, the young ones, black and white—sure, I made them all up. They're my children, so to speak.

RP: Your voice is represented primarily by the man who's been living in Greece and by the first person narrator in the second part. Why did you want to use both of these voices?

JW: The answer to that gets down to the heart of what the book's about. I would disagree with you a little bit in the sense that these voices are no more me than, let's say, the voice of Timbo, or the voice of the young man who survives the fire, or the voice of Margaret Jones who was a former member of my group—the group inside the book who parallels or figures the actual MOVE organization. My voice is the leader of the orchestra. My voice is the voice that pulls together all the characters within the novel, and everybody in the novel is a character. They have a role in a larger kind of context, in a larger picture. I'm offstage; I'm the person who's talking to you now and my life is in a sense part of the novel—but also very much offstage. People have a hard time understanding that.

RP: Even when you're speaking in the first person you feel like you're offstage?

JW: Yes. Well, maybe less offstage than I am at other places. But all the voices are fictional; they're voices that are made up to create certain effects within the novel, within the drama.

RP: That may explain why, even when you were speaking in the first person, I felt that the omissions were as clear as the things that you were saying. The things that you weren't saying were almost as interesting. Was that intentional?

JW: I was talking to one of my writers here at the University of Massachusetts today. I was saying to her, "a little more mystery, a little less history." That is, don't spell out everything for the reader. Don't give the biography—leave spaces. Let the reader figure things out. That's certainly a principle I bring to bear in my own writing.

RP: What do you think is the status of the African American man in the United States right now?

JW: One of them is directing our efforts in the Middle East. Another one I'm sure is right now being hauled away in the paddy wagon from some bar somewhere. The point is there is that kind of continuity, that sort of rainbow of faces, and types, and kinds. Too often when people ask that question they're really asking a lot of hidden questions. That is, they have their own idea of who the black man is and what the black experience is. Somebody who is really engaging that issue has to take in Colin Powell as well as the many brothers who're in prison or who're suffering as the oppressed at the bottom of the socio-economic ladder. So in my books—in my thinking—I try to look at the whole continuum.

RP: That's very much the story of your own life, too, isn't it? Just within your own family there's a Colin Powell and a brother who is still in prison, is he not?

JW: Yes, I have a brother in prison. But the Colin Powell—I don't know who corresponds to that.

RP: Well, I mean Rhodes scholar, PEN/Faulkner Award winning novelist, professor—that's pretty high up the ladder, I think.

JW: Yeah, but I don't have as many men as he does. I don't have as many tanks or airplanes or anything like that. Nobody's afraid of me.

RP: Oh, I wouldn't be too sure of that. Most of the reviews of *Philadelphia Fire* were really positive but, interestingly, probably the most critical one I read was from Ishmael Reed—who complained that you didn't follow through with the story about the MOVE house. Do you want to respond to that?

JW: Well, Ishmael was a little disturbed by that. So was Charles Johnson, who is a good critic and an interesting reader. But I thought they both, in this case, missed the point in the same way. With due respect, it wasn't a piece of investigative journalism about MOVE. There're lots of books that attempt to look at that organization—the history of that organization—and what happened to the people and biographies of the members. That isn't what I was after. The book is not even a fictionalized biography or history of the MOVE cult. It's a book about many things. To look at it and ask it to be something that it never purports to be—I don't think is exactly fair.

RP: If Cudjoe had found Simba [the boy who had survived the fire], what do you think he would have found?

JW: He would have found some aspect of himself. He would have found what he was looking for. That's what most of us find when we set out on some kind of quest, chase some sort of grail. We're projecting a loss or a need or an emptiness in ourselves and we're looking for it out there somewhere when, in fact, the most profitable journey is inside. We need people outside of us to trigger, to affect, and to change us—transform us. But I think Cudjoe would have found just what he was looking for and then the real fireworks would have started. Simba Munto, the survivor, would have been much more than Cudjoe bargained for. That in itself would have required Cudjoe to become a different person than the person he set out to be.

RP: Is he going to pop up later in your writing?

JW: Son of Cudjoe, or son of *Philadelphia Fire?* It all depends. Why not?

RP: I mean, since he didn't find him, it could happen.

JW: Well, he did find him. The book found him. By the end of the novel I hope Cudjoe has incorporated that part of Simba which is most important: that is, Simba's ability to survive, and his determination to do things his way.

Also, there's the consciousness that it's a very dangerous world indeed and there're lots of people who are not kindly disposed to him. He'd better learn to be a fighter; he'd better learn to create a new world because the old one was dangerous and falling down—on fire. I hope Cudjoe learned all that by the end of the novel. Also, Simba Munto, the lion-man-boy, is out there in the street. It's his voice that energizes the raps. It's his voice that's in the background of Philadelphia. It's Simba and his friends who are putting graffiti on the walls. They're the ones who might be responsible for the fire next time unless all that negative energy and anger are somehow transformed to useful purposes—purposes that are useful to them.

RP: How much of an inspiration to you in writing this book was just the idea of a fire? How much did it propel the narrative?

JW: The actual event was very traumatic and, as soon as I heard about it, as soon as I saw it on TV, I knew I'd have to write about it in one way or another. So it was central. But then, fire resides somewhere in all our consciousnesses and unconsciousnesses as a symbol of what we fear most, of what we most desire. That's a kind of immortality—the fire that consumes. But then, the phoenix rising from the ashes—it's figured in so many ways in our imagination and the unconscious collective lore. So fire just resides below the surface, just barely below the surface. Of course, because it's been used in literature so often—and I'm a teacher writing it—that's another point of access. I'm very happy that critics have made the link between *Philadelphia Fire* and James Baldwin's *The Fire Next Time*—that was important to me also.

RP: So that was something you considered in the writing?
JW: Sure.

RP: One thing that you do, both in *Fever* and in *Philadelphia Fire* that I like a lot, is to sort of juxtapose these rants with rational passages. Do you know what I mean by that?

JW: You think the rants are not rational. I think it's a different kind of logic. I think it's a way of saying the unsayable. I think rap music itself, the genre, is very clearly based in a historical reality as seen from the point of view of the people who are making the raps. Seen from another point of view they may seem to be rants. They may seem to be crazy and distorted and chaotic. But they are describing reality as perceived from their perspective.

RP: You said a minute ago that you were happy for the connection that was made between your work and James Baldwin's. When you think of yourself as a writer, do you think of yourself as a writer or do you think of yourself as an African American writer? Or both? I mean, do you think of where you fit into African American literature, or literature as a whole?

JW: Those are the distinctions that are important to other people. They're not really important to me. I see myself as an inheritor of an African American cultural tradition, and I'm very proud of that. Anybody who wants to understand my writing has to take that into account. The fact that James Baldwin wrote *The Fire Next Time,* that Charles Chesnutt wrote about a riot and a fire in Wilmington, North Carolina, and that my ancestors came from the continent of Africa—all that's important. There's also an extra-literary world that informs the writing: the voices of the people in my community, the voices of my relatives, the voices of the preachers when I grew up attending Homewood AME Zion church. And then there's a world community of writers like Chinua Achebe, and there's a world scene that includes the Third World and South Africa. As much as I have the power and the outreach, I'm operating with an awareness and a consciousness of all those strains. So, to think of myself in terms of an African American writer or an American writer plays into a rather provincial set of distinctions that cause more problems than anything else.

RP: You referred a moment ago to growing up going to the AME church. Are you much in touch with the kinds of people that you grew up with now, or are you drawing from memory when you write about them?

JW: I was in Pittsburgh and Homewood about three weeks ago and visited at least the current incarnation of Homewood AME Zion church. I saw lots of people in Pittsburgh as I always do—people that I grew up with who are a part of that community and who have never left. So I do have an immediate visceral touch that way. But the stronger touch is the touch of the spirit. Many of the people of Homewood who are most important to me are no longer alive in the ordinary sense, but they're part-and-parcel of the community in their spiritual presence. What they built, what they made with their movements and their bodies and their songs and their love—*that* I draw from, *that* is with me all the time.

RP: By "in the ordinary sense," do you mean they're physically dead, or that they have lost their spirit?

JW: No, I mean they're deceased.

RP: What are you working on now?

JW: Getting the semester over and the promotion stuff done so that I can start working on another book. That's the worst thing about having a book come out—it's a real distraction. It's a necessary evil but, boy, I haven't written a word in ages! That gets on my spirit pretty quickly.

RP: Is there a story eating at you?

JW: Well, stories I'm always writing so I've been working on some stories. But I haven't really focused on the new long work. I'm pretty sure it's going to be about South Africa.

RP: Have you gone yet?

JW: Yeah, I was there last February when Mandela was released. That was a special time and I want to catch up with that. I want to try to get some of that down on paper. I think I have a story kind of brewing around in my mind and I'll get to it.

Home: An Interview with John Edgar Wideman

Jessica Lustig / 1992

From *African American Review* 26.3 (Fall 1992): 453–57. Used by permission.

I went to Amherst, Massachusetts, on April 23, 1992, to talk with John Edgar Wideman on the UMass campus, where he teaches a graduate course in creative writing. Wideman's literary mapping and charting of Homewood's neighborhood streets and people indicate the complexities and paradoxes of contemporary American urban literature. In discussing his portraits of Homewood in *Damballah, Hiding Place, Sent for You Yesterday,* and *Reuben,* we explored the ways in which fictional, constructed landscapes can be read.

Lustig: You moved from Homewood when you were twelve, yet it's the place that you keep circling back to. I find it interesting that, despite all those years away, it's the primary place in your work, that you keep going back to it as defining *home.* Maybe you could talk a little about that.

Wideman: Okay, but let me start with a distinction. There is a neighborhood in Pittsburgh called Homewood. It was there before I was born, and probably when I'm dead it will still be called that. It's considered a number of streets, houses, population changes—people get old and die. It's a real place in that sense. Now, for many of the years between birth and about twelve, I lived in Homewood. Other times I've lived in Shadyside, which is a completely different neighborhood. That's the level of fact. The distinction I want to make is that, once I started to write, I was creating a place based partly on memories of the actual place I lived in, and partly on the exigencies or needs of the fiction I was creating. Once I began to write, to create, I felt no compunction to stay within the bounds of Homewood. Now how that fictional place relates to the actual Homewood is very problematic. And, depending on the questions you ask, that relationship will be important or irrelevant, superfluous.

If I were to tell the story of your life in my fiction, I might talk about your height, and keep you tall, but I also might make your hair dark, because I want a heroine who has dark hair. And I might know your parents well, or know just a tiny bit about them, but I could make one a sailor, and the other a college teacher, just because that's what I need in my fiction. People could then go back and say, well now, what did Wideman know about this young woman named Jessica, and how long did he know her, and how tall is she really, and what do her parents do? But all that might or might not have anything to do with the particular book in which you appear. So although I have lived in other places, the Homewood which I make in my books has continued to grow and be confident. It has its own laws of accretion and growth and reality.

Lustig: What I think is really interesting about the way this Homewood, in your books, is figured is that the post-1970 landscape has been in a lot of ways devastated. Your characters—and you, for that matter—talk about Homewood Avenue as it is now, as opposed to what it was in the '50s, or the '40s. And yet the way in which the people relate to each other makes it feel almost like a rural place, like a small town. I think that a neighborhood is an urban construct, so I'm very interested in the way that these people seem to interrelate as a small-town community.

Wideman: I go in the other direction. I think it's the people who make the neighborhood. That's the difference between learning about Homewood through my writing and learning about Homewood from sociologists. There have been interesting books written about Homewood, but the people make the place. They literally *make* it. Yes, Homewood Avenue is devastated, but when the character in "Solitary" walks down that street, she sees the street at various times in its history. So it's populated by the fish store, by five-and-tens. She remembers places that were there when she was a little girl. Characters do that all the time. They walk through the landscape which, from the point of view of some person who's either following them with a camera or looking at them from a distance, is just vacant lots, but the person in the story sees something else. What counts most is what the person inside the story sees. That's where the life proceeds; that's where Homewood has a definition.

In other places in my writing I talk about how the old people *made,* created the town. But they created it not so much with bricks and boards; a lot of them simply moved into houses where other people had lived. They created it through their sense of values and the way they treated one another, and the way they treated the place. That's *crucial* to the strength of Homewood, and it's something very basic about African American culture. Africans couldn't bring African buildings, ecology, languages wholesale, in the material sense, to the New World. But they brought the invisible dimensions of their society, of our culture, to this land. That's what you have to recognize: This world that's carried around in people's heads overlays and transcends and transforms whatever the people happen to be. So it's not anything that people in Homewood invented. To make something from nothing is almost a tradition.

Lustig: Home, what could be called territory or turf, in your books, is often shaped by streets. You know, some of your characters will sort of read a litany of streets. I know that's so in *Hiding Place*. That seems to me like the equivalent of boundaries or property lines in rural or suburban areas, like a sense of possession, or of defining your place, your landscape.

Wideman: Absolutely, and I'd take your point a step further. That litany, or *incantation,* is a way of *possessing* the turf. You name it, you claim it. There isn't that much physical description, I don't think, of Homewood. It's mostly the inner geography, and then street names as the most concrete manifestation of that geography. The street names are there, I think, because they have a magic. They have an evocative quality, and that's something that can be shared when you speak. There are streets, and when I say them to you and you walk down them, that's the opening. It's no coincidence that some of the great catalogues that occur in classical literature have to do with the names of the ships, the names of places. For sailors or voyagers or travelers, naming is a way, literally, of grounding themselves.

Lustig: Talking about streets, or a neighborhood, in connection with this whole idea of memory and memory links, and evocation, and incantation . . . what I find so striking is what you do with time, and how much of your work starts or is set in the present and then goes back, and back, and back. And a lot of time the *look* of the present is very different from that of the past, especially since urban renewal. You often refer to the effects of urban renewal as having devastated whole blocks or houses that you used to live in or live next to. I think that could be an interesting argument against urban renewal, because of the idea of memory, those memory links, the tangible memory links or the physical memory links, to the past.

Wideman: I don't know that it's so much an argument against urban renewal, because urban renewal is a big political decision, and lots of factors go into it—and some of the reasons for doing it are very good indeed. I mean, if you take that preservationist argument to its logical conclusion, then there's a good reason for keeping the slave barracks in the South behind the big house. You don't want to lock yourself into some ghettoized existence.

There's nothing essential about things; it's how people see them, how people treat them. You could have the same attachment to a shiny new house, if you really felt it was yours, if you felt you had experience in it. For instance, the house that the Tates live in in *Sent For Your Yesterday,* that's a big house, a roomy house. And there are obviously well-put-together staircases and stuff like that. It might even be a house that *had* been urban-renewed, at least remodeled, et cetera. And it's a perfectly good situation, although it's kind of haunted and scary, too.

Lustig: Well, I'm thinking more of urban renewal as it was conceived of in the late '50s and during the '60s, as it involved the razing of blocks and sometimes of entire neighborhoods.

Wideman: The impetus behind that kind of urban renewal was a simple-minded remaking of people by changing their external circumstances.

Lustig: Or slum clearance, as it was sometimes called.

Wideman: What that really was about was turning black people into white people, without a critique of what was wrong with white people, what was wrong with the world that blacks were being asked to become part of. That's the whole integration-into-a-burning-building kind of thing. That's why it didn't make any sense, and why it was devastating. Nobody asked what was important, what was valuable about the black community that shouldn't go, that should resist the bulldozers. There was just a wholesale exchange. We'll give you these external circumstances because we think they're good, because our lives are prospering. We'll plunk this down on you, and it'll become your world. When you examine it that way, then the real problems behind urban renewal become clearer.

Lustig: You say, I think it's in *Brothers and Keepers,* that your grandmother's house on Finance was your link to Homewood at the stage when that book was being written, the early '80s, and you were remembering the railroad tracks going overhead. I know this isn't a fictional work, but that image sticks out for me because it's very evocative, because I understand the sense of this place that is yours, that you're linked into through your grandmother, because I have that with two neighborhoods in Brooklyn that were home to me. I'd like to hear more about why it's Homewood, and not parts of Philadelphia, not parts of Laramie, that you write about. You've been in many places that you could write about as, figure as, home—many places in which you could absorb the stories. A lot of times it seems that your places are alive because of the stories that people tell about the places, continually, to keep them alive.

Wideman: Well, there's something simple going on here. Those elements of Philadelphia that I came to appreciate and enjoy, and the same with Laramie, I plug into Homewood. They're in there, although they're kind of disguised. If I met somebody yesterday who had some quality that I felt was fascinating, and it either reminded me of my grandfather or suddenly opened up some mystery that I had in my mind, well, I might stick that in. It's not like there's this well of Homewood experiences that I keep drawing from; it's stuff in the future that I'm also locating there. It has to happen that way, or else the work would become static, a moldy thing, nostalgic. The neighborhood, the place, is an artistic contrivance for capturing *all* kinds of experience, and it works to the degree that it is permeable, that things that happen outside Homewood continue to grow up.

Lustig: That makes sense. The idea of plugging in the different parts is an elegant way of putting the writing process, or the writerly process. But if we're talking about the neighborhood as sort of this artistic crucible for you, I'm interested in the environment that you create in your books; that is, Homewood. Am I correct in understanding that the environment forces some of your characters into situations? I read Tommy, in *Hiding Place,* as having been forced into his situation through an accumulation of circumstances.

Wideman: I think it's safer, and it's always more productive and useful, to look at the individual case. That's, again, the break in the fictional from the sociological. The play of environment versus character, versus the individual, to me is pretty meaningless when translated into the statistical terms that you use for gas molecules. You know, where and how they separate, how many will end up in this corner. That's sort of silly when you only have one life and your life pushes you in the way that it does. It's also kind of dangerous to generalize from one life. I want to examine the interplay of environment and character at the level at which it's meaningful, and that is the individual life. What part does biology play, what part does nature, as opposed to nurture, play? You can only answer that, and even then in a very tentative way, by looking at the individual life. I'm not making any case, except the case of the person.

Lustig: And so this play of the place, and the individual, is going to create different stories for each of the persons in that place?

Wideman: Exactly. I mean, it's not because Robby gave in, because something in the shape of Robby's life was the shape it was. I had other brothers; there were lots of other kids like Robby who turned out a different way.

Lustig: I understand. Let me ask you another question about *Hiding Place.* The last line of that book is, "They better make sure it doesn't happen so easy ever again." It's Mother Bess, you know, talking about Tommy's situation. I think that can be really interesting in conjunction with what you said about incantation, and litany. That line, for me, embodies what I see you doing with different memory links as stories passed between people, and between generations, because I think one of the most important things about this place that you create in this book is that it's generational. It's an established neighborhood that's generational, that continues to exist with links between generations. As a reader you wonder, what's going to happen in this place? What is happening with the new generation? I'm not asking you to say, here's what's happening, here's the news, you know, but that kind of line, coming from a representative of the older generation, not the younger one . . . as readers, can we infer that you are saying that, for these people, a memory link has got to be established, and strong, or else the nature of Homewood *will* be lost, as a place, as a home?

Wideman: I think that's fair enough, if I understand what you're saying. The learning goes in both directions: Older people teach younger people, and younger people also teach their elders. I wanted Bess's last words to reverberate. I wanted almost to make hers a kind of avenging, or a threatening, voice. The community has learned something, she has learned something, and now it's in the air, it's out there, that idea *should* be out there. And if that idea *is* out there, an idea that has a certain amount of anger, because of what's happened to this relative of hers and, knowing something about his life circumstances, the rotten deal he got, the love she has for him . . . these are things that are very powerful. They can only be allowed to fester, or be ignored, at one's peril. She's arming the community with a knowledge of itself which will hopefully open the door to a healthier future. The singer, or the storyteller, if he or she is functioning the way he or she should, traditionally, should arm, should enlighten, should tell you what's *happening,* tell you what you need to do, what your choices are. That's the stage I wanted to take Bess to, in that book—and, with her, the reader and the community. Bess inhabits the same world the little fairy who helps to burn things down in *Hiding Place* inhabits. Hers is a *blood* knowledge; it's very palpable, but it's also a world of the spirit.

Lustig: It's what you can call upon.

Wideman: Yeah.

John Edgar Wideman

Michael Silverblatt / 1993

The interview printed here has been prepared for publication from the videotape "John Edgar Wideman," *Lannan Literary Series,* No. 33, produced by the Lannan Foundation in Los Angeles, 1993. The interview was conducted on 6 April 1993 following a reading which the author gave in Los Angeles. Mr. Wideman received a Lannan Literary Award for Fiction in 1991. Used by permission.

MS: I thought I'd ask, because I read the essay in *Esquire* on the Los Angeles riots. It was an essay that had profound effect in the city. I wondered, has your writing changed in the aftermath of the Rodney King decision?

JW: I don't think it's changed one little bit. Maybe that's arrogance, but what happened last April is something I've been thinking about and experiencing in many ways before and after the event. It wasn't exactly news. And it wasn't something that I couldn't frame and contextualize and connect with the ongoing work. In fact, that's why I wrote about the uprising, because I felt that for me it was a natural extension of the kinds of things I was thinking about. The novel *The Lynchers* is about police and symbolic violence and the relationship of violence to revolution. These are not my themes—these are cultural themes, these are part of the tradition.

MS: That is one of the things that impressed me about your work. That the themes are your themes as well as the themes of the culture right now. Do you consider yourself to be an enunciator of the culture you live in?

JW: I hope not, it's a pretty awful culture. I'd probably have a sore throat or a disease. I think I swim in it, like we all do. And I think I am not the one to judge how much I'm immersed or whether I'm the vehicle or the thing itself. That's for somebody else, maybe, to look at me and say. But I feel this is, among other things, an exciting time, a perversely exciting time. Because it's so clear that what we think of as our culture, what we have thought of as our culture, is now problematic. If culture means a way of orienting a group or a society in a world so that you make sense of that world, so that the world can be passed on and be shared with a younger generation, if culture is supposed to do those jobs, then this one is not functioning very well. So it's an exciting time because I think we have, whether we like it or not, lost the controls—our hands are no longer on the controls. So the question is, who gets them? How do they get them? Is there enough of a vehicle left to even want to be in control of it? It's the younger people, those who haven't been entirely jaded or don't have too much at stake in the way things are now, who will lead the way—who will make these decisions. We've sort of dropped out. The only kinds of decisions our generation can make now, I think, are decisions about whether we leave a scorched earth or not for the young people to try to operate within.

MS: When I was reading through this book I found myself thinking *The Stories of John Edgar Wideman,* not stories *by* John Edgar Wideman. And I thought, in a certain sense these *are* the stories of John Edgar Wideman and his family and the people around him. More in a sense than many other writers, the works pooled from autobiographies and refer to processes of tape-recording and reporting that you've done. And I've wondered if you've noted a difference between autobiography, reporting, and fiction?

JW: I don't think there is much difference. I think, for instance, historians are probably novelists who haven't come out of the closet. Any reality, any creative reality depends upon a lot of arbitrary assumptions and stylizations and some frame, some ideological frame that a person imposes on their experience or what they think of as the historical experience of a country. Many people understand that much better than they have before. I learned that in some very homey ways because I wrote these about people that I grew up with, and they are a series of stories. And then, when I'd go back to Pittsburgh and get in family gatherings, weddings, and funerals, stories would be told—stories that I'd heard all my life by the generations who are older than I am. But then, in the midst of one of these recitations or narrations, I'd hear something that I knew I had written about the family—it'd suddenly appear!—either an incident or a character. And I didn't stop the person who was telling the story, but I thought, hey, this is getting interesting, isn't it? And this was particularly gratifying for me because, as a younger person listening to the older folks tell the stories, I was totally intimidated. I thought, Jesus! If I could ever have that kind of fluidity, if I could ever just sit down and make people laugh and cry and bounce up and down and have a good time the way my Aunt May could, or the way my mother can now, boy, that would be quite an accomplishment. If I could capture some of those things in my writing, I'd be a pretty good writer. And so I listened like a real novice. But then I watched the literate and the oral begin to mix and fertilize and cross-fertilize. And to tell the truth, I don't know the difference anymore. I'd code the stories or change them a little bit so I wouldn't embarrass people in the family. But then I'd forget what I changed. So there we have this great mixture. Those are the stories that are being passed on to the next generation. I think that mirrors what happens in literature at large or in society at large.

MS: I see your work as being—whether it's a memoir like *Brothers and Keepers* or something else—I see it as being part of one continuous strand, one continuous telling, a long ribbon. The stories sort of contain one another, shed light on one another, are in a certain way commentaries or responses to each other. The desire to tell something more deeply—an anecdote here, flowering into a story elsewhere. A character turning into another character in another story. I've noticed that some of your characters, like Loon Man, are two or three people combined. They shift and reveal glimpses of themselves. And I've noticed also that there's a strong shift between the sardonic parts of the novels and the more felt parts. I guess I wanted to ask you about—I don't know what to call it—cultural schizophrenia.

JW: Well, yeah. DuBois talked about double vision, African Americans having this double vision. I think that was a very suggestive and telling metaphor, only now it's time to revise it. I think having two sides—you're lucky if you only have two sides. There's been such a psychic fragmentation, and so much more input—and powerful input—from different kinds of technologies and different kinds of cultures clashing, that most of us are many, many in one. And I have a lot of superstitions, a lot of crazy things that go through my mind. Two of my fascinations are time and identity. Time and identity are these abstractions that I think you are referring to as you talk about some of the dichotomies in my work, and some of the abiding themes. The baseline for those are my interest in time and identity. And those two subjects are connected. I believe that the next real revolution in human consciousness, if we don't blow ourselves off the face of the earth, will be a readjustment of the notion of continuous personality. The idea that we are one person and we somehow have the ability to yoke all these warring impulses and hostile impulses up into one package and call it John Wideman or Michael Silverblatt, and that we have this terrible weighty obligation to make all these pieces fit into one whole. I believe that exerts a kind of supernatural force on us. It might be comparable or analogous to religion. Religion did a lot for our development from amphibians to whatever we are now. But there also is a time when human consciousness evolves a way of life without complete dependence on a supreme deity. That's a major time, a major hitch in human development. And I believe that when we get rid of this idea of continuous personality it will present the same kind of major shock wave. Because a single personality is, when you get right down to it, pretty much a kind of superstition. From that a lot of guilt follows, a lot of prejudice, gender confusion, and gender angers. If we can face up to and acknowledge and begin to use the diversity we find inside ourselves, then maybe we'll be able to start to tolerate diversity in the world outside of ourselves.

MS: These characters seem part of everyone, and that in some sense, too, it's not just that all stories are true, it's that all stories are one, that the places that go into stories and timeframes—I think in particular in these new stories, there is a piece on *Oedipus Rex* as retold in *The Gospel at Colonus*, that filters through and makes us aware that one story is a retelling of another—that we're all constantly coming back to the place we were where a tragedy occurs. In *Philadelphia Fire* there's a reworking of *The Tempest* as magic island stories. I found myself saying, yes, the place where continuity occurs is in stories. Stories are always the stories of other stories.

JW: Well, on the one hand, there are myths that are archetypes that we keep coming back to. That's part of the urge to understand who we are, and one of the vehicles by which we understand. Then there is the individual telling of the story which, I think, is just as crucial. Somehow there should be a dynamic between those two. The fact that the stories are the same story can be very deadening and very crushing. But the fact that I have the opportunity to tell it my way—that creates a little bit of space for me as a person, as an identity. We need to perform the stories. They'll inevitably be different because we bring different experiences to them. But we have to feel that we can perform the stories. We have to feel that we have a legitimate right to perform the stories. We have to feel that our versions are just as important as anybody else's because what I've learned is that, if you don't tell your own story, somebody else will tell it for you. They'll have an interest, they'll have a reason for telling it—and it won't come out quite the way you want it to come out.

MS: One of the things that moves me most in these stories is that many of them are about wording silence, or wording absence—the absent brother or a dead child or a missing child. At one point, I was blown away by a section of a story called "Back Seat" in which you put words to the silence of a relative, describing that silence and what it means. I found it to be so moving and so culturally relevant to the kind of enterprise in this fiction.

JW: All literature, I think—here goes a generalization—but all literature is about longing and loss, per se. What the writer—what any artist—does is try to make those things which probably are not accessible anymore. The whole act of reproducing something in another medium implies that what you would like to have there is missing. "Western wind, when wilt thou blow?" is an early lyric. It's a cry because somebody's not around. You want to hug somebody, but they're not there. That's kind of the beginning of the impulse to art. Substitute activity, I guess—something like that.

[Here the interviewer asks Wideman to read the passage from "Back Seat" beginning with "I once asked my grandmother Martha" and ending with the sentence "She had stripped them clean."]

MS: I think that's great and beautiful prose—overpowering. Tell me, you know at the end of something like that that you've done a good day's work, yes?

JW: Oh, there's no better feeling than to be in touch with the spirit of someone who's very important to you, someone you love. And this piece, "Back Seat," was kind of a dirge that I wrote very soon after—well, I began it when my grandmother was quite sick. I knew she didn't have much time. She was a special person for me. And there is that question of loss and absence and regret. But not really regret because I think I've learned through writing and reading that the way we look at time is rather insignificant, or rather limited. There is a dimension of time that is not linear. There is a dimension of time that is more like a sea—like a great ocean—and in that time all beings exist. You're just as likely to run into your great, great, great grandparent as you are to run into your children or the guy who lives down the street. That's the time that I think art sometimes allows us to enter. That's a capacity we have as human beings. To exercise that capacity is a real gift. That's what I feel when I can talk to my grandmother this way, or she can talk to me. We're on that plain of Great Time and it's a traditional concept. Many peoples believe in it, practice it. It comes out of West African tradition; Native American people have a sense of this Great Time. It's the West that has fractured time, has kind of tamed it and made it linear: beginning, middle, and end. Made such a great distinction between what is dead and what is alive. I think almost every great religion says nay to that simple linear pro- gression and has some set of ritual for moving people in and out of Great

Time. I think that's an important thing to recover. I've learned through the old people in my family that Great Time is where we have a sense of community and unity and being which can't be touched by oppression, by slavery. These are things and they, too, will pass. That's not a question of not staying on the barricades, or being passive and waiting for them to pass. But it's a view that we need sometimes. There is a greater arc of time than my life, your life. I think only the old people, and contact with them, can give you the strength that that Great Time provides for a single life—for this moment that any person's alive, any individual person.

MS: I fully believe that. I, too, grew up in a house with my grandmother who lived to be 102, and I think that I would not be the person I am if I were not in the presence of her memory. I think that even being in the presence of an older person when they're not speaking—when they're just thinking—if you've been with them for very long, you have some feeling for what they're thinking. And it enters you. I think it is an impossibly rich situation—it's not just beginnings, middles, and endings. I think that by losing extended families in America and American houses we lose so much of our past and so much truth.

JW: Well, one side of that is very germane to the problems that are occurring at this very moment a couple of miles from here. That link between fathers and sons, black fathers and black sons, has been mediated by the violence and the oppression that's so much a part of America. So a healthy conversation that has to go on between the generations is foreshortened, is mediated. That's not to say that there aren't plenty of fathers sitting with their sons and trying to talk to them. But there's this interference, this static. It's not only the father's voice that the son hears, it's the version of the father that the society has created: the fact that the father can't be a full citizen, the fact that the father can't as a birthright give the son full citizenship. So there is a metaphysical community and a reality that is denied by racism and oppression. Therefore, generations can't talk and the young people are floating free. That freedom is an extremely dangerous one.

MS: I wanted to ask a final question. At the beginning of your career you spoke of the influence of Joyce and Eliot, and I think that many American critics—in the absence of other standards—use collage as a way of talking about certain kinds of literary composition. They don't know how to talk about jazz or improvisation. I wondered if you'd talk about jazz and music and its influence on the way you structure your work.

JW: I can give you the two-paragraph version of that, or I guess I could just open up the books and start reading anywhere. Music: it don't mean a thing if it ain't got that swing. When I'm writing well, I want to be able to hear it. One of the things I do as I'm composing is read stuff aloud to myself and look for a kind of music, the music that I remember from my primal language. I think everybody has a primal language. By primal language, I mean the language in which you learn feeling. For some people, like myself, we're kind of bilingual. We speak a standard English, but we speak some other variety as well. It's usually that other variety that is our primal language—not because it's less sophisticated or less expressive, but because that's the language in which we learn to feel. And it's as much nonverbal as it is verbal. In other words, a mother rocking you, or the way a father walks away from you when you're a child, or the music that you hear when you're a child, or the sounds that somebody makes when they're crying or laughing—all that's part of the primal language. And that primal language is the one that, as a writer, I'm always trying to get back to. That's the one I'm trying to recover. I think the best writing comes from those who have somehow managed, whether they even consider it consciously or not, to move back and partake of that primal language of feeling. At that level language is a kind of song—a kind of heightened, sensuous, perceptible medium. I'm always trying to approximate that music in the stuff that I write.

John Edgar Wideman

Ishmael Reed / 1994

The interview printed here has been prepared for publication from an audiotape of a live event arranged and produced by *City Arts & Lectures of San Francisco,* 10 January 1994. Used by permission.

IR: I think if anyone reads your work they know that there's a poet in the work, in the novels, even in the nonfiction. How long have you been writing poetry?

JW: As long as I've been writing. But I don't write it seriously, so to speak, because I don't revise. I don't think of an audience or of trying to put things in perfect shape for publication. I play around for as long as it interests me and get it "sort of right." The fiction I try to get more than "sort of right."

IR: There are some people who say that the first draft is it. There is such a school of thought—I think possibly located in San Francisco—that says that the first draft is purer, being inspired and coming from the Muses. I would like to publish those two poems, that's why I'm asking about the poetry.

I'm very glad to be here with John Wideman. I've reviewed two of his books, *Brothers and Keepers* and *Philadelphia Fire.* I think they are extraordinary works and I think that *Philadelphia Fire* is one of the most remarkable books. I don't know if a term like "novel" can categorize it.

I want to ask you a question about the image of black men in some of the works. In *Brothers and Keepers* you say that "proving that one hasn't lost one's roots means boogie-ing, drinking wine, and chasing pussy" which I noted was the description of black male aspirations that got a former Secretary of Agriculture named Butts fired. The second part is, does the preoccupation with sex in *The Lynchers* among your working-class black male characters and a similar preoccupation with sex by your educated black male character in *Philadelphia Fire* and elsewhere convey to the white reader that black men are sex crazy—which is the stereotype about black men going back to Roman times—and are some stereotypes true?

JW: Well, the title of the last book of stories was *All Stories Are True.* A stereotype is a story so I guess it's true if I want to be consistent. The other side of that phrase is that none of them are true. It would be wonderful if every time an artist, particularly a prose writer, began a book, you could count on a kind of innocence in your readership, in your audience. But you can't. There's the burden of history. There's the burden of the language. So that becomes one of the impediments to getting said what you want to say. It makes the simplest kind of writing—from the point of view of a minority person, of an African American person—profoundly political. Because you enter into an ongoing battle, an ongoing controversy, and willy-nilly, whether you like it or not, your work is figured into that squabbling, that battle, whether you like it or not. I think it was Richard Wright who said that blacks and whites in America are engaged in a struggle over the nature of reality. How I dress tonight, the vocabulary I use on the first page of *Philadelphia Fire,* all those things are data, information that will be processed in this battle. This means that the writer has to maintain a tremendous kind of vigilance which is OK because it is a tough hustle and you should have that vigilance anyway. But it also means that you are not free in the best sense. It also means that people go looking for things in the writing as much as read it and there is where the problem is. If you bring the stereotype of a black male as a sex-hungry buck, if somewhere that resides in your consciousness—and if you are an American it can't help but be there—then there is going to be tension if, for example, I have my black character flirting in the back of a theater with his girlfriend.

IR: Why do you think that is? Why do you think there is such a fascination with black male sexuality? We see it in parts of the popular culture, politics, and criminal justice system. You remember James Baldwin's description of cops arresting black men.

JW: The pat-down.

IR: Yes, the pat-down and all that which he indicated had homoerotic overtones. How would you explain all this fascination?

JW: I'd explain it simply as self-fascination. We've always served as "body doubles" for our fellow countrymen in scenes in which they either do not want to be exposed or in which there is great risk; our bodies are substituted for theirs in the psyche, in the imagination, and sometimes in the real world. What was happening when Africa met Europe, in those earliest encounters? It was the beginning of the Renaissance, the end of the Middle Ages, and Europe was trying to sort out certain conflicts within its psyche and history. The questions of the duality of human nature, the angelic side versus the devilish side, the flesh versus the spirit, were being discussed and argued and debated. The Renaissance was a kind of attempt to salvage a certain definition of humanity, one that is harmonized and transcendent, one that has more angel than devil in it. That impetus in Renaissance art and culture was partly founded on the myth, on the illusion, that Europe's parent was classical Greece and Rome: The myth that those classical civilizations were formed by people who looked exactly like the people in Western Europe.

Among those myths and illusions that were positive were myths and illusions that were negative. The discovery of Africa was that Europe found a way to dispose of or project those sides of itself, of its character, that it didn't want to deal with. To quote myself, "Africa became a sort of rag upon which Europe cleansed its hands." Those sexual realities that Europeans couldn't accept about themselves it projected onto Africans. They included the untamable, the id, qualities that were shaking up, that were counterproductive to, this Renaissance sense that Europe was attempting to forge. Those elements got cast off onto black people. One analogy would be what is happening now as we try to find places to dump nuclear waste. This nuclear waste is, of course, a product of our technological civilization, our attempt to get better in a different sense. Back in that time the attempt to get better was a psychological business and Africans became a dumping ground for all the crap that could not be accepted. That's one way of looking at it.

IR: You said that there was a battle over different perceptions of reality. You mentioned yesterday in the [*San Francisco*] *Examiner* interview about white suburban kids adapting pseudo-urban styles. We know that some of these gangsta rappers are from middle-class homes. We have these gangsta rappers imitating a version of reality and the kids in the suburbs imitating the imitators. But this pervades the culture. You see the black style as what I'd call a shadow mainstream. You see our style on Broadway, you see our style in the movies. It pervades popular culture. Who is winning the battle?

JW: When people don't know that a battle is going on it's pretty hard to have winners. That's the problem. It's not seen as a battle. It's not seen as a competition. There's only one side. As long as this sort of ossified way of looking at culture as mainstream plus a bunch of peripheral activity in the minority cultures, as long as that is pervasive, as long as people bring that to their way of evaluating what is happening, then that's not a war, that's not a competition. So analyses are always crooked, corrupt. They don't get at the point.

IR: In *Brothers and Keepers* you discuss an encounter with a white kid who had heard of Big Bill Broonzy, the blues singer, and you hadn't heard of him. In connection with the last question, how did you feel a couple days ago when they were celebrating Elvis Presley's 59th birthday and claiming that he was the King of Rock n' Roll?

JW: I missed it. We're here sponsored by the Women's Foundation. I'm here in this part of the country mainly to watch my daughter play basketball. So I've been involved in Stanford's basketball game. I missed Elvis' big day, his coronation. I did see that for a cut rate you can go from almost anywhere in America to his hometown. So if you don't like this show, see your travel agent.

IR: In *The Lynchers* a character says, "I'm neither poor or ignorant. I'm doing all right and my children going to do a lot better than me. The Man knows we're here. And he knows we got something going. I know. Don't bother to Tom me. That's your bag. I know where I'm at. I'm not fool enough to wait for somebody to give me something. I'm going to fight and demand. But within the law."

Will self-reliance alleviate the suffering of the inner cities? And why aren't white middle classes and upper classes who receive government subsidies in the form of tax abatements criticized for receiving subsidies and entitlements and asked to practice self-reliance? Why are only black people being asked to be on their own and practice self-reliance and pull themselves up by their bootstraps? Why aren't they asking Chrysler, that big welfare queen?

JW: They *have* asked a couple of these car companies to practice self-reliance and they've fallen flat on their faces. I think self-reliance is a very suspect idea offered as a cure to anyone. Self-reliance justifies the capitalist mystique. That's the whole riff. If you succeed, if you gather a certain amount of the earth's resources or Berkeley's resources or your family's resources, then there is less for other people. That's a fact. Suppose you are able to tilt the table, to have everything roll off the end of the table into your mouth. The fact that you do it through self-reliance is not the issue. That's no better than doing it through some other means. What the issue should be is how you relate, how your self relates to other selves. Self-reliance should not be equated with self-interest.

The Civil Rights Movement epitomizes the tragedy of conflating self-reliance and self-interest. There was a spiritual side to the Movement in the sixties, but it got corrupted by the notion of self-interest. Now there couldn't have been a group of more self-reliant people than the blacks in the south who turned 360 degrees on their history, on the local oppression, on the stereotypes and the roles of blacks and whites in that part of the country who were able to integrate into their myths and into their struggle white kids from Barnard and Yale. The white kids who went down there were able to adjust to this agrarian, Africanized culture that they found there. There was just tremendous self-reliance and strength in a lot of people and that was always the core of the Movement. That was something that people could believe in. But then there was the simple notion "Why are we doing this?" "Well, we are doing this to get more, to get things." That's where the folks who were in it because it was the right thing to do and the folks who were in it simply to get more, only to improve their lives, split. That split was always there and it wasn't talked about.

IR: Are you talking about Black Power? Is that the self-interest part of it?

JW: Yes. When it surfaced, then it divided people into camps, which maybe they were in already, but it didn't give them a chance to sort it out, to see the connections. I don't agree with Stanley Crouch that Black Power per se is a villain, that the end of the Civil Rights Movement was caused by Black Power. Because Black Power was a very immediate, strategic move in the midst of that struggle, in a very complex time. Black Power is a very complex concept and I think Stanley Crouch oversimplifies it. Black Power is not the enemy. From Black Power doesn't automatically follow anti-Semitism, racism, etc. Those are historical developments that occurred in some groups after the point of the explosion of Black Power. But Black Power is not the demon.

IR: In another part of *The Lynchers* a character says to another, "You are the history they have manufactured . . . How many carbon copies of you walk the streets of this great nation? . . . You're that safe, predictable . . . [One day you'll get a glimmer] of what a clumsy, repetitious trap they've made black manhood and how eagerly, foolishly you've performed your paces." In another part, it says, "No matter how much we have incorporated these rules as our own, we know that they were forced on us by people who did not have our best interests at heart." A killer in *The Lynchers* wants to murder a woman because she is a puppet. In *Fever* people are regarded as chips in a power game. These passages imply that black self-reliance is limited by something called "they." The "they" forces program blacks and deny them free will.

JW: It's interesting to hear all these things I wrote and to hear them put in a context of some things that I'm still thinking about and some of you [in the audience] are thinking about. I know Ish is thinking about them. Many things were not as clear at the time *The Lynchers* was published—in 1973—as they have become now. In *The Lynchers* I was feeling, and I think the country was experiencing, a tremendous sense of frustration. Here I was. I had worked hard. I had managed to pull myself up by my bootstraps and attain a degree of self-reliance. I had a decent job. I had a family. I lived in a good place. I was among the privileged people. I had the world in front of me. I could do just about what I wanted to do. But at the same time I felt a tremendous void inside and a tremendous sense of guilt because those behind me, around me, hadn't seen much of a change.

This was true for a majority of people like me, for the people I grew up with. I couldn't understand that. I could understand some things about it viscerally, but I needed to really understand it. I needed to make sense of a society that would allow a person like myself to survive and achieve, but that was so determined to maintain a status quo that assured that I would be the exception, not the rule. Just thinking about that contradiction made me angry. To me the perfect metaphor which seemed to make sense was a kind of negative of that situation. Instead of seeing myself as the positive example and myself as being allowed to enter the mainstream, I turned that whole thing around and thought about the one who got lynched and what that meant to the group and how lynching and success somehow were like mirror twins and that if you looked at both of these exceptions then they gave you two different ways to see the mechanics, the systemic working of the society. Once I realized that then I was on my way. To answer your question more specifically, *The Lynchers* is a critique of self-reliance and it is a beginning of an understanding that no matter how "bad" I was, it wasn't enough. I wasn't surviving because I was smarter or tougher or better. I was surviving because of a lot of forces that I was ashamed of.

IR: In *The Lynchers* a character says that the police have made him sign confessions to crimes he hasn't committed. In *Brothers and Keepers* the Laramie, Wyoming police treat you as though you were a criminal. "No matter," you say, "that I wrote books and taught creative writing at a university." Also in *Brothers and Keepers* you say that the fact that a few twists and turns of fate landed you with the bad guys became a stark message to you about your own vulnerability. How much do you think that black crime statistics have to do with black men being railroaded by the criminal justice system and by politicians—we have one here in this state—out for votes and by the media out for ratings?

JW: I think there is a direct relationship. If you are realistic you have to admit that in a climate of racism being born black is already a crime. It has always been a crime. So it's only logical that sooner or later there will be a particular kind of punishment waiting for you. I think that it's that sense of doom, that sense of anticipation, in young people today that causes such anger and has separated them so absolutely from society, from the generation before them. That sense that you are fated to be a criminal, that you are a criminal already. I say this in total understanding and clear knowledge of the fact that maybe many of your kids, black and white and somewhere in the middle, are doing just fine, are doing well. There have been changes that have been positive. We can't speak in big generalities, but for generations in this country there have been people, mired in a class, who have always been beset by oppression and by poverty and the absolutely predictable ravages of the justice system. The justice system is set up in one sense to keep us separate, to control those parts of the population that offer a threat to property, to the status quo. Clearly that is what the justice system is all about. As long as that's the case and as long as far too many black people fall into that class, then the statistics are going to be the same. It becomes a question of which comes first, the chicken or the egg. Is it that the statistics push us into crime? Or is it the other way around? I'm arguing in a deterministic way that the statistics are self-reinforcing, the statistics are predictions that have a built-in inevitability.

IR: The FBI crime statistics have been criticized by a number of studies. For example, if a person is arrested more than once, that counts in the statistics. Another criticism is that the statistics cover 95 percent of the areas where whites live, but only 70 percent of areas where blacks live. So we don't know if that remaining 30 percent would impact on the statistics either way. We don't know if there would be a decrease or an increase, say, in the number of robberies. But according to victim surveys, which are considered to be more accurate, violence is down. Violence is down in New York—perhaps the lowest since 1936 using every index used by the FBI. Violence is down in California. Crime is down in California, according to the crime index, down 3 percent. In my town, Oakland, California, there has been a drastic reduction in crime. In East Palo Alto, which was called the Murder Capitol of the U.S., crime has gone down 86 percent. But the media represents crime differently. I watch so much television—I'm such a vidiot—that I've become a scholar of the media. That is how to turn one of your bad habits into something useful. I get articles published in the *American Journalism Review*. The media creates the perception that whites are threatened by this criminal underclass. When you look at reality, whites are probably safer now than they were ten years ago. Whites have more to fear from other whites than from blacks. Seventy percent of the violent crimes committed against whites are committed by other whites. And they don't even factor in women. I don't know why that is not a big issue. The leading cause of injury to women is battery and you don't see that covered every night on NBC and ABC. That is not considered sexy enough. Why are people so afraid of black people when they are more likely to be harmed by members of their own race? Maybe you've answered that already.

JW: I was starting to go back to what I said before, about the roots of the paradigm of race in this culture and society. I think it is better that people toss that question around in their own heads. What are you really afraid of? What is the basis of your fears? Nobody can answer that for you. These are the sorts of things that come to you when you sit down calmly enough, quietly enough, and clear some space and try to ask that question. What are you afraid of? Then if you ever get to that, then you can ask the question why. Clearly somebody has a stake in making you afraid of black people. Why is that? The answer to that seems clear. So your real fears are not the ones that you take to the polls, not the ones you use your pocketbook to try to alleviate. Because then you would perhaps upset somebody's apple cart. You might become a kind of rebel and not go along with things as they are. You probably have much more to fear from the FDA than you have to fear from all the gangstas in Oakland. I'm not going to settle for the choice of different colors of toilet paper. That's not real choice. What are the real choices in your life? What power do you have to make them? Those are the issues that maybe we should be concerned about. Take my daughter's situation. The national referees association has decided that they don't like the women wearing basketball pants that are too long or are too low on their hips. So there's a rule now. You can stop a game and make a girl go to the sidelines and pull her drawers up. Now that is the kind of stuff that we get rules about. Those are the kinds of things, the sideshows, that we spend our time on. Basketball is a great thing—healthy, breaks down gender stereotypes. Why isn't it more widely accessible in the schools? Why isn't women's basketball shown on TV? Why aren't the scores even reported? Questions that would get at the systemic problems of gender and sports aren't broached. So why are you afraid of what you are afraid of? What's controlling those fears? What stokes those fears? And who has something to gain from your false fears? That's the way I would twist that question.

IR: Orlando Patterson, in an op ed piece in the *New York Times,* criticized a recent mini-series that starred Oprah Winfrey and Maya Angelou. He said there is a tendency among the black bourgeoisie to romanticize the black underclass mother. He made that criticism because the movie, the mini-series, differed from the book because the criticisms of the mother were transferred to the father. The woman was held blameless for what happened to her and her dysfunctional family. Do such lines in your book hold underclass mothers blameless for their predicament and blame the problems of dysfunctional families on the male gender?

JW: I hope not. That's not what I think. That's not what I believe. Those are bits of drama, parts of a context in which if you read a little further or read something different you will get somebody answering that question or somebody representing another point of view. That's why the fiction is a lot different than the media because you are asked in a piece of fiction to hold in abeyance your judgment and hear all those voices. Then, given your own lights and your insights and your imagination, you are asked to try to put that stuff together. So I hope that the indictments that the women are making of the men sound true and are close to the bone and they're things I've heard and I'm recording them "from the life." But they're not to be taken straight. They're not attempts to do what an editorial does, which is more of a monologue. The novels, I hope, raise questions. That's the business of the novel, to raise questions, not to provide answers—which is funny because I'm sitting here tonight trying to provide answers. So I feel somewhat uncomfortable.

IR: In yesterday's *Examiner* an interviewer described your rage as "complex" [laughter]—as opposed to being raw, I guess, primitive.

JW: Give me the good ol' simple rage, the good ol' days, simple rage [more laughter].

IR: In your books your characters express their rage in various ways. Some of them becoming enraged at the least slight. Wally in *Reuben* becomes enraged when a stewardess offers him a pillow. In *Brothers and Keepers* you say that sudden flashes of fear, rage, and remorse could spoil a class or a party, "cause me to retreat in silence, lose whole days to gloominess and distance." When a white kid embarrasses you about your lack of knowledge about Big Bill Broonzy, a blues singer, you say, "I didn't hit him. I should have, but never did." Inside, you say in *Brothers and Keeper,* was a breeding ground for rage, hate, and dreams of vengeance. White reviewers and critics are always congratulating black writers for transcending anger. For example, when Toni Morrison received the Nobel Prize for Literature, a local newspaper critic congratulated her for going beyond the anger of James Baldwin and Richard Wright. It is fashionable nowadays for victimization-deniers to say that black male rage is an internal psychosis with no objective justification. How do you think black men should deal with rage and bitterness?

JW: Well, you should hit somebody [laughter]. And if that doesn't work, blow him away. Ice him.

IR: I mean, seriously.

JW: That's dead serious [more laughter]. Just the way you put that, Ish, was symptomatic and kind of funny, because you say that the reviewers had, in one breath, identified rage and anger in black writers. Then in the next breath they were complimenting somebody else for not having it. So basically what you have is somebody talking to himself or herself. Because there are very few reviews or critiques that really take the trouble to establish these assertions. Those are just assertions. It's just a circular monologue. I really get annoyed when people talk about rage in my fiction. You've picked out a couple of passages where I use the word myself. Rage is real. It's a very powerful human emotion. But people often ask me, "What are you angry about?" or "Why do you look so angry on your book covers?" I'm the Prince of Rage. It sells books, I guess, or it makes reviews. It's funny because on the back of one book—I think it was *The Lynchers*—the photo was taken on the roof of a building in Philadelphia. The photographer and I were on the roof. The sun was over the roof. The guy stood me so that I was looking into the sun. My mother always told me not to look into the sun with your eyes wide open. So I'm squinting when he takes the picture and I become the "rageful black writer."

You can't win. You never hear about the "rage" of George Washington and the other patriots. You never hear about Abraham Lincoln's "rage." George Washington had "reasons" for wanting to break away from the British and not pay the stamp tax and live on his plantation with his slaves. He had "reasons" for doing that. He was a patriot. He wasn't some white power rebel filled with anger. But Toussaint L'Ouverture, even Martin Luther King, bless his soul, was seen as "raging" about the condition of black people. The poor soul who shot folks on a train on Long Island. He was picked up and made to epitomize this notion of senseless rage. It's another kind of stereotype, a brand, like the "burly black brute," that is there in the culture and will be there to color somebody's perceptions—unless you work really hard to break it down, unless you work hard to change the language, to radically modify that perception.

IR: In *Fever* there is a passage which says, "No reason for niggers to be at the University if they weren't playing ball or coaching ball. At least that's what white people thought, since they thought that way, that's the way it was." You could be talking about any campus where black people are present. You have a connection with University of Massachusetts at Amherst which I call a hot campus. What are some of the pressures that you as a black male professor has had to face?

JW: Amherst actually is a pretty mellow place. It's a school into which many students from Boston feed and Boston has quarters virulently racist. That whole story has been written about. You probably know about the school desegregation problems in Boston. Some of the kids bring some of these attitudes into UMass. We also serve small town western Massachusetts communities. Some kids come into the school who really haven't seen black people who have a totally different lifestyle. They are candidates for a cultural shock, sometimes a prejudice. You have the archetypal situations. You have a small black faculty in a New England town with almost no resident black community. You have the really skewed numbers, 80-20 percent white to black representation on the campus and the numbers are even more skewed than that in certain areas. That's a peculiarly American mix that leads to all the troubles that are on the campuses across the country. I think that UMass gets bad press because we actually foreground our problems. People talk about them. People get upset. I think that's healthy. I think that's important. But when you try to confront the issues openly you get bad press. Since now we have a press that depends upon computers, every time there is another urban riot Massachusetts is stored in the memory board of the computers of all the reporters. So they punch up "trouble on campuses" and UMass comes on the screen and so they include it in their article about Podunk U. So it seems like we're always in trouble. I think we're no worse than most places and I think we're better because we talk about things.

IR: Do you find much "political correctness" on the UMass campus?

JW: It is a varied campus, but there's a very strong political correctness movement and a group of conservative faculty who make it their business to go after signs of political correctness. I still am not altogether clear about what that means. I don't think it means much of anything, in fact.

IR: The characters in your books address women in the same manner as the gangsta rappers. I could say the same about characters in my books or of any number of writers. Do you think that gangsta rap should be censored and do you think that in a society in which misogyny is widespread in popular culture, gangsta rap is being singled out and why?

JW: I think it's probably being singled out. I don't believe it should be censored. However, we have a real problem in this country because we pretend that we have a free marketplace of ideas, but in fact we don't have a free marketplace of ideas. We have a very few people who make decisions for millions of others and their standards and their ideas are forced upon us by the economic reality of the control they have over the media. When you have a situation like that, together with an educational system which does not equip people to think independently, then you have the ingredients for a disaster. You have the ingredients for contemporary American society. It is quite scary because we still hold up this myth of the educated citizen who by making choices can discriminate between the wheat and the chaff and the evil and what is correct. In fact the system runs through a kind of central bureau. It is not that the central bureau has an ideology. It is that the central bureau doesn't have an ideology. It runs simply on the basis of profit. That means chaos. There is no break. There is no break among the consumers because the consumers are either not educated enough or privileged enough to have a wide spectrum of choices presented to them either in schools or on the tube.

Who are the moguls? Who educated them? What are their qualifications? We make sure that people who drive buses go through all kinds of crazy tests and have to get stamps of approval. And yet some "blank" who decides what ten million people are going to watch on Thursday night, what do we know about that jerk? What do we require of him? I don't want a Communications Commissariat. I don't want a Commissioner of Culture. But we certainly have gone to the other extreme. Unless we begin to talk about some of these issues and talk about them not in terms of censorship, but in terms of education, in terms of the myth that there is some kind of family values operating at the center guiding us and look at the chaos directly in the face, then we are going to stay in trouble.

IR: This is the last question. There were a number of speakers at Rainbow Coalition Conference, held here last weekend to deal with black on black violence, who said that white racism—for example, widespread drug-related police corruption—has contributed to black on black violence. The media spin expressed by writers like Timothy J. McNulty of the *Chicago Tribune* summarized the Conference in the following manner: "Once the enemy was overt racism but African American political and social leaders who entered a three-day gathering Saturday turned inward, asking each other to do something about black on black violence." Do you think that overt racism is no longer a problem and that the problems that blacks encounter are traceable to self-loathing and nihilism, which is a line promoted by Cornel West, or black misogyny, the line promoted by bell hooks?

JW: I believe just the opposite. I think the paradigm operates so constantly and so consistently in this society that it has made most of us despair. The fact that we don't talk about it anymore is related to the same reason we don't talk about death and taxes. They seem inevitable. They're a given. So you accept the given and then you try to go beyond that and do something else in a sphere in which you might have some control. I consider our situation as a species of self-deception, a sticking of our head in the sand. You know what happens to your behind when you stick your head in the sand. I think that's the state we're in. We're very exposed, very vulnerable. It's not because things are better. It's because we've stopped talking. We've stopped trying even to identify who the real enemy is and what the real problems are.

Getting Under Our Skin

Patricia Smith / 1995

From *The Boston Globe* 19 January 1995. Reprinted courtesy of
The Boston Globe.

Amherst—As he negotiates the beamed den of his home here, John Edgar
Wideman is both gangly and sleek, moving like the basketball player he once
was. He is wary of interviews and grimly distrustful of the press, which
becomes evident in the way that he holds words in his mouth for long seconds
before releasing them into the air. Once he has committed to the exchange,
it's almost painful to watch him fling open and slam shut, beckon and forbid,
teasing with glimpses of himself only to snatch them back before they become revelations. His eyes build walls. His smile topples them.

Wideman has recently returned from a two-week tour to promote his critically acclaimed book *Fatheralong,* a tender exploration of fathers and sons,
a biting meditation on race, a love song to the author's own father. Even as
he celebrates a phone call from his mother informing him that the book is
No. 1 in his native Pittsburgh, he hisses about the hated book-tour regimen,
the system of "using a writer's flesh" to sell his words.

"I didn't go into this to become an entertainer. I didn't go into it to dance
around coast-to-coast and attend soirees, or to become a public speaker and
answer all kinds of asinine questions about everything from basketball sneak-
ers to single-parent homes. That's what happens—you get on talk shows and
somebody says, 'Well, here's our author, John Wideman, he wrote *Fatheralong,* it's a good book,' and the phone rings and somebody says, 'Well,
whatta you think about the Knicks?' "

Wideman laughs—an easy, inviting sound—and the wall topples. "Even
if the question is more relevant, it's usually more general stuff about blackness or about cities or about dope, whatever somebody thinks you ask a black
man."

John Edgar Wideman is not easily questioned, but the persistent can read
his lyrical, jolting prose in books such as *Philadelphia Fire, Brothers and
Keepers, Fever* or *Damballah* for answers tucked into their pages. Here is a
man who has given so much of himself in his work, celebrating and probing
the notion of family, writing of his brother and his father and his sons and

himself, shattering emotional barriers with each chapter. Yet he has retained so much. So much of his history, his screaming, is coiled in the tense body. So much of it lurks behind veiled eyes.

His brother is serving a life sentence for murder. His youngest son is serving a life sentence for murder. No easy answers. He feels the questions circling, builds another wall with his eyes.

Those familiar with the 53-year-old Wideman's work know that he often interrupts his stories—changes voice and mood and tense and rhythm—to wrangle with a personal demon. In *Fatheralong,* that demon is the specter of race. As he gingerly unfolds his father's life, there is an undercurrent of rebellion threaded through the story, a breaking with the program.

"I refuse to be victimized by race," says Wideman. His eyes harden, his hands strain toward fists. "I don't even think race exists. It's . . . a system of classification that doesn't exist. So when somebody talks to me about the black race or the yellow race, I just sort of nod or say 'Shut up,' 'cause I'm not buying it.

"I used to think black people were a different order of human being. When I was a kid I thought that being black meant I missed something, that in some ways I was on the wrong side of the fence. Other people ran and controlled the world, and the best I could do was get a little piece of it somehow. I don't believe that anymore. This country, this USA, is as much mine as anybody else's. I'm in a very different place from where I started, not only because of things I have come to intellectually, but because I feel that this is *my world.*"

Wideman does not deny that the idea of race is a potent one. It has power. It fuels other false notions. It controls human belief, human interaction.

"It's not race that has power over our lives, it's the way we are treated by people who are racists. It's not that there's no such thing as an African-American culture, people with darker skins in this country who catch hell. The notion of race itself is a bogus idea, a form of classification of human beings into more than one kind. Because of the pervasiveness of that notion—which is not a tenable notion because it can't be proved and because nobody really understands what it means—you have racism and a society built upon a myth."

There's no soapbox nearby, but Wideman's eyes have grown wide and gently crazed. His legs twitch, but he does not stand. This is a topic that he has lived with for 15 years, a ghost floating through his writing.

"You get somebody saying they want to build a school for black males and somebody else saying, 'Well, that's racist.' Both sides make perfectly good sense. So what's the problem? How do we get over that, talk about it, sort out two impulses that are contradictory, where do they come together? How do we negotiate this incredibly dangerous terrain of race? I don't know."

The man opens for a moment, then slams shut. Wideman has stumbled upon that terrain, stretched himself to move in opposite directions, temporarily lost his soul in that muddled area between black and white. Now a professor of English at UMass-Amherst, Wideman as a kid was the star student, the Peabody (Pa.) High School valedictorian, president of the senior class, captain of the basketball team. Full scholarship to the University of Pennsylvania, captain of the basketball team. Straddled the lie, roomed with white jocks, spoke the two languages. "It was like acting," he has said. His friends were long-haired dopers, well-to-do Jewish kids. Wideman sounded white, moved with their muscle. Rhodes scholar. Penn's first tenured black professor. Married a white woman. Professor of English at the University of Wyoming. *Wyoming*. Living the life. The life. Not *his* life.

"I had to spend so much energy and so much time in totally uncharted space, accommodating and making do. I even forgot sometimes where I was and who I was. I think that kind of amnesia, forced, both conscious and unconscious, is an interesting stage to explore and write about.

"Clearly, there was a lot of stuff I wanted. I'm very honest with myself about that. But I don't think I ever lost sight of where my heart belonged, which direction I would go. . . . That was part of the tension."

Wideman's rep as "a brother down with the other" was perpetuated in the award-winning book *Brothers and Keepers,* which told his story and the story of his brother Robby, imprisoned for life in a Pennsylvania penitentiary. In the writing, the author seemed to draw a stark line between his white, sanitized world of academia and Robby's whirl of drugs, petty crime and murder.

The door flings open. The wall comes down.

"You know, once upon a time in my life, I remember being fascinated to find that W.E.B. DuBois had written more than one autobiography, that there was a writing and rewriting of his life story as that life continued and the author changed. I think in *Brothers and Keepers* I oversold the idea of running away. I don't think I ever ran away from the black world in a kind of blind acceptance of something else. I made too much of a dichotomy between the white world and the black world—running from one, running toward the other. It's too simple. It's never that way. It was really more like a back and forth. Periods of immersion in one, then immersion in the other.

"But from the responses of a lot of readers, I guess what they heard—and that means, to some extent, what I wrote—was that it really was an either/or situation. Gray areas don't sell. That book continues to be thought of as the story of how one brother became a success and the other one failed. That was not my intention. I wanted my voice and my brother's voice, our lives, to come together so that you really couldn't say that one of us was successful and the other was not. There was a chord that was much more fundamental, much more interesting, much more compelling than any sociological profile we represented."

Wideman believes in storytelling as a way to preserve and rescue, to hold the family close. He sings forth ancestors and celebrates the living in a way that conquers the pain inherent in life. He believes, like Chinua Achebe, the Nigerian writer and critic, that the dead are those nobody talks about anymore and who themselves don't speak. So his stories must breathe, conjure voice.

"There's no hard and fast line between the living and the dead, and we have the power within us to imaginatively make contact. That doesn't make them alive—it makes a little bit of us dead. We break a barrier that is there for very good reasons: to protect, to save us from confusion. If you dare penetrate that, you've got to pay the price. If you invite the dead back, you don't know what they're going to say if they come, or how it's going to affect you.

"A writer has to take those chances. For me, writing isn't second nature— it's first nature, because most of the things in my life are organized around it. Of course, I'd toss all the books in a heap and throw the first match if it was a question of somebody in my family's life. But books are how I make sense of the world—and in some ways they come close to having the importance of family, because if I don't understand the world and don't move in it with any kind of confidence or grace or understanding, I'm no good to anybody anyway."

John Wideman's world is not easy to understand. It's difficult watching him try to twist it into making sense. The walls growing high, then crumbling.

In 1988, one of his two sons was convicted of first-degree murder. Touring with other residents of his grandfather's Maine summer camp, Jacob, 16 at the time, stabbed his roommate in a hotel room in Flagstaff, Ariz. The young Wideman told detectives, "It was not premeditated. It was the buildup of a lot of emotions."

The rending of Wideman's heart can be heard throughout his subsequent work. An elegant and powerful letter to Jacob ends *Fatheralong,* and *Philadelphia Fire* is interrupted by this plaintive crying out:

"Nothing is more painful than the phone ringing and finding him there at the other end of the line, except finding him not there, the sound of the phone call ending, the silence rushing in to fill the void words couldn't."

A brother gone. A son gone.

Wideman refuses to speak of Jacob directly, although the memory of his youngest is evident and pervasive. In his hands. The gently cracking voice. The slamming of his eyes.

"One of the subjects in *Philadelphia Fire* was the loss of children. But in all of my books—even if you start in 1967, when I wasn't married and had no children—there's a real concern about knitting up the generations and the loss of children, the loss of identity. It's not an obsession, exactly—but if somebody looks at the sweep of my work, I'm trying to figure out the answer to certain problems that are probably unanswerable.

"I guess it's as much about loss"—Wideman shifts uncomfortably on the plush sofa, wrings his hands—"and time"—his heart fills his chest, pounds almost audibly—"and the difficulty of holding onto things and the fear of losing them." The sun blasts through the window and cuts a clean line from his forehead, slanting toward his chin. His deep breath shudders as he searches for calmer ground. When he speaks again, he takes on an almost professorial tone.

"But for African-American people, loss is so tied up in parcel with the experience of the last 400 years. You begin with the separation of families of Africa, the transformation of families by the experience of slavery, the attempt to start up families again after slavery, after freedom, after the Great Migration. There's the disintegration, the attempts to hang onto each other and make a place for ourselves. And that tension is a very human story.

"There are so many ways parents and children can lose each other."

It's disarming, the way Wideman abruptly detaches himself, turns a personal hurt into a world lesson. His writing disturbs and unsettles in the same way. He is celebrated for the deft way that he leads us off the beaten path and into the wilderness, asks the uncomfortable questions, abandons us to struggle with the answers. His novels and memoirs are difficult undertakings, bedtime reading only if you like being rattled by your dreams.

The awards, the literary recognition, the academic and popular respect, all stem from a heady mixture of aloofness and accessibility, the exquisite way that Wideman arranges words toward a meaningful music. He has never been afraid to hurt himself. But it's not the recognition he seeks.

"You read reviews, and you read ten good ones, even those praising you to high heaven, and you sorta skim 'em. But then someone says, 'But on Page 37 . . . ,' and the whole process stops, you kinda glom onto that one. You mean I'm not perfect? You mean the book's not perfect? You mean you don't like me?

"I think the kind of writing I do means I have to be thick-skinned. I demand that readers meet me halfway, that they participate and think and open themselves up to confronting some stuff that maybe they haven't thought about before, some feelings they're not willing to own up to. To that extent, the very nature of what I do means if I'm not upsetting somebody, not getting under their skin in some way, what I'm doing is probably not working."

Wideman works his way under our skin. In his stories, we see ourselves, opening and closing, opening and closing.

The sun now sparkles across half of his face. The other half is in shadow. He sighs, squeezing all the air out of his chest. He is thinking of loss and discovery, the cycle of fathers and sons. In the evening, his daughter Jamila—an All-American basketball player at Amherst Regional High and now a star at Stanford—flies in from California. Life can be good. Life can be tough. "I know anything can happen," he says, "no matter how firmly or clearly I've sketched out a world in my head. Anything can happen."

In a 1985 *New York Times* interview, the author recounted one of the earliest lessons he learned as a child: If you look away from something, it might not be there when you look back.

So he tries it. He slams his eyes shut. But when he opens them again, the world—ugly, joyous, hurtful and healing—is still there. So John Edgar Wideman picks up his pen. And he deals with it.

John Edgar Wideman

Arnold E. Sabatelli / 1995

From *Passages North* 16.2 (Winter 1995): 43–56. Used by permission.

I leave Kalamazoo on a seasonably cool mid-March morning and head east, but before I reach Ohio, even, it's already in the upper 60s, and I slide the heater all the way into the blue. I have just finished another quarter of teaching. It is my fifth year out of graduate school, and I'm heading back to Amherst for the first time. I'm going back to the early chapter, the place that formally launched me on this whole affair, to see my former thesis advisor, John Edgar Wideman—author of twelve works of fiction and non-fiction and two-time Penn-Faulkner Award winner—back to the melodic voice I hear on the other side of a phone, now, only a handful of times a year, the voice I remember whenever I sit down across from my computer and chisel away at the novel, the stories, the poems I am always fighting to find time to write . . . back to interview him for *Passages North.*

I'm driving to work out the tensions of the quarter and to have plenty of time to figure out what I will talk about with John. I keep a tape player running on the seat beside me and speak loudly to make sure I'm heard over the rumble of tires. I've never done this before, but instead of coming up with cogent and provocative questions, I keep reminiscing—remembering reading stories aloud sitting around John's enormous fireplace, and later whacking at congas when John cranked Mongo Santamaria, those awful cramped UMass seminar rooms, John saying, "I feel as if I've given you the ball and you ran with it," after I published a story in a decent journal . . . things I haven't thought about in years. I'm realizing how strange it is that we so quickly leave our educational experiences behind us, especially when we delve head-long into academic life and the crap-shoot of trying to make it as a writer. I'm realizing that this trip back feels almost sacred, though I had never expected that.

I'm driving through the Berkshires under a full moon, going slow now because after twelve hours, I don't trust myself, and I've seen plenty of deer; it's still warm, and they know the remaining snow won't last, that things have started to change. I'm close to my old house now, in Williamsburg, where I lived for the four years I was in graduate school at UMass. I'm headed for Ashfield tonight to stay with old friends in their 100-year-old farmhouse. I pull in at the stroke of midnight, shaking, unsteady, and my friend greets me at the door. Soon I climb in under a pile of blankets. The cat, Cleo, curls between my legs and starts to purr, and I'm struck with how close I have always been to Amherst, to the life I left here, all the good people I got to know, all that I discovered in and out of class.

145

When I call him the next morning, John invites me to sit in on a graduate workshop. He thinks it will give me a more interesting angle for the interview, especially since I'm a former student. He is teaching again. Later he says, It's not enough for me to have an interesting story line or interesting character. I have a fascination with the medium itself, for better or worse.

John is thinner, older. He gives me a hug. His voice hasn't changed. His eyes haven't changed. The office hasn't changed; it is small and uncluttered, looking out toward the same 1960s concrete buildings I'd stare out at while he pored over some new addition to my thesis, waiting. Soon, class begins. John asks for a volunteer to read a few pages out loud from this week's story—a concrete starting point.

When teaching, my first rule is to try to be as concrete as possible, even though I might start out with a pretty complicated or abstract principle. Or, a very simple principle like, "what do you put in and what do you leave out" and "how can a story actually sustain tension or gain dimension from the reader's experience with this back and forth between giving and taking away, between omission and what's important to the story." Very quickly, I try to move from that abstract point to the story itself—the nuts and bolts of what's in the sentence—where the writer had a choice. . . . But until you get to the level of sentence or image, it's fairly hard to talk about writing in the abstract because everything is both right and wrong. You want to start a story with a punch, a bang. A good first line. Start right in the middle of the action; that's good advice. But it's also good advice to prepare your reader and make sure the reader has all the information that he or she needs to get into the story.

I'm in Michigan now, writing during the first really hot weather of June, having finished yet another quarter of teaching. I've got the tape, that liquid voice, and a written transcript, which at times seems so incredibly different than the audio. Everything is both right and wrong. *I contemplate these documents, these reminders of the actual event, trying to ascertain the nuts and bolts, the good first line, how to make this story ring true.*

The important thing is the dreaming of the story. If that's happening it's a blessed event because there's nothing else to consult. If you see a green sky and strange animals running around, and see the whites of their eyes, well, you begin to describe them, and that is what the process is all about. The dreaming's sort of a jump-starting or kick-starting the process. But how do you get past a point where the muse is not speaking or the voices are not speaking, and how do you get from there to the next point in the story, or is there a next point in the story? There are easy times and there are difficult times. The easy times are when the voices are present and they're present either because of some sort of luck or conjuring on your part. Sometimes the voices have to be coaxed into being; and I perform some sort of ritual to get their presence and to make them available. It's always a back and forth between those two stages—not a seamless back and forth, though. Sometimes I'm aware that the front brain is mostly responsible for the next line, or I'm putting that weight on the front brain. Other times, it's the old reptilian brain just kicking in. Sometimes it is a process of negotiation between them. Sometimes it's just a little dance they get going.

During workshop, John reads a passage he finds provocative. He likes the risk of the second-person narration. He likes the attention to detail, the genuineness of the voice. He turns to a passage where this quiet urgency is lacking, where the voice pushes too hard, where the second person draws too much attention to itself without an obvious enough pay-off. He is deeply serious, but at the same time gentle, encouraging. This is hard, important work.

In "Fever," I knew I had to have an ending that would try to pull together all the strains and all the voices that were part of it, and there were many different voices—18th-century characters, a contemporary writer sitting in the present-tense, various characters and kinds of rhetoric—and then I began to think about, well, how was I going to get the story back to Philadelphia? How was I going to tie up the MOVE situation? And then I started to hear this hospital attendant and hear him sort of bitching and moaning about working in a hospital. Of course, that connected with the nurses during the plague year, but it really was basically my brother's voice, because my brother had talked with me about working with very ill children, mainly, but also some older people in the clinic—that was one of the jobs he had—and I remember his voice. That was the key. I heard him fussing about his job, but also having tremendous compassion for the people he was working with, and I remember one story in particular about having to smoke a cigarette because the smell was so bad from some guy's dirty drawers—an incontinent person. Once I got inside that voice, once I heard my brother talking, I didn't have to think anymore about how the scene would actually connect with all the other scenes and voices in the story. It was a matter of just jumping on board. The voice was a kind of Gordian knot solution; it was the sword that cut the knot, *boom.* I stopped worrying about it.

John reads from a book review of a new novel in which the author doesn't use the letter e, *and asks what we think. The students are cautious. Is it just tricky, a gimmick, or is John suggesting there's something good, something valuable here? I remember that same feeling, wondering exactly what he thought about different stories. Once, he wrote out a short-short story on the board, a six-line story, and we realized his fascination with the intricacies of language in those few, simple words. I've never had an opportunity like this—to ask him what he thinks, how he does it, why he does it, what's in it for him. I'm scribbling down questions for the interview to follow while he teaches, subtly, about honesty in writing, about authenticity balanced with the need to take genuine risks.*

. . . It's just something I enjoy! Number one, I enjoy contemplating the medium, how subtle and complex and challenging it is to try to write narrative, and I have fun with that, and I like to read people who are challenged in the same way that I am by the medium, and, of course, I like to read books that are solving certain kinds of puzzles. I've always had interest in that very dimension—books as ways of solving problems that are thrown up by this great sea of words in language. And so, it's, to me, a very natural thing to be in the middle of a story, both concerned about the story as an artifice and the story as a challenge to this crafts-person at a work table. It seems to me quite possible to work in both levels at once; it's a challenge to work in both of those levels at once and invite the reader in to those moments that are intriguing to me because of who I am. And this take I have on writing, for me is just very natural. . . . One risk is that I'm going to get off into some things where I leave a lot of readers behind. But that just happens to be my propensity, my interest, my fascination, my bent, if you will.

This is not separate from the fact that being an African American I recognized early on in life that I have a special stake in this language all of us Americans use—because the language, for me, was always a minefield. I had to learn not only what people were saying, but also what was behind the words. I had to learn very specifically in my upbringing to deal with the great crevices and gaps and traps in the language which I would very definitely fall into if I only listened to what people were saying. There was always something that they weren't saying; there was something more that they might be saying; there were whole areas of experience which were essentially closed out for me—certain things that people would say to me, certain words they could say, certain tones they would use—so I became preternaturally aware of the multiple levels of speech and speech acts. How a person was looking at me. How loud they were speaking. . . . Any speech act contains a level of combat or war—who's running the show, and whose language is it; who's boss? That's buried in the most mundane kind of exchange, and if you're the person who can get your ass kicked as a result of making mistakes about these very subtle nuances and registers, then it behooves you to learn them quite well. The next step is to turn the language to your own needs. I realized this was serious business, and that if I was going to be successful, I had to not only learn to use more than one register of language, but to be fluent in them so that I could find my own spaces, so I could use the language and somehow personalize it, take it back.

On tape, my voice sounds balky, uneasy, though at the time I felt perfectly at ease, delighted that John would take an hour and twenty minutes after class to talk through the most intimate details of his craft with me. Listening, a professor too, though always the wide-eyed student in awe at the book-a-year pace, at the incredible range and intelligence of John's own "sea of words," I know all of this was said in other ways when I was a student proper.

I think when you wake up in the morning you begin to construct narrative; each human being begins to construct narrative. This is not a secret. Lots of other disciplines have caught on to this and have found very abstruse ways to talk about narrative as it applies to psychology, abnormal psychology, sociology. . . . Story has been as useful to many of these disciplines as computers. So, they're taking this very ancient way that people connect with one another and themselves and looking at how the process works and it provides insight into both the social and the hard sciences. So, yes, story is a primal structural device in both people's individual identities and group identities, national identities, etcetera.

One of my first insights into this was when I began to read French linguistic criticism—as much as I was able to understand of it anyway—and then the American followers. When I began to read that stuff in the late '60s, it became clear to me that much of what I was reading was also comprised in, and articulated by, the folklore conventions that I was also working with and trying to figure out—that is to say, a blues singer or a preacher in the African American tradition interrogated many of the same matters as these French estheticians and narratologists. And in my practice as a writer, I was working in many similar and parallel paths. So, it seems to me that without a doubt, a really good oral storyteller has a very comprehensive grasp of the complexity of what he or she is doing. It's experiential. We internalize at a very early age rules of language in order to make sentences, and it would seem to me that if you try to make more and more complex kinds of objects—a word being the simplest—and move up to phrase, and move up to sentence, then move up to paragraph and move up to something as complex as a whole story, well, then you're internalizing other kinds of rules. I think it's only natural that when you internalize these rules some of them become part of your conscious repertoire, so you're also learning to manipulate and play with them and be silly about them—in the same way that the jazz musician interrogates traditional, conventional music.

Immediately after the interview, I play the tape back. My questions seem insignificant next to the responses. Before I leave, I say, "God, that was great, tremendous," and John says, "Well, it's not always that easy to talk about these things. It was easy to talk with you because we have that history and fondness," and I'm still riding that flattery and jolt of energy right up to this moment, trying to compile all this, somehow, wanting to express the whole spectrum of responses, of all these present tenses colliding in the concurrently static and fluid moment of the writing. . . . Are themes emerging? Complicate; never accept easy or "bi-polar" answers. The writer illuminates the complexity, then goes about solving the problem in the only way possible, through the experience of the story, the craft, the art.

There is no single African American experience. Some are born with a silver spoon in their mouths and their problem is to get it out; others have nothing, and the problem is to fill their mouths. In my work I'm saying that writing, any art, has something to do with the culture, and given certain formations of African American culture, yes, key issues—oppression, poverty, violence, for instance—are foregrounded whether you like it or not. But there is always more to a group than its sociological profile. More than what you see from outside. Language is a terrain or field of combat where identity and high-stakes stuff are at risk in the most ordinary exchanges. Think of

Russian peasants speaking to the nobility, all kinds of Patois and Creoles where you have colonized people and an imperialist government. Think about language and class in America. Certainly people are now full speed into investigating language and gender. So, it becomes respectable to talk about a woman's language or poor peoples' language. After all, each of us and all of us are born and have to learn a language. That's a very vexed proposition, because you are not simply learning a neutral language. You're learning certain forms of submission and dominance, and you're learning what the world thinks of you. And as you get to be a more skillful speaker of the language, then it's starting to learn things about you, and it will start to judge you and put you in certain places. So, for any individual, the language is this big, whale-mother-sea that you have to learn to swim in. The answer for some people is that they don't speak at all. In other words, they are suspicious of the language. Others become aficionados of it. "Race" highlights and focuses these issues. If you are African American, you have not only the natural dependency of being young and stupid and starting out in life, but you must deal with structural and social formations that are intended to keep you in a certain place and to forbid you to move beyond your given status.

In class, most students come down against the novel without the letter e. *It draws too much attention to itself, too silly. I suspect John doesn't fully agree, but I know he won't just tell them what he thinks. He pushes them, says, "But the first time a caveman pointed at something and gave it a name, that must have seemed pretty silly." Later, I ask, "Can writers help us negotiate the 'whale-mother-sea' of language?*

Well, yes, I think so. We have many examples of just how that works, both implicitly and explicitly. Ralph Ellison talks about these things in a very eloquent and non-racially coded language, but within that he gives you just marvelous examples of vernacular and idiom at work, and how they are able to perform a kind of magic to give his characters a space within a world very threatening to them. And he himself, by mastering the language, has worked out a space so that now if you think about the American novel, and its possibilities, you have to deal with Ellison. So, yeah, there are all kinds of examples.

And this goes back to folklore, because folklore also enacts some of these liberating strategies, both in its form and content—a whole genre of stories about Ole Massa—and often these stories turn on tricks with words or an overall kind of eloquence or ability to pull the wool over somebody's eyes, and that genre leads directly, over time, to what now I think would be epitomized by rap: a way to use language to control space and control your relationship to dominant culture—a tradition and conventions are built out of protecting the speaker and empowering the speaker; at the same time, teaching you how to keep The Man off your back. And accomplishing this in a way that transcends race, because the lessons embodied in rap are lessons that kids all over the world have picked up on. The Beatles, by mining only a small seam of the power of rock and roll and rhythm and blues, transformed a generation. I think that same kind of transformation is now at work as rap proliferates and spreads across the globe. I was talking with a German woman who said she went to her grandfather's birthday party somewhere in rural Germany, and his great granddaughters sang a rap birthday song to him. So here is this old German guy, and he doesn't listen to WIBG, but here's this cultural thing coming at him, and he was delighted by it, loved it. You just never know what's going to happen next.

Then a hard question, that I decide to phrase by telling a true story about a very recent discussion I had with an African American graduate student of political philosophy at the University of Michigan. He viciously criticized Wideman for trying to keep a foot squarely in two different worlds—for writing about the ghettos of Pittsburgh and for having attended Oxford as a Rhodes Scholar, and now being a part of the academic/writerly establishment. These, for him, were contradictory gestures. For John, it sparked a long near-monologue which he used to extend and deepen practically everything he had said up to that point in the interview.

It took me a while to figure out how much a part of the problem that kind of formulation is. It's based on a really false premise, a confused idea about culture and a confused idea of what constitutes American or African American culture. So when somebody says something that bifurcates that way, if there is time and opportunity, I try to slow down and explain to them why that's an inappropriate way to talk about things. Really, there is so much more interplay and interconnection in culture than that, and it's very dangerous to characterize a fluid interchange in a bi-polar way. You quickly get into biology and archetypes and racism when you do that. The well-meaning critic says, "Wideman is one of the best black writers of today," and I'll stop and say, "Thank you, but now what the hell did he say; what does that mean?"

Is there really such a thing as black writing apart from the fact that you may be able to identify the writer's African ancestry? For a writer what does that mean? Is there something that follows from that bloodline? You can employ Aristotle's definition of tragedy, and it can be useful. The problem would be when somebody says, "Tragedy is this, and only this definition Aristotle worked out." You go from description to prescription, taking something and asserting a rigidity or absoluteness about it. It's inductive versus deductive. Whenever I hear either/or choices, the hair goes up the back of my neck and I think, oh shit, this is a selection process; I'm being pushed to the left or to the right. What is usually much more interesting is the middle ground. How do these supposed opposites really relate to one another? Whether you're talking about nature and nurture or black and white or men and women or old and young. As a thinker, as a writer, what interests me is overlap, how things relate to one another, not whether or not they relate to one another. And what discourages me, and it's what stultifies people, is when you begin to believe those categorizations and think that they are really two separate things and not a continuum.

This continuum of connecting, almost connecting, refusing to connect, denying connection, etcetera, is a constant tension in my work, given the fact that often in the Homewood books I'm talking about a group of people who basically are just beginning to emerge from a kind of rural peasantry, coming from the south to the north. Their stories are really pretty simple stories: the plot lines, what happens to them, the kinds of problems they have with one another. But at the same time, there is a tremendous degree of complexity in their lives. I have tried to cultivate a high degree of sophistication in the way I tell stories and try to learn a helluva lot about how stories are told and how other people tell stories—other writers, other cultures—because as I look at my people, like my grandfather who came north in 1888 to Pittsburgh, and my other grandfather who came a little earlier from West Virginia, as I looked at their lives and learned more about their lives, there was no simple set of techniques, no simple story form, which would contain them. They kept bursting out of those. So, I was pushed to seek forms and levels of sophistication that were commensurate with what I viscerally and emotionally understood about their lives as well as what I understood with the front brain.

My process of thinking about my grandfather begins with a kind of blood identification; I remember sitting on his shoulders, and his smell, and the roughness of his chin. I remember the shirts he wore and the sound of him spitting into the spittoon. I definitely remember his voice. I remember hearing gospel music and the sway of his shoulders. This is all absolutely viscerally available to me when I think "John French."

On the other hand, I know that he was a man who had tremendous respect in the community and at the same time he was a gambler—not a church guy, but a street guy. I know that people still tell stories about him. He cultivated his own set of very pagan standards that made him unique, and made my mother a very staunch yet compassionate Christian. I understand that he operated in a world continually erecting barriers, and yet within the cage the world had built around him, he developed tremendous tolerance and humanity and compassion. He was a very proud and strong man, yet when he wanted to eat Chinese food, he was willing to go to the back door of the Chinese restaurant. He was friendly with the Chinese guy who ran the restaurant, and sometimes the Chinese guy would come out back and sit on the steps and eat with my grandfather. John French—knowing white people wouldn't patronize the joint if blacks sat inside next to them—put it this way: "Lee has to feed his family."

How do I get all that complex social/political thinking down in a story? Well, I better work my ass off. I better bring to bear the finest instrument and the most subtle instrument I can to even begin to try to tell his story; and then when I think of the music of the language he spoke, how do I get that into what I'm trying to write? It's the nature of the experience that sent me to school.

I've been steering a little throughout, but I don't need to. He's deep into this now, speaking in a way I've never heard him speak before, yet nothing he has said, nothing he says surprises me; it had been transferred experientially during my four years of work with John. I want to hear about the effect this has on audience, on the accessibility of writing, but that's where he's heading, anyways.

I think anything that you do really well, the better you do it, the more intrinsically you push a particular medium, the deeper you penetrate into the medium, your audience is going to start to shrink. The power of art is that you have somebody like Shakespeare or Giacometti or a Michelangelo or a Bach, and they push a particular convention or cut into that medium in such a way that, on the one hand what they're doing is so marvelous, so awesome, that a group of specialists grows up who are still trying to figure out what the hell is there, and on the other hand, people begin to imitate what they think a Shakespeare or a Bach or Ralph Ellison might be doing, and even the watered down versions that these people come up with please many, many folks, and rightfully so. You have this dual operation that on one hand is sort of shrinking, that the better it is the fewer people can really understand it, but maybe, if it's really good, it has a great expandingly outward flow that invigorates in unexpected ways and on many different levels. Many are called but few are chosen. It's not supposed to be something anybody can do. But the very best work keeps alive the notion that there is something worthwhile in achieving at the highest level.

That's the purpose that a Michael Jordan serves. After a point, he serves the medium. He helps you see that while it's all well and good to play and have fun, there is something more than that that you can learn. This thing can transcend. Then, all the little games that you or I might play in are all that much better, because we've seen the light and the light has shown us where we can take this. The metaphor breaks down because the writing game is very different from the basketball game. There is no agreement on the height of the basket, the length of the playing field, whether you should keep score or not . . .

I ask, "Who are the Michael Jordans of the writing game?" and here, again, the responses are both expected and unexpected, pushing toward a larger problem that lies behind the question.

I really like the one that I'm reading. I treat that question like I treat the question "Which of your books do you like the best?" The one that I'm working on because that's the one that's alive for me and the one that still might be the great one because it's not finished yet. What appeals to me is the process. What appeals to me is the chance I have to try to do it again. When I look at other writers, they excite me when they open doors, show me new ways to think of things I haven't thought about before. Not because they play the perfect game, but because they keep my interest in the game piqued. I can read a book that might do nothing but some crazy, one-shot deal, but that is more important than a book that may be, overall, ten-times as good but doesn't do any particular thing better than has been done before.

When John teaches, when he writes, he always pushes you toward the unsteady footing, the more complex way of approaching the problem, what-

ever it may be. In a recent article, "Beloit," Rick Bass says that not enough teachers teach the "heart beneath the heart" of writing. I'm realizing that John, somehow, took me there right from the start as a writer and a teacher. John found a way to teach that, or, as Bass puts it, "Writing cannot be taught; it can be learned," and he found a way to make me want to learn about it. This interview is a part of a puzzle for me, a map, a problem I need to solve—not the text, but the whole experience. . . . I remember that some students had trouble with John's teaching. They wanted the specific answers to be provided, the workshops to "fix" their stories. In what ways does the teaching of writing extend beyond those small seminar rooms? How do teachers of writing not "give away" what sustains them as artists? For me, John answered these questions already; by giving what some might charac-terize as "less" in a workshop, by keeping his distance and "teaching" the attitude, the tone, the love, by inviting you to take possession, he gave more; and he managed to teach by the tremendous example of his craft—the re-markable books that even through personal tragedy, even through the poten-tial pitfalls of overwhelming success as a writer, kept coming, and keep coming.

So I am pushing for a form here, a way to contain it all, to transfer the depth of emotion of the experience, and still, in these, the most direct and explicit words I have ever exchanged with John, I am aware of the implicit levels. I realize that these words are very much directed toward an old stu-dent, a friend, a former intramural basketball teammate, a young scholar/ writer hungry to make his mark on the world. I realize, too, that these words go out to African American writers, to all writers and readers. . . . I drive back to the midwest, leaving the Berkshires behind, putting my recent past back into the drawer of memory. I realize that Amherst has always been, will always be, "viscerally available," that moments like these will wedge them-selves permanently into me, and with luck and hard work will find their way out through my art, through my own efforts to harness and take control of the "big whale-mother-sea" of language.

In my new copy of Fatheralong, *he writes, "Arnie, Stay in the Struggle, John." Toward the very end of the interview, he says,* I wish Nike would start an ad campaign where they showed someone just doing leg curls or some-thing and then showed someone slam dunking and saying, "It takes a million of these to do one of these." *He goes on to characterize his "motto as a teacher" in the following way.* As a teacher of writing, I would say my job is empowering people. Why? Because the way we're taught language in school most of the time and most people's relationship to the language is, it's this big powerful thing out there and you don't own it. It's not you, or an extension of you, but it's something other, something else. I want to empower folks to feel the intimacy and reciprocity of the language. I know it was a long, long time before I had the slightest idea that the language was mine and that I was a part of what might make the language important. And what I would like to do is make people reconnect and feel that the language does belong to them, that they can do things with it and can make things with it, that it's an expressive medium in which they can expand and learn things about themselves.

I feel reconnected at several levels, not only because here, at last, is a formal, literal account of the kinds of things John teaches, often more subtly, to his students—the "fluid interconnection," "the middle-ground" of all exchanges, the reawakening and revitalization of things that will always be central to my teaching and to my writing—but also because of the generosity and intimacy that John showed during my brief return to Amherst.

Interview with John Edgar Wideman about *Fatheralong*

Michael Silverblatt / 1995

The interview printed here has been prepared for publication from an audiotape. The interview was conducted by Michael Silverblatt for the weekly radio program *Bookworm* on KCRW Radio in Santa Monica, California. The interview aired 2 February 1996 over National Public Radio. Used by permission of *Bookworm* and the producers of KCRW.

MS: What does the title *Fatheralong* refer to?

JW: I memorialized a mishearing. When I was a kid one of my favorite gospel songs was "Farther Along." But I heard that as "Fatheralong"—one word with "father" being the operative part. When I heart that song it made me think of God the father and my natural father. In fact, it was a word which made me feel how large the world was, how small I was as a child, and how there were lots of presences in that world that I did not understand. Also, the song was one that I heard my father sing often in the house. My favorite version of the song was Sam Cooke singing "Farther Along," but my father was right up there with it. He had a beautiful voice and he sang all the time, not only that gospel song but all kinds of songs, around the house. So the word combines a feeling of transcendence, a feeling of a child's smallness, a love of my father, the love of music, and lots of questions that a young kid has about where he belongs and who's out there in control of this mysterious world.

MS: The book is mysterious in a certain way. It begins with a meditation on race. When we finish that preface, we turn the page and discover a very specific incident: The difficulty of visiting Pittsburgh where your parents lived and being at your mother's house unable to see your father because they have been separated for years and have difficulty being in each other's presence. One immediately senses that this small incident is being used to stand for something much larger. Could you speak about the general and the personal in this book?

JW: My father was available to me physically very little in my childhood. He simply wasn't around the house. He held two or three of what we called "piece-a-jobs" in order to make do when one good job would have supported us. It meant that I didn't see him. He wasn't around, he was absent. Then at about the same time I went away to school my mother and father had personal problems and it meant that my father and she were separated. So he wasn't around at that stage of my life either. All this didn't mean that my father and I were estranged, but it meant that he was invisible, he was absent. The love that I felt for him and the love that I felt he had for me—I had to hold these things in my imagination. I had to create it—I had to construct it—without his physical presence.

MS: You say that the marginalization of the father stands for the whole issue of race. I wonder if you could say what you mean.

JW: As I examined my relationship with my father, I didn't mean to try to make a neat metaphor and use that as a way of directing the reader's attention to how African Americans are marginalized in this society. But almost inevitably, almost without my consciously thinking about it, the language of exclusion, the paradigm of exclusion, began to direct the pen, direct my thinking. After all, here was a man with whom I was connected by blood and time and experience, but it became to my benefit to pretend that none of those connections existed because his presence and his personality were a kind of inconvenience. So I saw myself treating him the way I had been treated, the way African American people had been treated over time.

MS: You mention in the second chapter that almost every relationship with the father—rejecting him, emotionally lynching him, embracing him— stands for a movement of racial politics.

JW: Yes, because for me there's a kind of bedrock of learned attitudes and conditioned responses that characterizes this culture, and probably other cultures as well. It's a very, very deep and to some extent metaphysical method of handling "the other"—what frightens us, what appeals to us, that attraction and repulsion. There are probably psychic mechanisms which nobody can name, certainly not me, that create a paradigm or archetypes that control our handling of "the other." What was fascinating to me as I wrote was that I reproduced these attitudes. I reproduced this construction of the other in my attitude towards my father. As I foregrounded that in the writing, I was in fact researching and analyzing a general cultural response.

MS: You compare the relationship of writer Richard Wright to his father with the relationship of writers who come after Richard Wright to Wright himself. The literary father needs to be rejected or overthrown. Is there a literary father in your own work whose influence you've been wrestling with?

JW: I think it is a whole passel, or a whole posse [laughter], of literary fathers, beginning with T.S. Eliot. I would insist on the generality rather than the individual writer, because somebody like Eliot still informs and is still very important when I think about literary influences on my work. I haven't abjured him, I haven't cut myself away from his influence. But the whole notion in English literature or the received literature that is taught in colleges and high schools—the idea that that covers the territory, that those famous authors who appear in the anthologies are the ones who are taught; the idea that in order to be a writer, you somehow have to fall in line and imitate and reproduce what they produced—that's the father I've wrestled with. That is the collective psyche or consciousness that I've very consciously worked away from.

MS: When you talk about Achebe in the opening of his novel *Things Fall Apart* as telling father legends or father myths, is that an alternative to the European tradition, or just another father to wrestle with?

JW: Achebe's an interesting writer because he set out to write a novel about his people and Ibo culture. His notion of novel is a fairly traditional one. But because he's a genius, he transformed it. His infusion of cultural material from Africa in itself wouldn't have been that much of a break-through, to funnel in new wine in the old bottle of form. But it was his sensibility, his switching of perspective, putting an African sensibility at the center of the novel, that's the most striking—as well as using cultural items, the language and the spiritual perspective of Ibo culture. He represents a writer who was very important to me because he legitimized a different sort of content. But he was smart enough and good enough so that, when he used this different content, it began to affect the form and enlarge the form.

MS: I want to bring up something that happened to me in college when we discovered the writing of Amos Tutuola. I had been in a school where John Barth was the writing teacher. To discover this extraordinary storyteller from Africa, Tutuola, was a real event. It was Barth who brought in Tutuola's first book, *The Palm-Wine Drinkard,* and he was exploring Tutuola's subsequent works beyond the first one. Then one day he came in very disappointed and told us that this individual style of Tutuola's was not in fact a literary style, but simply the way Tutuola spoke and that these were transcriptions. It was as if a style that is forged, like Joyce's, was inherently preferable to a style that was natural, a transcription of the world. This I think has been the dichotomy between the European inheritance of literature and an oral inheritance, stories that are written versus stories that are told. Do you have any feelings about that?

JW: That's an interesting story. It's almost like saying that I'm going to take down all my Velásquez paintings because somebody figured out that the guy simply had an astigmatism [laughter]. That's why those people look the way they do. Or get rid of Giacometti's people because somebody figured out some biological trait that the artist had which determined that everybody looked skinny to him. So I wonder about that. I'm very suspicious of that reaction and sort of disappointed by it. Barth was doing everybody a great favor. You could make parallels between some things he consciously figured out that he wanted to do in his books and what Tutuola was doing. Rather than discarding a whole body of work because it seems natural, I think that one should ask the question, "What does natural mean?" Tutuola's work represents an historical tradition and conventions that had been worked upon, fashioned, articulated, and made more precise over time in the same sense that Mr. Barth or Mr. Joyce or Virginia Woolf sat down at a table and worked through various options for a literate tradition.

MS: This brings up the whole issue of what literary society makes of what it decides to call "naive." To suggest that an oral literature, because oral, is therefore necessarily naive, seems to me to be the kind of marginalization that you're talking about. In other words, it's marginalizing the other because it's unknown. I'm sure that Barth came to know much more—this was just a random example. But to assume that an oral tradition is therefore a naive tradition, that it doesn't have its own sophistications, that there isn't a whole wealth of alternative meaning in a more casual, less written, art, seems to me a refusal to understand a culture.

JW: I think somebody would have to be deaf and dumb to reach that conclusion, and uninformed about how oral cultures work. After all, *The Iliad* and *The Odyssey* are products of oral literature and everybody wants to jump in line to claim the Greeks as the father of their literature, at least all European cultures do. For me the models of eloquence that were most important— I'm very clear about this now—were the women in my family. I was lucky enough to grow up in a household of women. Not only did they pamper me, take care of me, and make me feel that I was the center of the world, but they talked all the time to one another. In that context I learned to listen, because they were addressing things to me. The speech was coded so that I wouldn't understand everything, because they were talking about their boyfriends, about my uncles, about my father. They didn't want me to understand too much, but they weren't going to shut up either. So already what I was observing and hearing was a very flexible and fluid kind of vernacular that could assume a register that would exclude "Mr. Big Ears" (me) who wasn't supposed to understand everything. The people who were using that vernacular could make that kind of flexible switch. It's fair enough to say that I lived in an oral culture, growing up in Homewood around talkers—the barbershop, women at home, the preacher on Sunday, the preacher on the radio, the music. When I became a little older, as a teenager, there were the talkfest competitions like "the dozens" and "signifying," those male rituals of talk that made our group what it was, gave people personalities and status. If you lived in that kind of culture, you realized first off, very quickly, that there are good talkers and bad talkers, and a mile in-between, and some were very good talkers indeed. The joy that the very best talkers bring is a kind of ecstasy.

MS: The book begins with stories of fathers, but by its last chapter, time is conflated in an opening legendary paragraph, and suddenly the book gives way to stories of sons, stories that you tell of your son. I wonder what the difference between father stories and son stories are for you.

JW: I imagined the book as a kind of great arc. Part of the effort was to return to South Carolina, to this little town called Promised Land where my grandfather was born and his father and his father on back. I wanted to go with my own father and investigate that place and see if we could recover the names of Widemans that had been lost and root ourselves in that region. That was one direction I wanted the book to move. But the whole point of this investigation was to speak to my sons, to preserve for them, and to create for them, a sense of belongingness, a sense of authority, and to demonstrate to them how much a claim they had to this land and to their identity. So inevitably the arc had to lead to sons. To answer your question more directly, there is a circle and a flow. There's no difference between the stories of the fathers and the sons. They feed from one another and they go back to one another and they depend on one another. In fact, the racial crime that might be one of the most horrendous is that this cycle of communications that allows fathers to become sons and sons to become fathers has been interrupted—has been mediated—by voices that are antagonistic, hostile, to that process among African American men.

MS: You say that all paternity is questionable, that the rhyme "mother's baby, father's maybe" becomes inevitable for a black man in American culture. Can you explain that?

JW: It has to do with this mediation that I was just trying to discuss. When you ask the question "Where do you come from?" I think the question you are really asking is "Do you belong here? What right do you have to be here?" And that's a vexed question for African American people. Trying to answer to that question opens up the past of slavery and oppression and all the issues of division and whether or not black people are in fact equal to Europeans or Asians, etc. Asking that question means that paternity is being questioned. In fact, in a way somebody's playing the dozens with us. We're being undressed in public when that question is asked. It's a literal question. I have blood of Europe and Africa in me. Why is that the case? What does that mean? The social pathology that has been forced on the black community by oppression means in fact that many kids don't know who their fathers are, or, if they know their names, they don't know where they are. Or if they know their names and know where they are, they have no visceral relationship. So in that sense it's a very real and trying question.

But I think it also goes back to the larger issue, the more encompassing issue, and that's that for all Americans the questions, "Who is your father? Where do you come from?" are problematic. We've been struggling with that. One of the most basic themes in American literature and art and culture is "Are we legitimate?" Have we made an impress upon this land? Does American really mean something, other than the power to make a whole lot of money, get big muscles, and push other people around?" Are we more than our material or technological culture? And if we are, what is it? Do we find our roots in England? Why the obsession with English culture? Why do we learn the English classics to the exclusion of other literatures of the world? There are some very big questions there.

MS: One of the central images in *Fatheralong,* at least for me, was the image of the jailhouse, when you go and pick up your father at the old age housing development where he lives. You say it reminds you of the structures of prisons. You mention later that your father was unable to bring himself to visit your brother in prison. Your own visits to different jails counterpointed by visits to your homeplace seemed to structure the book. I wonder if you could talk about prison and paternity because to many Americans right now paternal structures in themselves are read to be imprisoning.

JW: There's almost nothing I can add. You've cut into the symbolic structure of the book. All I can say is "Amen." I'm glad you're making that kind of reading and certainly it connects with what I was trying to do. But unfortunately for me, in my particular life, jails and prisons are not metaphors. They're actual, factual barricades and walls that I have to deal with. It became incredible to me as I wrote this book how many times I literally crashed into those walls. But if you think of America's relationship to the Africans who were brought here beginning in the 16th century—if you think about that, it's quite clear that one reason we were brought here was simply to be used and then be discarded.

One of the primary questions of the culture is, how do we control these Africans? How do we use them without allowing them to break out of the very utilitarian and self-serving purpose that we brought them here for? How do we keep them in the box? How do we keep them on the plantation? How do we keep them on the farm? How do we keep them in the inner city ghetto? That's the perpetual problem. All sorts of metaphysical and material remedies or solutions to that problem have arisen and using that perspective, that lens, one can obtain a whole analysis or picture or rendering of American history.

MS: A final question. This book which is very much about barriers seems within itself to break down barriers, and listeners to this program know that usually I talk to novelists or poets. You're primarily known as a novelist and short story writer. This book involves essays, bits of sociology, meditation, italicized projected legends, father stories, son stories—I wonder if there's a literary strategy in the breaking of forms similar to the breaking of barriers?

JW: If there's anything consistent in the body of my work I think it's that impulse to yoke together those things that other people have sundered. Not only have they sundered them, but they have set up rules that say you can't yoke them together or you shouldn't or it's best not to. Not only has that been a dimension of my literary life, that's been a dimension of my personal life.

An Interview with John Edgar Wideman

Renée Olander / 1996

From *AWP Chronicle* 29.3 (December 1996): 1–8. Used by permission.

John Edgar Wideman is author of thirteen books, eleven fiction and two nonfiction. Among his honors are a MacArthur Award and two PEN/Faulkner Awards for the novels *Sent For You Yesterday* and *Philadelphia Fire*. In 1995, his prose work *Fatheralong* was a finalist for the National Book Award. He recently edited *The Best American Short Stories 1996*. Mr. Wideman lives and teaches in Amherst, Massachusetts. This interview took place while he was at work on *The Cattle Killing,* just published by Houghton Mifflin.

Renée Olander: *Brothers and Keepers* is the first book of yours that I read, and I was riveted by it, largely because of my own experience with a younger sibling, and then it occurred to me that given the size of America's prison and jail populations, your story is relevant to a huge number of people, maybe even an invisible majority, whose family members or friends are caught in the criminal justice system.

John Edgar Wideman: It's a universal story. Almost every time I speak before a group of people someone wants to share a story. Usually it's a conference of some sort. One person or another will come up to me and feel comfortable telling me the story. Everybody from Ed Bradley doing a *60 Minutes* piece to the last time I was anywhere and met anybody. It's a universal story that gets a lot of play. And it's not a "Look at my brother over there and me over here" kind of story—it's that "there but for the grace of God go I."

Olander: Do you ever feel overexposed in your writing?

Wideman: Well, I may choose to show you the wound on my arm, but not the wound on my leg, so in that sense, it's very calculated. Not totally. Certainly, not totally when the writing takes over or a story takes over or the unconscious takes over. But on the other hand there's a degree of exhibitionism in any kind of writing, and there's also, I think, a tremendous urge to conceal.

Olander: So is writing chiefly an exercise in artfully revealing wounds?

Wideman: Call it a wound, a disturbance, something we wish to change, something that makes us start moving around. Life starts with a wound.

Olander: Could we talk about *Philadelphia Fire,* especially the last section, where the main character, Cudjoe, who has a sort of authorial voice, seems a little obsessed with self-definition, and he says, "Why this Cudjoe then, why am I him when I tell certain parts, why am I hiding from myself?"

Wideman: One thing it's about is process, artifice, convention. I can't help but feel—let me back up and start in another place—I'm very suspicious of . . . I'm very suspicious, period. I think I learned my suspicion in the womb or at the breast. Even things I love to do I'm suspicious of, so for me, being a writer, and wanting to make things, I bring a very powerful, I hope healthy, skepticism into the process. One way to translate that abstraction would be to say, "Okay, here I am in Amherst, Mass., writing these books about Homewood, a black, economically depressed community in Pittsburgh—what's all that mean, what do all these words on the page have to do with that reality, and if I'm really bothered by that reality—of Pittsburgh—it exists now, this moment, my people are there, my relatives are there, and suffering various forms of oppression and danger and pain, why don't I do something about it? What's it mean to make stories up about it? What's it mean to, in a sense, exploit it in a narrative or a poem?" And these questions and that kind of split mind, that kind of divided mind, is a voice, is a part of me I've never been able to quiet, and it comes through as a sort of explosion of doubt and skepticism that is part of everything I do, for better or worse. And it's one thing that keeps me from writing traditional narrative, because I frankly don't believe in it, the tricks of it, the conventions of it only carry me so far and then it becomes transparent and I get dissatisfied. Therefore I'm very restless as a writer; I'm trying new things, changing narrative voice, looking for different forms, combining forms, looking for things people haven't written before—material, content—it's that restlessness and suspicion and skepticism that I think accounts for a lot of the formal qualities.

Olander: There's a way in which you seem to be a writer's writer, in terms of the issues your work brings up, the conscious looking at story, the issue of exploitation in telling a story, and the connections between books. Are the Cudjoe in *Philadelphia Fire* and the Cudjoe in *Reuben* related?

Wideman: Same name.

Olander: Yeah.

Wideman: [Laughter] Well, Cudjoe, number one, was a very common name, it's like John, that was used in slavery days. It's also a West African name day. It's an echo of its time. There were lots of Cudjoes around. But in both cases, they point backward. But it's a conscious thing; they could be related. In a new novel I connect those two characters. As a writer you're always giving yourself more room.

Olander: How about the exposure of your family? In the Homewood trilogy, and in the other books, fiction and nonfiction, there are characters whose names are the same as some of those in your family, or fictionalized names but experiences that overlap those of your family, and there are references to your wife, Judy, in several books. Do you talk to these people, for instance, Judy, when she appears in a book, or is that ever problematic?

Wideman: Well, I don't live in a vacuum, so people tell me what they think. Fortunately, it's never been that much of a problem. However, there are specific issues. For instance, in *Brothers and Keepers.* My brother in prison is essentially a hostage; he's in a hostage situation, so I can't bad-mouth the guards, I can't reveal certain things. Even though I set up standards of frankness and candor about the book, I just can't say certain things. There are other situations like that. With family, what I try to do is have fun, that is, give glimpses of people, tease people, retell stories, even bring skeletons out of the closet, but in such a way that I don't embarrass or hurt anyone—and I do that by mixing things up, making composite characters, signifying, that is, obliquely referring to something that people in the know would understand but other people wouldn't, people outside the family. This is a kind of coded allusiveness, and I have fun with the code because few people really know how to crack it. People think they understand when they see a character John French, and aha! Wideman's actual grandfather is John French, and just like the actual grandfather, this character was born in Culpeper, Virginia. So what? I still have the power to play that image, that character, in any direction that I want to, and if someone is hung up by the literalness or someone loses their way because of the literalness, then that's their problem, not mine. But I don't want to hurt people, so I'm very careful. My rules don't always work, and I make mistakes because, as any writer does, I take liberties with other people's privacy. It may be that writing about people is by definition a kind of encroachment, so there's always a danger, but I try to minimize it, and that's all I can say. My intentions are good.

Olander: So do the people who appear in your books, or the people from whom you draw characteristics for composites—do they generally read your books?

Wideman: Well, they read those parts they believe are about them [laughter]. I really don't know how much people read; I'm surprised sometimes—my Aunt Geraldine, my Aunt Martha—they're not people who read "literary" fiction, but they're both very intelligent and read a lot. And they read my stories, the ones that they like; they don't feel compelled to read them all, but certainly I've had conversations with them about bits and pieces. I don't expect anybody to read everything or pay attention to everything. My mother's a very close reader whose opinions I seek—I want to know what she thinks. She's very insightful; she's a novelist *manquée* because she's so observant and intelligent. I wish I had some of her abilities to catch the way a person talks.

Olander: You say that in one of your books—you say you envy her.

Wideman: I'm envious of the storytelling ability of lots of members of my family; I don't consider myself a good oral storyteller. What I do is just kind of a shadow of what the good storytellers in my family do; they do effortlessly in conversation what I'm still struggling to do in my fiction. I feel towards them as I do towards musicians: very humble.

Olander: It seems to me that story, the power to tell a story, and what constitutes a story is a theme that runs through especially the last four or five books—in *Philadelphia Fire,* Timbo says "it ain't fair to start telling me a story then just stop in the middle"; Reuben says it's "his own story he's avoiding by listening to this one he invents"; *Fatheralong* mentions a white professor who has the "power and privilege to tell [your] father's story"— and there are lots of other examples—issues of genre and form are central to your work.

Have you heard what critic Noel Perrin wrote of you: "He certainly writes books called novels . . . what they really are are myths—generally of the biracial society" and that "if Wideman were a novelist, he would be a seriously flawed one" and that *"Reuben* has no real plot" or active scenes, but that your books instead interweave myths and superstitions and dreams—

Wideman: That's his story [laughter]. Well, if one translates *story* as plot, or a plotted narrative, then a lot of things that go around with the title "novel" on them wouldn't fit; so then that's just kind of arbitrary. There are books that I love that are basically plotless—for example, *Ulysses*. So that's just nomenclature. But I think I like what Perrin says, because I'm looking for something in the writing that goes beyond the storyline, and I think that's a tool, and a plot is a tool that the writer can use to draw an audience into a kind of conversation, but that's it. Once you do that, then that's when the excitement, the real action starts—meaning the dialogue between reader and writer the language focuses and exudes. The idea of the novel as a kind of energy source. It's a kind of kit that the reader goes to and tries to make something out of, and a really good writer puts all sorts of materials in there, and also instructions on how to make things out of it, and that's the exchange that I think is central to fiction, that I want to participate in as a writer and reader.

Olander: Do you have a reader in mind as you write, an image of an audience you hope to reach?

Wideman: At times in my life I have. When I was younger I always had very specific voices, and that is a sign of a younger writer. It means that writing for you, or for me, is an imitation of something that's already out there, something that pleases you, something that turns you on, and you're trying to reproduce it in some way with a little twist of your own voice. But I think that over time, something else happens and you begin to talk to yourself, to talk to the other books you've written, and the voice becomes much more internalized. Maybe you lose some of that grand ambition which is part of being a beginning writer—you begin to settle for what you have, and to listen more closely and pay more attention to your own voice and its energy and whatever its limits might be. It's like other things in life—I'm 54 years old, so I'm probably not going to be an Olympic-medal ball player—there are a lot of things that I'm not going to accomplish, so that makes me less interesting to myself and to other people, but it allows me the kind of freedom to run around the block at my own speed, with the body and mind that I have, and live with that, with fewer illusions, get the mileage out of it that's realistic, and I don't think that's any kind of hunkering down; it's probably a positive step.

Olander: I'm not always sure of your audience targeting. In *Fatheralong*, for example, there's a lot of usage of the second person, and as I read it, I thought that if I had not read the previous books, some names and allusions might be confusing, but also it seems that sometimes the second person refers to some abstract white power structure or participants of it, and sometimes the authorial voice seems to be addressing himself, and then especially in the last section of the book, that "you" seems to be the author's son Jake—does that sound right?

Wideman: Well, *you* read it, and I'm sure that, rhetorically, the "you" is structured in different ways at different times, but I'm not quite clear on the question, how that implicates the other books.

Olander: Well, maybe it doesn't, but I wondered as I read what you were assuming about your readers.

Wideman: At times in *Fatheralong* it's a meditation. And if I were to do it over again, I might slow down a bit and fill in some of the blanks, that is, make clearer some specifics that have to do with why, with people, with times, with places; there are a lot of truncated stories or pieces of stories that a reader might have a difficult time placing, identifying exactly, because *Fatheralong* doesn't give them enough information about those incidents, and I have a couple in mind. But because it is a meditation, and because I didn't really want to tell my story, but make it our story—and when I refer to *our* story, it's the collective story of America—that caused me to shy away from being too particular, although I used my life and people I know and things that happened to me to demonstrate many things that are significantly bigger. I like the idea that at times I get sort of in the middle ground between essay and fiction; I think some of the things that I'm happiest with are when I turn that kind of ambiguity into something useful to myself. And that has to do with a question you asked earlier about actual people's names that appear in the fiction. As I write more and more I find the lines eroding between the imaginative world and the "actual" world, and in fact, I'm persuaded intellectually and emotionally that those two worlds hook up and are joined, complement—in fact, exploring that, those connections and that interface, is probably one of the major projects of the second half of this century's writing. People who are using words like "constructing reality" or concepts like "constructing personality" or "constructing gender" are beginning to spin off in very specific directions or disciplines, if you will, trying to figure out and then deal with some of these same ambiguities—the personal life, the public life. We understand a little better as a society and as a culture that we can be almost anything, and that's a tremendous freedom, and really scary business, so we're pushed toward lots of different directions, and the fiction I write I hope is playing in that territory.

Olander: The critic Bernard Bell said that a "major underlying theme of your work is that what we think we are is at least as important as what we are."

Wideman: That makes sense.

Olander: But back to this issue of audience—in *All Stories Are True,* at the beginning of that book the audience seems to be clearly not black, not part of the family, because of what is explained about the family or about being black in America, but later in the book the audience becomes one that is part of the community almost, and there's much less explaining; and in *Fatheralong,* where there's a very directed "You tear down people's homes and move them out to an urban wasteland. . . ."—are you supposing that that "you" is going to be a white audience?

Wideman: I think what I'm supposing is that if the shoe fits—and "you" is a way of, I guess, gently pointing a finger without really pointing a finger.

Olander: Not too gently!

Wideman: [Laughter] It implies just that "you" better pay attention, that I am addressing "you," but there's also room for the person who hears it to also sort of slide out as well.

Olander: Throughout your books there's a very powerful fist, there's a lot of real rage.

Wideman: Well, *you* can be very much *in your face,* and if it works, it works because I'm referring to something that you can't deny. If I can get that sort of relation with the person who's reading, then I've captured them. In other words, when you use you, it's a kind of device that defines the audience and in a sense pigeonholes; it's a kind of allegation. And it allows me to—or it's a vehicle for—projecting assumptions, my assumptions about the reader or any group that's being addressed, and in that sense, it sort of reverses the naming business—it's the shoe on the other foot in a sense. It's not so much that I am being interrogated, but that I'm interrogating "you." It's an important stage in African-American writing, in any writing when you stop battling and fighting with the definitions that are out there—somebody else's that have been imposed upon you. You have a firm enough sense of the world that, in your work—stories, essays, whatever—you are presenting a picture of the world which contains assumptions and a definition of what the "other" is.

Olander: One last audience question—in *Reuben,* which seems to me to be your darkest book, with some very disturbing characters, especially Wally, who is a misogynist who continuously thinks or speaks of women in degrading terms—

Wideman: A misogynist? I think he's a very dangerous person, a very unhappy person, and I wouldn't want to necessarily get close to him—man, woman, or child—and that's part of the problem, for him; there are an awful lot of things he's not in control of and he takes it out on other people. I'd think of him more as a misanthrope, but not exactly—no, no, I wouldn't think of him as a misanthrope; I'd think of him as someone driven, and look out if you get in his way.

Olander: As I read that book, and I'm sure this says something about me, I kept thinking that a male audience would enjoy it more, that it's a very male-oriented book, because the language puts me off—the language in Wally's mind whenever he thinks about particular women or women in general seems to me unrelenting in its degradation of the female. And then also there's basketball and the language of sport—and neither of these are necessarily exclusive, but—

Wideman: Right. My daughter plays basketball. But—who's Wally? Wally's one of the guys, he's a jock, he plays ball, he went to school on that ticket, he's a predator, that's who he is, so that language and sensibility take up a lot of the time and yes, you're in that world. On the other hand, women are also major characters—

Olander: There's Flora, Kwanza, and Toodles—

Wideman: Take Toodles, for instance—actually I saw Toodles as a kind of goddess, and I saw the book as a kind of mythological tug-of-war for Kwanza's soul, between a male principle and a female principle, and a female principle wins out. There's the literal battle where the dragon is slain, somebody is restored. In that scene, *Reuben* is kind of allegorical—there's the myth of Osiris, the Egyptian myth that underlies and gives you the kind of plot-line, or story-line. But I wanted it to be optimistic; I wanted that last scene to recall Michelangelo's ceiling, especially God touching Adam. That was Reuben and the little boy—

Olander: Yes, but Reuben's future is endangered by his legal troubles and his age, his diminishing powers; how good is he really going to be for Cudjoe?

Wideman: Reuben's indestructible; that's my take on it. Reuben's also a kind of god—nothing's going to happen to him; the particular form he inhabits at the moment may disappear, but he'll be back, he's a principle.

You know, I write these books and I'd be in trouble if I had to take a test on them. You know, the characters often began with names of people that I know, the people I was basing them on, and that's really who they remain to me. At some point or another to protect the innocent or whatever, I change the names, and those are very superficial: I mean, I try to make the names interesting, I try to make them work in terms of the rhythm of the prose, and sometimes bear a kind of metaphorical meaning, but they're really in a way arbitrary; I don't remember them most of the time.

Olander: At the beginning of *Fatheralong,* you say the words, or concepts, of "race" and "racism" "are equally predatory, one just wears sheep's clothes," and yet issues of race are unavoidable in this society—do you think the construct of race has broken down any, or is any less pernicious than it was, say, 20 or 40 years ago?

Wideman: Well, things are always changing. There are a lot of assumptions in that question—what somebody's really asking when they ask that question is has there been a kind of linear progress, from awful awful old days to a little bit better now. And I would say, number one, that's the wrong question, because any place you cut into American history, you get all kinds of situations—you had black people and white people living together, families, making babies during slavery days; you had black businessmen who were very successful at the turn of the 19th century in Philadelphia; you also had awful things going on at all times. So I would think that, in a way, the question is not very useful; it just reinforces the idea that there was a then and a now. The scary thing about race relations is that no, they haven't changed very much at all—the pendulum swings back and forth, but we're still in a state of denial. We still think we need the concept of race to understand ourselves, and it's with the concept of race that we try to make sense of ourselves and our world, and it's a bogus concept; it's a concept that doesn't get us a very deep understanding of who we are, what we are, or what our country is now, or what it has been.

Olander: Yesterday I walked around Northampton, and I noticed that I didn't see any non-white faces; as you go about your daily life here in Amherst, are you continuously conscious of race?

Wideman: Yes—the simple answer is yes. But also because I'm a student—I look for things, and not necessarily bad things or negative things; I'm just very finely attuned, and that's something that is a heritage of being an American, a black American. And while some of it I can kind of lay off with, "Well, that's what I do, I write about these things," other parts of it are overt and make me racist, like everybody else, because here I am, what am I doing? I'm admitting that I'm very conscious of race, that it plays a part in my perceptions, et cetera, et cetera. Now I think one can do that, one can be conscious, one can study something, without being crazy, without necessarily hating what you're looking at, or using that as some kind of hammer or club to hurt other people. I mean, I'm very wary and observant of white folks, what they do, how they act toward who you are, and you don't necessarily have to be a racist when you do that; it just may be a survival technique, it may be a necessity. You may not harbor any particular anger; on the other hand, you're always on the edge of anger.

Some things have changed; most haven't. This is a bad time, frankly. It's a bad time because it's a frightened time. Whenever the populace at large is frightened, like any individual, you sort of regress—you're less charitable, more suspicious, more selfish. If you begin with prejudice, and if you begin with anger, those things get worse. So this is an awful time. And we're also involved in a kind of redefinition of race right now—it's not a totally new definition, but it's coming to mean very special things; there's a really scary identification between a young black male of a certain class, a certain geographic area, and being a criminal. This is very scary—because that kind of identification does exactly what the more virulent kinds of old-timey Ku Klux Klan white superiority stuff did; it's the foundation, it's the building block for a whole world view. And I think that's very definitely happening. There are aspects of the construction of black identity that are too depressing—

Olander: Do you have any thoughts about the upcoming, or ongoing, presidential politics/candidates?

Wideman: [Laughs] From the ridiculous to the sublime. I was reading a piece that a friend of mine wrote on Colin Powell—so far that's what's interested me most: the possibility that Powell might run, what that might mean. All that had a kind of edge. My main feeling is a real sadness with this country—what is it, two-hundred-some million people now? That we could even on our worst day contemplate as a candidate for one of the major parties an old man, far past his prime, who has not had an idea in a long time, who's gone through various kinds of upgrading of image, who appeals most to the most oppressive, aggressive, backward-looking elements in the society—it's completely unhealthy. I mean, I don't want to get personal, but if this is the best we can do—if we pin our hopes on, and put the hopes of our children in, the hands of these sorts of mediocrities—we're in for deep shit.

And then the costs of an election now—in fact, cost is one of the reasons certain kinds of people end up running—the fact is the whole process is controlled by money. It's just the offshoot of a society that is controlled by money interests. And the election is just going to be another advertising campaign. We all know that it doesn't matter what the product is—it's just how you advertise it and how you get it before the public. That democracy has fallen so clearly to this level is pretty frightening. It's not even a question of ideology, it's simply a matter of a populace that can't discriminate between what's real and what's fake.

Olander: Sometimes I wonder, who are these people who support a Bob Dole, or a Newt Gingrich?

Wideman: Yeah, it's the affliction of—well, "the Empire is dead"—I mean, we're still gloating over the fall of communism, and we haven't noticed that we've also fallen. Maybe not as far yet. We still have life, but what kind of life is it? The idea of free enterprise, the open market, stuff like that— pulling yourself up by your bootstraps now is a matter of winning the lottery.

Olander: Do you rely much on an editor or editors as the books move toward publication?

Wideman: No. I have a couple of friends who read. For my first couple of books, I was very lucky; I worked with a man named Hiram Haydn, who was the editor of *The American Scholar.* Hiram was the godfather of my first kid, Danny. Working with Hiram was a very profound and useful experience. To have someone who thought about my books, who thought about them as a fellow writer, who could project himself into the books and fight me about words and understand them well enough to actually make a good case when he disagreed with me—that was a wonderful experience but I haven't had that since he died. I don't know how much I need it now; some people might say a lot, but I don't know. I have to make use of the readings of readers who also happen to be very good friends. I'm looking forward to working with a new editor, Dawn Seferian, at Houghton Mifflin.

Olander: Do you have any favorites among your books?

Wideman: The one I'm working on is always the most exciting. It's sort of like kids; even if you did have favorites, you wouldn't say that aloud because you might hurt the others' feelings. Writing is a work-in-progress;

when one book's done, it almost passes completely out of my mind. I don't reread them; I don't think about them very much except when I might go somewhere to read, or someone writes a critical article about one and I might go back and think about it and revisit it. But it's the writing, the present-tense writing, that keeps me going; it's the process, and the process is always focused on the book in hand.

Olander: What are you working on?

Wideman: Well, I just finished, or am that close to finishing, a novel called *The Cattle Killing,* and I've got some smaller projects too; I'm trying to get a new book started, a new novel. I've been very lucky, thanks to a MacArthur grant, so I teach only one half of the year.

Olander: And you teach just one class?

Wideman: A seminar—and I really like to do those, so that's getting paid for having fun. It's twelve people max, and then I'll have some dissertations that I'm directing. It actually does get busy even with one class, even though I speak from a spoiled perspective; we have to admit students, which means we have a hundred-some applications to read through, and they all have writing samples in them. It gets busy at this time, and on the average I may have four dissertations, and then the class and other administrative stuff because we run the program, as most writers do. But I'm certainly not complaining.

Olander: How does your teaching influence your writing?

Wideman: It keeps me alert. Unless I was a total hypocrite, I couldn't look at other people's writing and criticize it and push them to get better and fuss about commas and quotation marks without applying that same kind of scrutiny to myself.

Olander: Do you give any sorts of assignments?

Wideman: It's a graduate class, and people are there in theory because they want to write, and I've seen their writing before they come so I know they're able to write, so I don't make assignments. What I try to do is create an atmosphere so that what they're trying to do is taken absolutely seriously and we can interact with one another in a seminar situation as sort of colleagues, people engaged in the same enterprise. What we talk about is the writing produced by people in the seminar, and that's usually enough. Of course, as teacher I have special responsibilities; with thirty years of writing and publishing, I bring a different take on the manuscripts than other people do. Sometimes we read other writers, and I might make a crazy assignment just for fun, but most of what we do is read one another's manuscripts and talk about them.

Olander: Do you ever show your work to the seminar class?

Wideman: Again, just for novelty, every now and again. But when we read things, they're always anonymous in the workshop. In theory nobody knows whose piece is being read, at least till the end, and then the writer has the choice of identifying herself or not.

Olander: Do you know Annie Dillard's *An American Childhood?*

Wideman: It's on my list. She and I have crossed paths in a number of ways. The Homewood Public Library, for instance—I walked to it with my Uncle Otis, and she was driven by her chauffeur.

Olander: You know you've been called "the black Faulkner" and the "softcover Shakespeare"—do you read criticism of your work?

Wideman: I wish there were more criticism; what there is mostly is book reviews, short-takes—I know those quotes, yeah, the ones you asked me about. And I don't want to be ungrateful, but they're a kind of broad brush.

Olander: Do you have literary heroes?

Wideman: When I answer that question—well, I don't answer that question, and I don't answer it because it takes attention away from the real stuff; the real stuff is the day-by-day writing process. And citing individuals as heroes or whatnot is like foregrounding an all-star team instead of foregrounding the game. I'm interested in the game, and everybody's a player. So I could conceivably read one of my student's manuscripts, and learn as much as I might learn from reading Toni Morrison. It's not so much that I like individual books or writers, but I like what they've done, and I like a passage from Toni Morrison, I like a passage from Russell Banks or Jamaica Kincaid, or Ralph Ellison, or T. S. Eliot, you know, moments and pieces, and sometimes whole books, but all books are essentially, as Giacometti says about sculpture, failures. Their art is not perfect; there's no perfection. So rather than think of all-stars, rather than think of personalities, I think of moments of the art that we all share. That's what turns me on.

Olander: What do you read?

Wideman: I read everything; I read lots of things. I'm a pretty voracious reader when I'm in a reading phase. History, biography. I binge. For instance, I was wondering why American poetry was focused so intently and in a way so narrowly in New England in the 1960s and 70s and maybe even the '80s, why a handful of poets all from the same place, who essentially knew one another, et cetera, et cetera, how they all came to be so important and sort of took over—so I systematically read a lot of biographies and studied that stuff. And that's what I do. For a while everything I read was about South Africa—I was interested in it and that's how I do it, when I have the leisure and the time. Every now and again I go on a crusade to try and catch up with younger writers, for instance, who have gotten some attention or whose books are selling a lot. Every now and again I'll force my way to read through a best-seller list—I usually don't get too far with that project. And sometimes it's an individual writer. Because I teach, because I do my own writing, because I have a family, because I have administrative work around the University, I sometimes get behind on my ideal reading list. Everybody will have been talking about *Remains of the Day,* Ishiguro, and so I'll say, who is this guy? So I'll stop and read his work. But I like to read all sorts of things—I have been reading French critics, sort of philosophers of language, interested in personality construction—a couple of books by Baudrillard. So I construct reading lists—that's what I do.

Olander: Do you ever read aloud as you write?
Wideman: I don't read to myself, but I hear it; I read aloud to Judy.

Olander: I don't see a computer or typewriter—how do you produce?
Wideman: I don't type; I never learned to type. I write by hand.

Olander: Who types your work?
Wideman: Judy did until recently. Now Beth Berry, a former writing program secretary at U-Mass, does.

Olander: So you read your drafts aloud to Judy, and she typed them up until your most recent books. How much feedback did she, or does she, give you? Would you change directions based on her reactions, or is there any degree to which you'd call any of your work collaborative?
Wideman: Yes and no. Judy's been in law school now for five years and had to give up typing my books. But up until five years ago, she would type the rough draft. Then she had to give the job to someone else. She didn't want to give it up—and I didn't want her to give it up. I give a lot of credit to her for her thoughts and reactions. On the other hand, what I was really looking for when I read to her was approval, a pat on the back, a green light. She was not neutral, but there was not a lot of substantive criticism going on. But the transition away from her typing was hard to make—she was crucial

in terms of support. I'd give a hand-written draft to her and then it would be real. There was a reciprocity, not all quantifiable, a spiritual and emotional bond. With short stories there was much more editorial input because she received scripts so raw from me. I guess I would call the work on the short stories cooperative.

Olander: Do you ever have dry spells where you're worried that you might not write?

Wideman: Yesterday. In between sentences. It's a sort of occupational hazard. Some days I'm afraid, and I don't want to stop. Other days if I've written something I'm really quite happy with, there's both the fear that it'll never happen again and the urge to say screw it—why should I worry about it happening again? Just stop—this is good, so put it down and do something else: build a house, dig a hole.

John Edgar Wideman

Derek McGinty / 1996

The interview printed here has been prepared for publication from an audiotape. The interview was conducted for the *The Derek McGinty Show* and American University public radio station WAMU in Washington, D.C. Conducted and aired on 9 October 1996. Used by permission.

DM: John Edgar Wideman's new novel *The Cattle Killing* is one of those rare books that craves, nay demands, the reader's full attention and concentration, because Wideman's first-person narrator is actually any one of several people and, if you skim a paragraph or miss a turn of phrase, you might get lost in one of the transitions. *The Cattle Killing* takes us through the minds and the times of a contemporary novelist who seems to be reading this entire book to his elderly father. The story proper takes place mostly in the last part of the 18th century, though, where a black preacher, a blind white woman, and others provide their vastly different perspectives on the racism and the other hypocrisies of the time. "Haunting" and "powerful" are the words that critics are applying to this latest novel by Wideman, who has 13 books to his credit. He also edited *The Best American Short Stories 1996.* He teaches in Amherst, Massachusetts, and he joins me here in the studio. John Edgar Wideman, good to see you again.

JW: Good to see you. Beautiful day here in Washington.

DM: Indeed it is. I was looking at this contemporary writer who is talking in the first person in the first part of the book which is all in italics and I thought, "Why, that must be you!"

JW: Well, if it's not me then it's somebody real close [laughter]. *I* might even mistake him for me. The trick is, Derek, that any character in a book is always created—partly a real model but always you have to begin from nothing and make it on the page. So, yes, a lot of the characteristics are mine and they're my thoughts and I have a father who lives on a hill in Pittsburgh and I did go to a conference in Pittsburgh and I did walk from a fancy hotel up the hill past the demolished black neighborhood that was called The Hill to my father's senior citizen's high-rise building—all that did happen. His apartment had been flooded. All those details are true or accurate, but then there are lots of things in it that are not true as well.

DM: Like what?

JW: I didn't take a book up to him. I *thought* about taking a book up to him. I wished the book was ready to take up to him [laughter]. There are changes in time. The event in Pittsburgh occurred recently—two years ago. It was a literary gathering of people who teach creative writing. That happened one year and then another year I was in a downtown hotel and took the long walk up to see my father. So it collapses different times and experiences.

DM: The idea of taking the novel to your father—almost for some kind of approval, I thought—was an interesting one. I wondered if you had ever done that, read to your father and said, "This is what I've done. What do you think?"

JW: That's one of those things I wish I had done. He's heard me read, because he's attended public functions. But as far as the two of us sitting down—I've never tried it. I don't know why. I wish I had and I still have the opportunity. But somehow or other it just didn't seem the thing to do with him. And why is that? I wrote a book called *Fatheralong* in which I tried to understand questions like that—why there are certain kinds of intimacy that are okay between black fathers and sons and why others seem forbidden and how necessary it is to cross those lines and open up towards each other in all kinds of ways. But it's one thing to write a book and it's another thing to live your life.

DM: We talked about that very book here. It's been a while, I guess. Did you begin to cross more of those lines after writing that book and after going around talking about it for weeks?

JW: Sure. In fact, the book couldn't have been created without my father feeling that he wanted to talk to me about things that he'd never talked to me about before, without me asking the questions. The book was actually made possible by a kind of breaking down of barriers that occurred over time.

DM: Let's talk a little bit about this book. You get into the current Pittsburgh which is suffering from the same kinds of problems that a lot of big cities are suffering from. You describe a murder in the beginning and then there's this plague-ridden Philadelphia in the late 1800's. What is the connection you see between those two?

JW: The connection is that they both exist at the same time as well as existing 200 years apart. They exist obviously in my imagination. They exist in that book. Everybody understands that. On the other hand, I think that there are levels and dimensions in which those two time periods collapse in terms of the individual imagination, in terms of feeling, and actually in terms of the repetition of events. Now the plague that is besieging the city is AIDS. If you think about it, in the popular imagination, who's blamed for AIDS? Where did AIDS come from? It came from African. It came from black people, people of African descent. That is the myth. Even if it's true in an etiologic sense, in an epidemiological sense, in terms of science, the way it was perceived in the public imagination was not as a microbe, but as one more menace that the black body contained. So you have that parallel.

You have the parallel of what's going on in the big cities today. That is, there are actual people who live there, real human beings. Those people are doing—we're doing—everything we can to improve the situation: fighting to make our homes safe, fighting to make the streets safe, fighting to raise the kids, fighting so the kids will survive. All that energy is going out of black people to save the city and save themselves. Yet we're seen as the perpetrators of the violence, as the perpetrators of the drug trade, as the people who are destroying the city. That's a perfect parallel to what went on in the 1790s during the yellow fever plague. So these things don't go away. In fact, the distance disappears very quickly in terms of the basic relationships between white and black in this society.

DM: I'm curious about the yellow fever plague. It was not something I knew much about. What hipped you to that period of time and made you see these parallels that you describe?

JW: I studied 18th-century literature at Oxford. That was my field. I chose that field because I knew nothing about it. I had a single course in college. I was fascinated by some of the writers, like Fielding, Smollett, and Richardson. I got just enough of a taste of it to make me want to go and study it intensely at Oxford. So I did that for three years. I lived in Philadelphia as a student and then as a teacher. Philadelphia partly is an 18th-century city. You walk down near the waterfront, Front Street, and you have the Mint and Independence Hall and the Liberty Bell . . .

DM: You have these really narrow little streets.

JW: Alfred's Alley. It's like you are *in* the 18th century. So I got a kick out of that, walking around and feeling that. Ben Franklin was like the presiding saint of the University of Pennsylvania and one of its founders. There was this funny little guy in his panty hose and short pants and long, swallowtail jacket on a statue [laughter] and I thought about those sorts of things.

But even more so, emotionally, what drew me to the period was the idea or the fact that at the end of the 18th century, America was coming into being. The Revolution had actually been fought in the last quarter of that century. People from all parts of the world, all kinds of people, speaking many different languages, were now collected in this land mass of North America and they were all becoming Americans. Just a day before, a week before, they were something else. They were Germans, they were Dutchmen, they were Frenchmen, they were Englishmen. You might have written down their identity with a hyphen. America was coming into being. They were losing a sense of foreignness. It was becoming their country. They were Americans.

Now there was one group of immigrants for whom that wasn't happening. In the American South it was clear why it wasn't happening. But in the north where there were many free people it wasn't happening either. Africans were not becoming Americans. It was an unrequited love affair—and I say unrequited love affair because the African people, the African-descended people in Philadelphia and New York and Massachusetts, wanted to become Americans. They were doing the things all the other foreigners were doing—raising families, trying to earn a living, learning the language, changing the language, taming the land, building the buildings. We were doing everything that the other Americans were doing, but we weren't allowed to become Americans. I've always thought that I wanted to know more about that. Emotionally, I wanted to know how it felt to be left out that way. Intellectually, I thought that if we understood that period better perhaps we would understand this moment better, because we're still living through the same kind of denial and lack of love exchange.

DM: This book—more than anything to my mind—is about, like most novels, relationships. The important relationships, how they come across in this book, are many times across racial lines. I thought the George Stubbs part of the book, the interracial marriage—it was not known by the folks where they lived that this couple was married—was very interesting, how you brought that out, how it was explained how they had been able to survive together over a period of time.

JW: That sort of thing is based on historical examples, of course. But it's also quite fascinating because what it does is call into question things that we take for granted. You take the average white or black American and they have a very distorted, very limited, simplistic view of the history of race relationships. That view is that somewhere around the 1860s slaves were freed and then you had integration. Before then, black people lived in one corner over there, singing when we had time free from work. But basically black people were slaves in America and white people were free. But that's not the case at all. There were all sorts of relationships between whites and blacks—commercial, romantic, political, military. It's that kind of hidden and unknown history that I think a novelist can profit from and so project and communicate in fiction.

In the book there is a black man living on a farm somewhere in Pennsylvania, a man who was born in Africa but who in fact was taken away from Africa by British Methodists. He was taken to England because these preachers wanted him to become a preacher. He was an apprentice, put in a seminary. But that didn't work out, so he had to go to work in a slaughterhouse. Then he migrated to America. That is an unusual and striking life history. What it emphasizes is this man's humanity, the possibilities, the potential. He had to learn English, he had to learn Latin, he had to learn Greek, in the seminary. Then he winds up working for a rich man. Then he crosses the ocean. He falls in love with a white servant girl. There's a mixing of class because she is an ignorant European woman. She's a beautiful red-haired woman, but she comes from a different world in so many ways than he does. So they wind up in Pennsylvania on a farm. Most of us have no idea—I certainly didn't—that those kinds of relationships existed.

DM: Talk about what they had to do to survive on that farm, though.

JW: When they first appeared in the environs of Philadelphia, the black man posed as a servant. The story that they floated around, the way they jived people, was that her husband was on his way and the black man was a trusted servant and he was her guardian while she settled and looked for property. Then, while they were looking for property, they spread a further rumor that the husband had died, had a heart attack on a crossing. That happened all the time. It wasn't easy to get from England to America. So they had that cover. He did the buying and selling in town. They purposely chose a farm that was very remote and that was how they looked to other townsfolk, as an aristocratic Englishwoman with a black servant who was helping her on this farm.

DM: Two things I'd like you to discuss, one minor and one major. He discovers that because he was a servant of a white woman he got treated economically as though he were white. As a black he wouldn't have received the same treatment in terms of what he could buy and sell and what he got for what he sold.

JW: Exactly. He talks about the "peculiar arithmetic." He's trying to school this young black man who arrives on the farm and who's the main character of the novel. They're in a wagon one day and he says to the young black man, "When I sell this wood I'm going to sell it as Liam the slave of Mrs. Stubbs, because then I'll get top dollar. But if I say that we're just two black men and don't identify myself as a slave and we sell them this load of wood, they'll give us about maybe a fifth, maybe a quarter, of what they would pay to Mrs. Stubbs' servant." So that's the "peculiar arithmetic" that underpins the economy of the time.

DM: Did you study about that? Is that historically accurate?

JW: Yes. It's very accurate. That's what I mean about time collapsing. I know that. My grandfather worked for people in Pittsburgh in the building trade. He'd go into the paint stores and tell them that he was buying the paint for Mr. Charlie and he'd get one price. If he went in as Harry Wideman and asked about the paint he would get another price. He'd have to pay a much higher price. I saw that work and this conversation between the African man and the younger African American boy in the 18th century occurred between my grandfather and myself in twentieth-century Pittsburgh.

DM: The other thing that I wanted to bring up is that living that existence ate the guy up from the inside. It destroyed him in a way over a period of years. He found himself retreating into himself trying to play the slave.

JW: Exactly. One very concrete cost of their secrecy was that they couldn't have children. What would the townsfolk have thought [laughter] if this little beige kid comes in one day on the back of the wagon? So that was a cost. For the novel it is a symbolic cost. It's a suggestion of the predicament that African American people find themselves in. If you are an orphan, if you are not a full citizen, and you procreate, what is the fate of your children? For the African man, for Liam, it was this same problem only with an exponent behind it, intensified. Because he knew if he brought children into the world they were going to get crushed. They were going to get wiped out. He knew that. There was no doubt about that. In fact, he made the choice. Rather than submit my children to that kind of danger, I just won't have any.

DM: You mention your main character. He's the preacher as we find out as time goes along in the book. Reading about this I find out that he's A.M.E. Zion Church founder Richard Allen. Is that right? Is that who he represents?

JW: Richard Allen served me as a model. I try to make it clear that he's not Richard Allen because at one point in the book Richard Allen himself appears in his own voice, in his own church. Richard Allen has talked his parishioners into leaving the white church where they're segregated and put into a little corner and not allowed to participate in the governance of the church or decide the rituals or what they sing and where they are continually insulted. Richard Allen has talked his folk into leaving and starting an independent church which was, in fact, the first independent black church in the North. But Richard Allen is a very religious man. At that moment in the book—and it's a long soliloquy, a stream-of-consciousness—he's reached that point where he thinks, "Okay, they're going to go with me to this new building. Hooray." But he's such a man of deep faith he begins to wonder, "Is God going to go with us? After all, we're leaving the church, the sanctified holy place, that's been here awhile. When I go down the street, is God going to come with me?" So I do interject that real person, but as a matter of fact the young man in the novel who's the main character—who's never named which is why we have to describe him each time—is modeled on Richard Allen's life. Richard Allen *was* an itinerant preacher. He did have a brother who was a sailor. He and his brother did in fact buy his mother's freedom and then bought their own. Richard Allen was involved in the plague in Philadelphia. He's the one who organized the black nurses and undertakers who eventually saved the city. My character and Richard Allen share lots.

DM: What made you decide to make him the main character? What led you to Richard Allen?

JW: I believed that, with Richard Allen being the deep soul that he was, his heart would be the kind of theater where all the emotions I wanted to have the novel exemplify could act themselves out. It's a novel about faith. It's a novel about faith and the American experiment in democracy. It's a novel about faith in God and traditional religion. It's a novel about faith in African tradition. I thought that Richard Allen had an authenticity and solidness that would make his decisions about these things meaningful.

DM: It seems to me that your book has almost a hypertextual context to it. I say that in terms of the World Wide Web. Things happen and they are linked back and forth in a very fast way and sometimes the hyperlinks are not immediately obvious. Did you think about that at all?

JW: I think that is an interesting description. Since I'm technologically illiterate [laughter] I've never thought of that metaphor. But [more laughter] it seems to work, it seems to work. I think more in terms of music and sports, but, yeah, why not? Why not come into the 21st century? I'm a person of this time, I know about these things. But Ishmael Reed said something once about comic books, about the fast cuts in comic books, and the fast cuts in movies. You go from one scene to another. If you're about 40 or 50 years old now, when you were a kid you grew up on comic books and TV and movies—visual arts—and you're used to taking these giant cuts. You have a character walking down a snowy street one day and, blip, the next day he's on a beach. You don't ask how he got there. The movie doesn't have to show you the train or the bus or buying the tickets. So we're used to those kinds of quick cuts. It opens up a lot of possibilities for the novel which I try to anticipate and use.

DM: Why did you give your main character what seem to be epileptic seizures?

JW: In a way he had to have them. He forced them on me [laughter]. I can answer these questions. I can pretend that I knew. I can pretend that these are things I figured out beforehand. But writing is like a lot of artistic activity. The unconscious works. The characters speak to me. They have an independent existence. The fits—I don't know whether that is something I figured out on my slide rule or whether my character just fell down one day and started to kick his feet and make funny noises. But I do know now, *after* the book, the purpose that they serve. This is a book that is located as much in the immaterial world, the world of spirit, as it is in the world of things, of the material world. I think there is an access that epileptics have to a spirit world which is very powerful and unique and I wanted to take advantage of that.

DM: He says that he gets a tremendous clarity of thought and feeling after he has these fits, as you describe them, and this is what leads him to do some of the things that he does later on.

JW: It gives him a kind of power, doesn't it? It gives me a power in the sense that I live so much in my own imagination and in my books. That world starts to become real to me as I give more time and more energy to it. I sometimes pay less attention to what is going on immediately outside—don't read the newspapers, don't watch TV. For the epileptic that access to a privileged spiritual world is a kind of doom in a way, but it's also a great privilege. I know a man who is an epileptic and he said that there is nothing worse than waking up and finding yourself slobbering and rolling around on the ground. Somebody asks you your name and you think you are saying it. But they can't hear you. There's nothing more humiliating and terrible than that. My friend has come to cure himself through diet and lots of different kinds of work—some medicine, some work with his own body. So he doesn't have fits very often. In fact, I don't think he has had one for four or five years. He says that, as humiliating as it is, he misses them.

DM: No!

JW: He misses them. He wouldn't want to go back, but he misses them.

DM: What does he miss?

JW: He misses that ability to escape. He misses what he saw when he was in the midst of a fit. That's what I try to capture in my character. I call it the "clear seeing," when the world makes absolute sense, when you're not nervous, when you're not anxious, when you're not worried about what's going to happen next. But things just fit.

DM: How do the spiritual and the physical worlds intersect in *The Cattle Killing?*

JW: In a way, it's a love story. The narrator of the story is in fact telling the novel to a woman who is very, very ill. She seems to be on the edge of death. But when he goes to tell the story—many stories really—that he makes up, she seems to revive. So the whole act of storytelling is a way of keeping her alive. Because he finds telling the story so necessary, she's keeping him alive. That seems to me a kind of nice definition of love. Through what you talk about, the stories that you tell, you make each other up and you keep each other alive.

DM: It's so funny to talk to you about this book, because some of the things you said are things I did not pick up in reading it. Before the show you pointed out to me that you can't rush through *The Cattle Killing.* Of course, I have to rush through them all because I have one night to read them. But it is important to take your time and try to pick up some of these things you're talking about.

JW: We live in the sort of world where everything has to be consumed immediately. I don't go to fast-food places, not because I am morally against hamburger [laughter], but because when I'm going to sit down and eat, I want to take my time. I enjoy it. I don't want a pill that fills me up. I want to enjoy it, savor it. Particularly literature. The books I like most are the ones I can read a couple of times—and read a page and think. But we don't allow ourselves time for that.

DM: But in a culture that does value stuff that can be flown through, and there's a great bit of that, what do you think when you say to your readers that, hey, you have to take your time with *The Cattle Killing.* Are you afraid that it will scare off some readers?

JW: I try to be upfront with readers and say, "Here's the kind of experience I'm going to offer you." Very early on in the novel you figure that out, because there are not a lot of the conventional hand-holds, even in terms of punctuation. So the reader can't whip right through because there are no quotation marks. When does the speaking stop and the narration start? There are no conventional markers of time. The novel isn't set up in a way that, when you look at a page, you see, "George said" or "Mary said." You can't read it that way. You have to figure out how I'm expressing that kind of communication.

DM: Was this intentional on your part? Or was this just how it came out?

JW: A little of both. As I read novels growing up, there were certain parts of them I didn't like. I thought that quotation marks were ugly. I thought it looked like a kind of disease [laughter]. These little funny, curly things all over the page. So I had an attitude about that. But also the more I wrote, as a kind of challenge, what I wanted to get into my writing was the same kind of fluidity and speed and motion that I have inside my head, in my thoughts—a stream-of-consciousness. Also I wanted to capture the energy and the force of oral storytelling. Now when you're listening to someone telling a funny story, you don't see periods and quotation marks and commas. The person doesn't supply those. That's supplied by the body, by tone, by somebody's eyes, by changing the inflection of the voice. Master storytellers can do that and take you all sorts of places. And that's what I want to do with the stream of my prose. I want it to work on the reader the way a good storyteller works.

DM: I read one of your short story collections, I read *Fatheralong,* I read this book, and I think one other book, and you deal with issues of race quite often. Yet I read an interview where they asked you if you considered yourself a black writer and you said no, because you said you didn't think that word meant very much.

JW: I'm sure you're right, and I probably shouldn't have said that if I answered no [laughter], because it just confuses people. You say that and somebody is already half-way down the room, saying, "Did you hear what that brother said?" What I should have said was, "Well, look a little closer at me [laughter] and ask me that question again." I mean, from the fact that I'm of African American descent, nothing follows. I could write mystery novels, I could write in Victorian English, I could write like the guys on the corner write now, I could write travel books. Nothing follows from the fact of my African American ancestry. Writing is not reflex, is not biologically-driven. Well, in some ways it is biologically-driven. But it's not determined by race. I want to make that clear.

DM: How much of it is determined by culture, though?

JW: Culture is the key. That would be the next thing I'd say. I'd say I probably prefer the designation "African American author" because that seems to imply culture to more people. "Black" seems almost to be a fighting word, and that is why we use it, and should use it sometimes, because it

expresses a collectivity. It expresses something about politics, it expresses
something about inequality, and so it's needed. But when we're talking about
art and literature, it's culture. There's an African American language. There's
an African American history. There's an African American identity. Those
are captured in many fine works of art and we need to talk about that and
understand that. That's my tradition. That's where I live.

Listener/caller: In the process of writing this novel, was it sometimes
difficult to balance the purposes of history, which weigh so heavily, and the
emotional development of the individual characters?

JW: Absolutely, because I wanted those two things to blend and come
together. Too much reference to history dates the book and makes it a kind
of antique, would make it a conventional historical novel. In other words, it
would be a book about something that happened a long time ago.

DM: A period piece.

JW: A period piece, exactly. I didn't want that. I wanted it to be a piece,
period [laughter]. I wanted it to be happening right now. I wanted you to feel
it. I wanted your guts to be inside the guts of the characters and that's the
whole point of it. If you don't feel something about what you're reading, if
you can't identify, if it don't have that swing, then it don't mean a thing. So
you've pinpointed one of my problems as a novelist, blending that immediacy
of flesh-and-blood characters with the historical reality.

DM: Talk about the historical reality. You go back to this South African
historical context with the Xhosa tribe and the "cattle killing"—which is
what the book is named for. Was this a true part of history? Did this actually
happen? Or was this something that you took some license with?

JW: No, I wish it hadn't happened. Not only did it happen there, it happened here. Some of you might be familiar with the Ghost Dance, that kind
of epidemic that overtook the Plains Indians at the end of the 19th century.
About forty years before that the Xhosa people had suffered exactly that sort
of pressure from outsiders who had been fighting with the Xhosa for 150
years trying to push them out of their traditional lands. It took a terrible toll
on the tribe. A prophet arose, a Xhosa prophet, a young woman. She said,
"If you kill your cattle, the Europeans will disappear, they'll be swallowed
up by the sea, your ancestors will return, and the ancestors will bring endless
herds of cattle, and life will be paradise forever after." The people were so
beaten up and so desperate that that sounded good. In historical fact, the
Xhosa began to slaughter their cattle, the result of which was a weakening of
the tribe. They doomed themselves to becoming second-class citizens in their

own country. The point there was, if you believe the lies of your enemies, that's the surest way to self-destruction. If we give ourselves a little bit of imaginative license, we understand precisely how that moral fits this moment, our moment in time.

DM: How did you decide to make that the central thematic concept of the book, when it's not that big a part of the book? The main character we've been talking about, it's his story that's the main part. This is something that you refer to only every now and them.

JW: Well, for many reasons. I see the young woman that the narrator is in love with as a spirit from Africa; she's an African spirit.

DM: This is the woman who he sees walking up to him early on in the book?

JW: She reoccurs as the servant of the blind woman. She reappears as a servant in the house of Mr. and Mrs. Thrush where the narrator goes to take some news. He meets her and they have long conversations. They have a little romance. This African spirit is the one he tells his story to. She's the one he's trying to keep alive. He makes the mistake of thinking that the bodies she tends to inhabit are really her. But the spirit is much more than the bodies.

DM: Once again, I'm catching up on things from hearing what you say that I didn't catch as I was reading the book. Right at the beginning of the book three's a section where you talk about this old African spirit.

JW: First of all, the book is dedicated to my daughter, Jamila, and I say that she came here with one of those old beautiful spirits that has been here before. Then you go on and get an ethnographic note about a phenomenon that the Ibo people in Africa call the ogbanji. An ogbanji is a kind of evil spirit who gets set up in a woman's womb and destroys the new life that comes into the womb. This will keep happening again and again. A woman will miscarry until you get this ogbanji out of the womb, because the ogbanji eats human lives. It's a kind of spirit that can pass from body to body. Each one it goes into it eats up, destroys, because it's so powerful. It's almost immortal, it's almost a god because it's so thirsty for life. It's just too intense inside a person. So you can exorcise an ogbanji through certain rituals. The Ibo people have rituals for that. Now my man, the narrator, comes across a spirit that's not necessarily evil, but she has the same power as an ogbanji. She can transport herself from body to body. She uses those bodies up. That's why when the narrator is talking to this woman he believes he loves, he's afraid her spirit is ebbing, that she's going to die.

DM: Which she is, but the spirit is not going to die.

JW: Yes, as long as they talk, then the spirit has energy.

DM: I don't know if you are familiar with all the work of Octavia Butler, but she has written a book called *Wild Seed*. One of the characters in it is an African person who at the age of thirteen realized he was a spirit like that. He began to take bodies, one by one, and within six or eight weeks he would burn them out and have to move on to another one. In a sense he was immortal. I wonder if both your stories came from that same evil legend that you're talking about.

JW: Well, we all draw from the same pots when you get right down to it. That's an old idea. It comes out in vampires even. But what I'm trying to do in this book is to avoid the sort of sensationalism of *Dracula* and break it down so it has meaning to us all. If you've been lucky, you know about people whose spirits are so strong that, even when the person dies, they continue to have an effect. If not in one's personal life, then think about someone like Martin Luther King who still is with us—as long as we venerate his ideal, as long as we understand where he was trying to take us—and continues to exert a tremendous force. So we're not talking about spooks and vampires. We're talking about something that's very real in our lives, the way that we're connected to our ancestors, the way that we're connected to their wisdom and their strength and their guidance. We worship our ancestors in this country. We just don't like to talk about it. We think it's superstitious. We laugh at the Africans because they are benighted and superstitious and worship their ancestors. Then we look at that mountain in the West and we have these four presidents' faces carved on it. We have their faces on the money. We have the big story of American history which is all about secular saints, people we should be like. Like George Washington, if you chop down a cherry tree, admit it. Any culture worships its ancestors. It's just that in America we deny that in general and we almost prohibit African Americans from forming that kind of relationship with the ancestors.

DM: I wanted to change subjects for just a minute and ask you about a fascinating piece you wrote about pro basketball player Dennis Rodman in *The New Yorker*. You seemed to be trying to understand the guy in a way that other people have not.

JW: Well, he started on my S-list [laughter], because my first exposure to Dennis was when the Chicago Bulls were playing against Detroit six or seven years ago when he was a Detroit Piston and Detroit would always beat up my boys, the Bulls, and Dennis was one of the villains. And I didn't like the way he played. He seemed to be a dangerous kind of player—a lot of enthusiasm, a lot of physical activity, but he didn't have any cool, he didn't have any style. I thought he was actually a kind of a thug on the court. I didn't like that at all. I remembered guys like him who I played against on the playgrounds. They didn't really have a game. They just basically got in the way. You had to be careful, because they were all elbows and knees and awkward. Even if they weren't trying to hurt you, since they didn't know the game, they might hurt you.

DM: Yes, I remember guys like that. You really didn't want them to check you, and you really didn't want to check them.

JW: No, you didn't want them around. But, on the other hand, they added something to the game. So I had Rodman bagged that way. And then, things changed. And sometimes I'm even patient enough to change with them [laughter]. I changed my opinion. I began to respect his ability more, and began to be curious about his rebelliousness. He became an underdog because a whole lot of people were picking on him and his attitude. Then I got in his corner and started to think, "Now, where is he coming from?" Then when he finally became a hero—that is, he put on a Bulls' uniform, my team's uniform—then I had even more compassion for him.

DM: He became sort of an antihero, didn't he?

JW: The strange thing about it is that here's a guy who, from a certain perspective, is poison—poison in terms of being a role model, of the work ethic, of going along with the program, of all those all-American values that the league tries to project. Now to me that had to make him a good guy [laughter]. These are attempts to sentimentalize the game, to steal the fire of the game.

DM: Really?

JW: Yes, because sport is one of the few places left where legitimate effort and individuality is honored or should be honored. We want to turn the players into lunch pail guys and good soldiers. That's a whole different value system and it tames them. It connects them to factory work, to the industrial society, and to the corporation, when, in fact, when you look at it another way, sport is a testimony to anarchy. Sport is a testimony to freedom, to individuality, to being allowed to do your own thing. If you do it well enough and hard enough, you can survive and make an imprint.

DM: What's the idea of attaching a mythical significance to the struggle between David Stern, the National Basketball Association Commissioner, and Dennis Rodman, who likes his own type of outfits and colors his hair and all that?

JW: That goes back to the days when I was in college or even before that, when the worst thing you could say about a basketball player was that he was "playground." I can remember very distinctly times in college and in high school making a move, going to the basket, trying a shot and hearing somebody say, "Playground move. You gotta get that 'playground' out of your game." That was meant as an insult. Now we have the whole game trying to approximate the playground, what the playground does—and those values have been incorporated into pro ball and college ball. Now they're trying to teach people how to play playground, and if you don't have that playground verve and ethos your teams are not going to be successful. So it was a personal insult to me and to the game when people talked about basketball in the corporate sense. I see that war still going on with Rodman. The league and society are trying to take away the power of spontaneity and improvisation and self-invention that sport offers and make it serve different ends.

DM: Dennis Rodman has any number of interesting defenders who think he's a character in a game that maybe needs a few characters. I wonder what your final take on him is as a person and on some of his antics. Is he a media creation or is he just being himself?

JW: Well, there's a certain point where you never know [laughter]. You have to ask Dennis—and he probably doesn't know. What we *do* know is that whatever act he has fashioned is working. It is profitable for him, he seems to enjoy it. So—"Will the real Dennis Rodman please stand up?" I think if you ask that question, you'll hear about four chairs in the room [laughter] all scraping at once.

DM: [More laughter.] That's a pretty good one! It's so funny to go from talking about very serious literature, which this book is, to something like basketball. Is that an interesting dichotomy at all to you?

JW: It's just the way I was raised. It's just been my experience. It's fascinating that we become known for one thing in this society and then that's our bread-and-butter and it's pretty hard to establish credentials in some other area. Of course, in another way, if you become famous, you automatically become an expert in every field. But it's a business that I have had to face all my life—that is, people trying to characterize me because I'm an African American. For example, being in the cafeteria on the University of Pennsylvania's campus and identifying myself as working at the university, somebody will ask, "Oh, in the Athletic Department?" [Laughter.] Just that automatic jump.

Benefit of the Doubt: A Conversation with John Edgar Wideman

Bonnie TuSmith / 1997

BT: Last year you took part in a symposium on your work at the University of Tours in France. Can you tell us something about the experience? First, who were the participants and audience?

JW: I had more than one audience. One day I met with two undergraduate classes. There were at least two hundred or so French students—mostly undergraduate and some graduate students. It was just general give-and-take. The next day was a more formal program: six presenters—well, five. There were supposed to be six but the German never showed up. And then either four or five papers given.

BT: Was it a mixed audience or were they mostly French?

JW: They were all French. Michel Fabre was the main organizer. He's an international figure in literature by now. A man named Claude Renaud was the person who organized most of my stay there. I spent most of the time with him. I think they intend to publish the proceedings. The last I heard Charles Rowell [editor of *Callaloo*] was going to publish it in English. Well, the papers were in English—at least I understood them so they must have been in English [laughter].

BT: How did responses to your work differ from those in the United States?

JW: How did they differ? I was very pleased because they were serious discussions of the writing as writing. Not that they were done in a political or social vacuum. There was much more attention to language, structure, form—to the writerly dimensions of the work. The French do some things very well. They do close reading, or textual analysis, very well. When one's work is subjected to that, it's very interesting. One person talked about the image of balloons. Certainly, it was enlightening to me because I hadn't planned it that way. The continuity of the figure of the balloon—not just in one book or one chapter but throughout the range of three or four books, bouncing back and forth from *A Glance Away* all the way up to *Philadelphia Fire*. So this person had clearly paid attention and treated the work with great care and seriousness, and a writer recognizes and appreciates that.

The other papers had the same kind of close reading, as *explications de texte*. People sometimes get confused and think of that as artsy or noncritical, but it can be extremely critical—people writing about race and gender and using techniques of textual explication of genre. There are good ones in all countries but I think that the French are very canny. I liked a piece that a man did on *Brothers and Keepers* where he talked about the figure of brother and the double, brothers and doubles and mirrors, etc.—very intricate reading. Another woman talked about a piece that just doesn't even get talked about in the States, a short story called "Surfiction." I guess surfiction was a natural for them because *Surfiction* is the name of a magazine ant it's edited by a Frenchman. I talked about Foucault and other French writers in that contemporary tradition in France—it's kind of woven in the story in the sense of game playing and trickery. The French critic who wrote about that story did a lot of work on Charles Chesnutt—on the roots and sources of the story. Frankly, I've enjoyed very little of that kind of serious treatment in this country so it was quite gratifying—special to me.

BT: I've been struggling with my students to get them to do that, to read with more care. When we study other languages—Spanish, French, and so forth—we learn the skill of explication as an essential part of the acquisition of the language. But in the teaching of literature in English the careful attention to the complex uses of language is taken for granted—as if it were just a natural extension of basic literacy.

JW: Yes, and there's very few organs that seriously treat literature in this country—shamefully few. I'm not a great reader of periodicals so I should be careful of what I say, but I try to keep up and I talk to other people who do read them. Most of the time a writer is subject to what amounts to a book report—a summary of the action and then "I like it" or "I don't like it" in so many words by the critic. If you're lucky, maybe on top of that is spread a little attitudinizing about what you should be doing, or where's your subject, or what should be your subject, or why somebody else wrote about it better than you did. You know, stuff like that. A review, if it's longer than five hundred words, can sometimes be a platform for the critic to expound his or her own ideas about the subject you're writing about. Seldom does a critic hold back his or her own ideas or politics and say, "Let's just see what *this* story or novel has to say. Let's give it the benefit of the doubt and let's look at the world on *its* terms and closely scrutinize and figure out what those terms *are* before we hit it with the hammer of judgment." I don't think that posture, that kind of treatment of books, is very prevalent. It seems rare.

BT: What about the French audience, the participants? Did the lack of first-hand experience with American culture become evident?

JW: There was an extreme amount of give-and-take. The people who presented the papers certainly knew what they were talking about. Because they were smart people they chose areas in which they *did* know something. But, it's easy enough to get footnotes. I read Turkish novelists, Yugoslavian novelists, Greek novelists—novels from four hundred years ago. I do that with the help of dictionaries, glossaries, criticism. I think I find what I need to know about the culture. I wasn't around in eighteenth-century England, so there are certain terms I don't know—certain ordinary, everyday facts of life that I don't know. But my *reading* of the really good books is not encumbered by that. If I think the book serious enough I do work and find out the cultural material that's necessary—and that's the approach of the French. They have the advantage, of course, of being on the outside of our culture, so they form an independent judgment as they go along. Sometimes it could be kind of funny—*we* might question whether Jerry Lewis is the greatest American filmmaker in comic history [laughter]. Or maybe that's some kind of particular French humor—I don't know. Other people can miss some obvious things. However, the French are generally well-informed. They study things. Sometimes, when you study something you make gross errors. But you also have particular kinds of insight.

BT: And the undergraduate students?

JW: The undergrads were a little more naive. But they certainly knew a lot about American pop culture. There's definitely an international pop culture. You'll find New York Knick teeshirts in Kazakhstan. The Kazakh kids don't know all the players but they know about the NBA, some of the teams—things like that. There's an international culture which makes some of these questions a moot point. Anyway, when I read a novel, for me the point is to *learn* about a different world. If everything was familiar, then, in some ways, what's the point? The point is to go into territory that's unknown—where you do flounder a little bit and need some help. That's fine, that's why you go into it.

BT: Also, what does it mean to you that the first symposium on your work took place outside the United States?

JW: Well, I wasn't surprised. It's a tradition. Baldwin was first picked up outside the country in a serious way—his work, that is. And it goes back much further than that. The Shakespearean actor Ira Aldridge, sculptors, opera singers, African Americans in many different arts had to go to Europe to be recognized. Leontyne Price. Of course, opera is slightly different— that's where everybody goes to prove they're for real. It's a great tradition so I'm not surprised—disappointed that's still the case, but not surprised.

BT: In your preface to *The Best American Short Stories 1996,* you repeat an African saying that's also the title of one of your books: namely, "all stories are true." Would you briefly explain how this saying summarizes for you the purpose and role of storytelling?

JW: Even though I've written a collection of stories and individual stories under that title—and pondered it—I still don't exactly know what it means [laughter]. That's the attraction. It's mysterious. It has so many twists and turns. It's almost like you can say you know what $E = MC^2$ means. But, to understand what it means, you also have to have a grasp of physics and all the details and ins and outs. So there's so much energy packed into that phrase. Although it's clarified and illuminated much for me, it still remains mysterious. Obviously, it refers to a kind of relativity—that each person's voice has weight and force and a corner of the truth. In that sense it's pro- foundly democratic. And this is *real* democracy.

In another way the same phrase suggests infinitely receiving mirrors— because of the relativity implied. Okay, all stories are true. You tell me a story in which George Washington's a hero; somebody else tells one in which he's a villain. Now, which is it? You tell me you love me one day and you tell me you don't the next day. Now, which is true? It gets really intimate and personal as well as says something about history. When you get right down to it, *knowing* the fact that all stories are true is as much a place to begin as a conclusion, because it doesn't remove the necessity for sorting through the evidence—of working through the stories. What I like about it in particular is that it decentralizes the truth—it fragments the truth. It puts truth in the light of multiplicity, of voices as a kind of construct that you can't arrive at unless you do have a mosaic of voices. I like that, actually.

BT: I want to tell you about an experience I had concerning storytelling. I used to attend weekly meetings conducted by the Women's Studies Program of a university. At one particular session, they were planning a women's conference so they went around the room to come up with ideas for the theme of the conference. Finally, I suggested storytelling as a common theme. What happened was that a couple of women walked out of the room. I had no idea this would happen. This was one of the oddest experiences I've had in academia. All of a sudden there was this division in the room. It seems that the minute you talk about stories and storytelling some "feminists" somehow assume that you're bashing theory and, thus, bashing them.

JW: Yeah, "story" has that suggestion—it's like "folklore." That's an old cleavage in the discipline as well. When I was at Penn there was a Folklore Department, and you definitely wanted to be in the English Department. What's interesting, though, is that if you look at literary theory in some of the English departments today, the central concepts come out of folklore: people like Clifford Geertz and Dell Hymes who, in discovering other cultures, turned up notions like speech act and representation, and how to describe a speech act. All this stuff is filtered back into the center of the most hard- and scientifically-minded English literature courses.

But, anyway, yeah, storytelling is considered soft. Storytelling is soft as opposed to hard—not analytical enough. Those are very limited notions. Again, if you look at things like physics, like neuroscience—people are talking about narrative. People who are trying to understand mental disease—aphasia and problems with the mind—are using ideas about story and storytelling. Everybody talks about narrative—from astronomers, to physicists, to behaviorists. To me, if you were to stop and define a human being, one definition would be a storyteller. I mean, you *could* put it in other ways—like a creature that lies [laughter].

BT: Same thing.

JW: Yeah, same thing.

BT: Here's a heavy duty question. In *Fatheralong,* you discuss the "paradigm of race" as a European invention. How would you define this paradigm and why should it be overturned? If this were overturned, how do you perceive human relations to be different? What does your analysis tell us about prejudice in other cultures and other periods of history? This is an involved question, I know. Maybe you can give us a "capsule version" of your argument.

JW: Well, the argument is pretty simple. If you try to determine the independent existence of race, what race is, you'll find that it's very difficult to verify—whether you're talking about biology or sociology. Race is a construct. It's a cultural, social, and political construct. As a construct, its purpose is to demonstrate or to sustain the dominance of one group over another. I think that is its purest essence. Now, that's not to say there are no differences. I don't think you can look at an African, a Korean, or someone from Finland and not see differences. The differences are real.

But race gives a meaning to the differences. Race is a particular way of evaluating the differences. Every theory of race I've ever heard of—because that's what we're talking about, ideas about what these differences mean— seems to me very quickly lead to hierarchical differentiations among various types of human beings for the purpose of establishing one as better or superior to the others, or for establishing one or more as inferior. I think that's how race, as a concept, has worked as far back as I can trace it. It's almost a way of establishing a kind of preeminence. In many languages people have a kind of race notion even buried in their own name, in their own language, where a people's name often means The People. They're The Ones, and everybody else is The Other. But, I begin with the notion that race is constructed to establish and sustain a superiority over others—that's its purpose.

BT: Wasn't there a concept of race before European colonization?

JW: There may be, and I might have misspoken. But I think that my definition is more functional than historical. My point would be that if you study the history of any people in terms of cultural contact, when something like the concept of race evolved—whether it's called that in Japanese, Chinese, or whatever—its purpose would be the same cross-culturally. I would like to know if in some cultures it is different. For example, if Koreans and Japanese would sit and talk about one another and the user could refer to a generic concept of *person*—Koreans are one kind and Japanese are another— without implying superiority or inferiority. I'd like to know that, to tell you the truth. It would be encouraging to know that perceived difference could actually be neutralized. Whatever culture in which that was true would be quite different from the West.

BT: In your recent talk at Northeastern University you made the statement that in some ways your brother Robby has paid the price for your success. Can you explain what you meant by that? Several people asked about this.

JW: It's a somewhat reductive statement, but I do think that it makes us think. It moves from the individual to the systemic. You have a culture which dooms a lot of people to second class citizenship in the West. The mechanisms that buttress, that perpetuate racism are the same ones that allow a certain number of people in a minority group to float up to the surface and succeed. In other words, there are certain kinds of safety valves in a racist or apartheid system that actually can be seen to function as much for the equilibrium of the system as they do for the benefit of those who happen to get the advantages.

A simple example would be prison guards. Maybe it's good to have black prison guards, so the system works to train black prison guards and they do a little better than other black people. Their success is, on the one hand, great for them, but the job they do is to keep the black folk in line. They are like the overseers during the period of slavery. Now that's a gross example. When you talk about middle class, and middle-class success for a certain percentage of black people, then it's a little more subtle. But the same kind of systemic forces are at work. You look at one side of it and you see black achievement; you look at the other side of it and you see a safety valve. There might be role models, so that there is not complete and utter lack of hope that might have revolutionary potential for the masses. Every colonial society has created this sort of buffer, a middle class of natives to help the colonial society work. So, why is America any different? Why should we look at segregation and integration apart from these other models that are quite clear?

BT: I think that when you make a statement like that—about Robby and you—it can work on several levels at the same time. The ramifications of the "difference" are quite clear. But some people still ask why you say that because they can't imagine anyone saying that.

JW: It's dangerous, too, isn't it? I mean, I got where I got not because somebody handed it to me, exactly, so I don't want to be in the position—by a statement like that—of slamming achievement. Because then why bother? One conclusion of what I'm saying is, okay, don't aid and abet the enemy. Don't piss on your brother. Then what? Be a hoodlum, be a crook, join a gang, prey on your own people and society? No, that's not it. I don't see myself as simply a safety valve, a creation of the system to help keep other people oppressed. That's one way of seeing things and I think it's necessary to see it that way so you don't get confused.

But there are other ways that I see myself—as an individual. Other ways that I see of pulling yourself up by your bootstraps and then, using that leverage, that education, that money, that renown—whatever you achieve—as something that you then can push back into the system and work for change. But if you don't recognize the ambivalence of your position of success then you may be in trouble. You may not do some of the right things, the correct things, to make greatest use of—for yourself and other people— the advantages.

BT: The next question is something I'm especially interested in. Can you comment on how color is used in your works in relation to human perception as well as to "race"? I'm very interested in how you handle color, especially your impulse for creating the albino character. You meditate on color. For example, in *Sent for You Yesterday,* remember John French's brogans where there are layers of paint and the narrator ponders over what's underneath the layers? There's a similar thing with Mrs. Stubb's skin in *The Cattle Killing.*

I think they're quite profound meditations on color. I'm interested in all aspects of color and the creative process.

JW: Well, it's not all conscious, that's the first thing I'd say. There are probably many different dimensions that change over time. For one thing, color is marvelous, it's beautiful. Color has mystery, allure. So I want to take that back, I want to privilege color—what's special about it. This has a lot to do with identity, with pride, with Black Is Beautiful. We do *see* it so it does change things and make things quite attractive. I don't want to give that up. At the same time, color is a badge and used against *us*. So I have to recognize its history in that way. Again, it's very charged and very ambivalent. That means that as a writer, I work hard to stipulate, to contextualize color—to diminish the negativity and to assert what is positive, what is ongoing, what is potentially enlightening about color.

I'm interested in its aesthetic dimension aside from the social evaluations of dark being bad and light being good. I want to break down the notion that black and white have anything to do with actual color: you know, one's the absence of color and one's the presence of all colors. So, really, black and white have nothing to do with color.

Then there's the history of color, how it has worked in the African American community. How—in a sordid, sad, shameful way—race and color prejudice was imposed on us and internalized—*both*—inside the African American community. My grandmother was what we call "color struck," and that meant that she didn't like dark people—she didn't think they were good looking. She was really taken by light, "bright" people. She herself could pass for any race. So there's that. Then there's also the *sign* of blackness as brotherhood, as community, as soul brother. Founding a political movement based on the notion that black is beautiful. And then in between there is the whole notion of the rainbow. That black and white have nothing to do with what we really are anyway. That, in fact, if we use our eyes we can invent and discover that actual color, what is actually out there, is something that is intriguing, romantic, intimidating, scary—full of possibilities.

BT: Do you remember why you chose the albino character, the albino image in *Sent for You Yesterday?*

JW: Because albino throws everything into chaos. Particularly an albino with African features, or who culturally is an African American person. That throws the whole system into chaos. Like Gary Cooper or Paul Newman with a vernacular brogue, wearing a big hat and singing like Harry Belafonte. It's throwing the whole thing topsy turvy, showing how arbitrary it is and, at the same time, how dangerous it is—enclosing and claustrophobic.

BT: In my book on community in ethnic American literature I noticed that, of the eight creative works that I wrote about, seven had some reference to albinism—either an image or a full-blown character. And that study has nothing to do with this subject. So I became intrigued. I figured there must be something happening for writers to be using albinism as a literary trope. I published an article called "The Inscrutable Albino"—as opposed to "the Inscrutable Oriental," you know. Since your albino character Brother Tate plays a large role in that essay, I thought I'd get your views on the subject.

JW: Absence of color throws the whole system into shambles, because if we are to be classified by color, what do you do with a person whose body denies color—it's transparent. Then the primary way of ordering human be-ings—the primary hierarchy—is destroyed. I liked that. Yeah, an albino could be seen as a freak of color. But then, what would that mean? It's also a kind of locus. A lot of interesting stuff.

BT: I'd like to explore your take on human relationships further by focus-ing on a statement in your work and in your comments that seems central to me. In a 1983 interview you said that possibly the most valuable inheritance you had was your grandfather's philosophy of "giving the other guy the benefit of the doubt." In *Brothers & Keepers,* published a year later, you wrote that your mother "had exhausted her reserve of understanding and compassion" after Robby's friend Garth died. How do you think about your grandfather's motto today?

JW: Like any principle, it's honored as much in the breach as the obser-vance of it. I wish I could be more like that. It's an ideal, that's all. Simply an ideal. The other side of that principle, which I also cite in my books, is that you do that—you give them the benefit of the doubt—until they persist too long and then you go upside their head [laughter]. It isn't the Christian turn-the-other-cheek. Or, you turn it once and if you get slapped on that cheek too then you'll have to look out for yourself. So it isn't a passivistic thing at all. Well, it *is* passivistic because it's a suggestion—a mantra—to mellow out, to see a larger picture. To treat the other person as you would treat yourself. But it doesn't say that there is, as basic human beings, some kind of goodness that would necessarily respond to turning the other cheek. It says that's the first response. Maybe it's the response that goes on the second or third or fifth time. And maybe with your children it goes on forever because you can't help yourself. But, there's a real reason for the ideal—at least in my way of interpreting what my grandfather said. I know he interpreted it that way, because he was respected tremendously but he was also feared. So watch out if you push too far.

BT: This notion depends on reciprocity. Otherwise, you just get taken advantage of.

JW: And people don't learn.

BT: Ever since I ran into this quote over ten years ago it's been really important to me. The idea of giving the other person the benefit of the doubt—and we're basically talking about a longer view, I think—is a guiding principle that I learned from your works. That doesn't mean that I'm not a fighter, that I'd let people walk all over me. But it's really important to keep the idea in mind—especially when times are really bad. I don't like to jump to conclusions about people if I can help it.

JW: Well, here's a perfect example and I think I've cited it before. In Homewood where I was raised and where my grandfather was kind of a legend there was a Chinese restaurant and my grandfather knew the man who ran the Chinese restaurant. I think they were maybe gambling together. But he knew him. The man started out with just a little kind of a kitchen in which he shoveled out food and everybody ate the food—and it was *successful.* Eventually the Chinese man moved his restaurant to a slightly different part of town. When he moved there, John French couldn't go in—because if he went in then it would discourage the clientele there. But, he would go in the back and sit on the back of the restaurant's steps and eat while having long talks and chats with the man who owned it. Somebody asked my grandfather about it. What he said—I don't remember the Chinese man's name so you'll forgive me if I say—was, "Well, Mr. Lee has to feed his family." So, my grandfather did not take the short view of prejudice but the long view that they were both subjected to a kind of racism. Because Lee wasn't the enemy, they were still friends. It wasn't humiliating to sit with Lee and eat in the back—that's saving something to get over on the enemy. It's a story that seems to embody that philosophy.

BT: When you get older does it get harder?

JW: I think you could get to the point where you say, well, I've been giving the benefit of the doubt a long time [laughter]. This worm has turned some turns! That's one way. Nah, I think my grandfather got more mellow as he grew older.

BT: Now I've got a few questions on your latest book. There's a statement early in *The Cattle Killing* that it is "not exactly a novel." How would you describe the kind of book it is?

JW: I think what I mean is that it's a very ambitious novel and that it will include games, genres, techniques, and demands on the reader that are a mixed bag, that maybe most readers don't associate with reading a novel. So it's a warning label—it is a warning to give me the benefit of the doubt that I know that I'm going to be asking things and trying to do things that are not ordinary, that are not traditional.

BT: That's a good way of putting it. In the prologue to *The Cattle Killing* the speaker introduces the image of the destruction of cattle herds by the Xhosa people during the 1850s in South Africa in response to a false prophecy. In what ways do you see this event as an appropriate central image for the book?

JW: I named the book *The Cattle Killing*. It seems to be very resonant. It seems to include all the pieces I needed to include. There is a lesson in it very clearly. The cattle killing is emblematic of the very simple lesson that if you believe the lies of your enemies, that is a sure path to destruction. Once that is said, once you realize that that is one of the morals of the event of the cattle killing—the national historical event—then that idea yokes the contemporary scene of the novel as well as the eighteenth-century scene. During the plague there were lies that were told about black people and in the twentieth century there are lies about black people and the danger is in internalizing them.

BT: I'm curious about the creative process. When you first learned about this historical event, was there something about it that immediately fascinated your writerly mind?

JW: Yes, although I didn't know exactly where it was going to take me or exactly what it meant. But it sure did get my attention—like that phrase "all stories are true." I had been peeling away at it, sorting it out—but it did grab me. In some ways it did grab me as immediately relevant to the contemporary moment. It has hit other people that way, too. When I told my mother the story of the cattle killing, before the novel was written, she said, "Mm mm, that sounds just like today, just like what's going on now. All these young people out there dying, what's happening today. That's some story." To her it clicked at once.

BT: There's also a remarkable parallel to Wounded Knee—in American Indian history—in terms of a people making themselves vulnerable as a result of believing in an apocalyptic prophecy.

JW: Yes, it's mentioned somewhere in the novel—at least I meant to men-tion it [laughter]. Only a few years after the cattle killing in Africa, there was the Ghost Dance in the American midwest—precisely the same kind of cul-tural phenomenon. A prophet comes along and says that if you perform this dance, the white man will go away and it will be paradise again—things will go back to the way they were. So the people embark on this suicidal ritual in order to change things. It was just a kind of dance of death that took place before history turned people into second-class citizens, destroyed the culture. It has happened in other places as well—it has happened in Asia. There was some sort of false prophecy and people believed in it and had their strength, their culture, jerked out from under them. There are a couple of books about this phenomenon.

BT: When a people believe in their dream visions—in a literal way like that—they're extremely vulnerable?

JW: It's like anything else—the life of the mind, visions, the words of prophets, politicians, leaders. They can all be right or wrong. All dreamers are not good dreamers. All dreams are not good dreams.

BT: In *The Cattle Killing* there's a scene where the eighteenth-century black preacher encounters a young African woman carrying a dead baby who walks into a lake. It isn't clear whether the woman actually drowns or not.

JW: Well, she keeps coming back. But not in that particular body—in others. In the book I think it's important to distinguish between spirits and bodies. Bodies are sort of shells or vehicles. I know this might escape people, but to some extent a body is meaningless except for the spirit that animates it. The spirit that animates it is stronger and has a life apart. So what we follow through the book is what is set up in the little epigraph beforehand that says that there are certain very powerful spirits that have so much energy, so much force, so much passion that they are too strong for bodies. They use up bodies, pass on to another one. I believe something like that.

BT: How much do you leave up to the reader to decide what to make of incidents like that of the drowned woman? The reader is faced with a juxtapo-sition of at least two levels of "reality": historically factual information—like the plague and the cattle killing—and this kind of spiritual presence as well.

JW: I depend immensely on the reader to process the novel, to make sense of it. It's not a kaleidoscope, although it has some features of a kaleido-scope. You turn it this way it looks one way, turn it that way it looks another way. That's what I want. But it's not random. There are certain ways of getting through it that I try to push the reader into. There are paths. Some will make more sense than others. Those are the ones that a reader will have more success with. The reader will plot those, follow those. But, it's not real big on conclusions. It's not real big on answers. I don't think that is the role of novels. Novels should ask questions—questions that are like Chinese boxes, questions that bend the life and the energy that you or I have. We set out questing to deal with these questions. If there are any answers, the answers are examples, a witness of a given life, i.e., a story. That doesn't close down the quest. That doesn't close down the question. It just means that that's *her* story, it's *his* story. I would rather have my books end that way—testifying to the fact that, if you pay attention to this powerful witness, there's something to be learned from the way he or she approached this question.

BT: There's a passage in *The Cattle Killing* that asserts the power of stories to persist and to "save" us "If someone is listening." You often comment on the relationship of the storyteller to the listener. Can you elaborate on this issue—especially on the implications of the word "if"?

JW: Well, I'm not always certain that people are reading my books. I'm not always certain that anybody is listening to my outcries. There's powerful evidence that suggests that there is not a lot of communication among human beings. We keep doing the same stupid things over and over again to one another as individuals and groups. We heard the roar of pain of the Holocaust, and that has been just a few generations ago. We have forgotten it already. What could be louder and more intense, more horrific, than that outcry? But it gets lost. We start forgetting quickly. We didn't hear it when it was loud and alive. I see that, I understand that. I don't think there's any guarantee that life will persist or that society will turn towards justice. I *hope* so. I look at a person like my mother who has tremendous faith in that vision. I think about that. It makes me pause and wonder—and hope. But I don't necessarily have her faith. I don't have her faith all the time. So I sometimes wonder if anybody ever does listen.

Do we listen to ourselves? I know I can sit and make moral or ethical, practical decisions about what I want to do, who I want to be, what I want to write, then look back—like with New Year's resolutions—and think, "Whatever happened to that idea? Whatever happened to that reform?" Here I'm treating that person the shitty way I did before. So, do we listen to ourselves? No. It's always a war, it's always a battle, it's always a struggle. Stories are ways of highlighting and identifying the struggle and reminding us that it's important at some point to stop and render an account and an accounting. Stories persist and work in that way.

BT: The last section of *The Cattle Killing* consists of a letter written by the son of the narrator-author to his father. In his letter the son comments on the father's book which he has just read. What was your purpose in bringing the author's son into the story?

JW: Well, it works—in terms of the plot, the circling of the plot. Also, I don't want to write books—no matter how dark the vision, how uncompromising—that suggest to my children that their lives are meaningless. I want to write books that suggest that there's a place for them, and that there's some way that they can use the lives that they can give—in an important and positive way. So whatever has happened to me, however I see the world, it is important to me to pass it on. One of the reasons I work hard is to pass on something useful to them. It's a record of some remarkable things that I hope they may be able to do something with, make something of.

Also, my son is a writer. So it's a literal passing of the torch—in a kind of playful way. It's acknowledging what he does as a writer—someone who's embarking on a lot of the same things I'm doing. It's also a parable about texts. It's a parable about actual life, the fictional life, invented lives—about fathers and sons who invent lives for one another, generations who invent lives for their ancestors. All that comes into play. It's also a kind of carnival of texts—of letters, novels, reminiscences, research, historical documents—and how those interact and click together at certain times for readers, writers.

BT: You're referring to the letter, supposedly historical, that was written by an African during the 1850s describing the cattle-killing event, and that the son has discovered by chance in the British Museum? The letter that's included within the letter the son writes to his father.

JW: Yes, that's what I mean. That is one of the texts that's involved in all that. When I say the section is a "carnival of texts," I mean all of the pieces that come together in the last four or five pages.

BT: [Laughter.] You make the reader *work* to pull all of these threads together.

JW: [Laughter.] But that should be *fun!* That should be, "Oh! Oh! Oh! Look at that!" "Oh! What's this?" "Oh! What's that?"

BT: [Laughter.] It'll be hard work for the kind of reader who expects to be given the "It"—the ones who say, "Tell me, quick! In five minutes or less."

JW: [Laughter.] Well, they wouldn't have made it that far. They would have been lost in space by then.

BT: Some readers have a sense that they have to work so much harder in your later books, such as *Philadelphia Fire* and *The Cattle Killing*. In fact, a reviewer for the *New York Times* wrote that with *The Cattle Killing,* you "may have ventured beyond [your] readers this time out." How would you respond to this?

JW: I wouldn't. [Pause.] It's beneath my [laughter] dignity. Everybody's entitled to his opinion.

BT: Do you have any sense that your more recent books are becoming less accessible?

JW: No, I would hope not. As a matter of fact, I think there's a lot more in *The Cattle Killing* that's more visceral, less of a head trip, than some of the early work. I think there's much that has more immediacy. There are some sexy scenes. There's stuff that you can get off on if you're not treating it as a crossword puzzle. If you treat a book as an intellectual exercise, if you don't swing with the language, don't get off on the stuff that's the meat of fiction—the sensuality of the scenes—if you're so busy searching for some kind of meaning and significance, instead of experiencing the language and what's going on with the character, then you'll have a very abstract and intellectually alienated feeling about the book. You'll miss the parts that are the fun parts.

As a culture, as a population, we have a lot more success experiencing music. We go into music in a lot more relaxed way than we go into reading books. Sometimes it's the critical stance, it's the critical habit which dulls the senses and causes people to miss things. Yes, there's an intellectual sub-stratum, there's an intellectual seriousness about what I write. But I'm not stupid. I know that the only way I'm going to intrigue anybody enough— entice them enough to get at some of those points—is to provide a surface, to provide a play: a sensuous, rhythmic experience of language that has a first appeal, a primal appeal. Once you're entertaining somebody then you can also instruct them. But you don't begin by scaring them away. At least that's not what I try to do.

BT: In my graduate course on Chinese American literature, in noting how writers deal with painful and difficult issues we've been discussing the strategy of "charm and disarm." In a conversation I had recently with the writer Gish Jen, who has this incredible sense of humor, she mentioned that she was worried that people were not taking her seriously. I told her that, in my view, humor is one of her greatest strengths and she should just go with it. The serious message is still there. It's also true, though, that readers can just be entertained and not deal with the serious issues. I try to teach students that they need to read at different levels at the same time. They need to attend to more than one feature of a literary work.

Those at my university who heard you read from *The Cattle Killing* said that they had the kind of experience you were aiming for—getting into the rhythm of the language, visualizing the opening scene in the contemporary Pittsburgh neighborhood. They commented on these characteristics of your style. They really picked up on the rhythm and beauty of the language. Some of the younger students—even though they were not very familiar with your work—were saying, "Wow! That was powerful." They immediately connected with the reading—how the language worked, your voice. It really pulled them in.

JW: That's a problem, you know. People are so alienated by their education—or by lack of education—from the reading experience itself. They start reading something and there's an unfamiliar word, a different kind of sentence, or a transition that's not a very ordinary, conventional kind of transition and they get worried. They say, "Oh, this is not for me." Or, "This is difficult." And then they stop. If only they would just let themselves go through it and not be pushed out by being intimidated . . .

I mean, it's funny. Kids have taught themselves to listen to this rapid rapping that, unless you really work at it, listen to it six or seven times, you don't know what the hell they're saying. But you get an ear for it. You get an ear for very complicated rhythms by listening, by exposure, by not expecting that it will all be there the first time—even in pop music.

Here the head of racism rears up again. This is particularly true for minority kids—for all kids, really—but particularly minority kids. The minute certain signs are manifest, signs of an abstruse or unusual vocabulary, or certain kinds of sentence rhythms, certain transitions or elisions, the response is, "It ain't for me. This is not the book for me. This is not the straight-ahead, straightforward, old-fashioned narrative of black vernacular. So maybe this is not for me. It's for *them.*" Shying away. And that's a crime.

On the other hand, there are white readers who expect a certain something from a black text—an African American text—and if they don't see it immediately, if it's not the voice from the ghetto, then that turns them off. There are these anticipations, stereotypes in the reading experience that are alienating people from their reading, from the potential to learn from the reading.

BT: I think this is where experience with other languages is very helpful. For example, recently I was teaching a Chicano novel, *Bless Me, Última.* I said the title character's name with the correct Spanish pronunciation. I said

"Última" with an accented long "u" and my students pronounced it like
"ultimate" with a short "u." This happened repeatedly. They didn't even
attempt the Spanish pronunciation—it was so foreign and alien to them. Apparently, they were used to blocking out unfamiliar sounds. They seemed to
be afraid of that foreign territory.

This approach to language also affects what they get from their reading.
So I often ask them to read out loud passages of whatever I assign when
they're home. And then in the classroom, we try to *hear* the language as well
as interpret the text—to experience the writing fully. But in other classes
they don't do that. They're only looking at words on a page. It's strictly a
cerebral, intellectual thing. There's no experiential aspect. I think that de-
tracts from their ability to respond to the complexity of a text. They feel they
have to get the meaning, *the* meaning, in a few minutes, or they lose interest.
It's because they're not calling on all of their faculties.

JW: Yes, and faculties that they use unthinkingly in other situations.

BT: In a 1988 interview you said that "language aspires to the condition
of music. Music seems to me the medium that comprehends all others, because music can be silent."

JW: That's pretty fancy, isn't it [laughter]?

BT: Yes, quite impressive. Then there's Alice Walker's statement in a
1973 interview when she said: "I am trying to arrive at that place where
black music already is; to arrive at that unselfconscious sense of collective
oneness; that naturalness, that . . . grace." Both of these statements identify
the nature of your mutual craft. Would you care to elaborate on this notion
of writing as music?

JW: It's an interesting coincidence that Alice Walker and I both shared
the same editor. That was how I met Alice, through my editor. He sent me a
copy of the galley proofs for *The Third Life of Grange Copeland*. His name
was Hiram Haydn. He lived on the same street as Charles Chesnutt in Cleve-
land in 1900. His career went all the way back, continuing through the 30s
and 40s. So there is that connection between Alice Walker and me at the start
of our careers. That's just a literary footnote.

What I want—and probably what Alice wants—is both the support and
resource of tradition, but at the same time the independence and respect that
music has earned. But I would go even further. Nobody asks the question,
"Is Dizzy Gillespie the best black jazz trumpeter?" In sports, nobody asks
the question, "Is Michael Jordan the best black basketball player?" There's
not that hitch in people's thinking. They'll say, "Dizzy Gillespie is the best

jazz trumpeter" or "Michael Jordan is the best basketball player." Period.
But I don't care who you are—maybe it's beginning to change with Toni
Morrison and the Nobel Prize for literature—the question "Who is the best
black writer?" still has a kind of resonance. People think they understand
what that means. People still make that distinction. You can be the best black
writer, but that doesn't mean you're the best artist. You can be a really good
black writer, but that doesn't mean you're a really good writer. We need to
get that monkey off the culture's back.

BT: What about writers using the term "black" to identify their connection with an African American tradition—especially with music?

JW: When we're talking culture, that's one thing. Certainly, there're
some differences from the mainstream that African Americans share. Just as
other groups are aware of certain cultural differences that they share. Hindi.
Thai people. There're differences that are not socially constructed—they're
physical, outward differences. Then there're some that are not physical or
cultural. They come from an individual's imagination.

So I'm very happy to be someone who embodies in his work an African
American tradition. But that means a cultural tradition. That doesn't mean
that an African American is biologically determined and that this will determine how I write, what I write. There's a distinction. One vision is accumula-
tive. You can talk about traditions, conventions, influence. In the other view
you're talking about something fixed genetically: essentialism, which is a
cage. Cultural identification makes a lot of sense to me and I want to be
understood as being in a tradition—an African American cultural tradition.

BT: Your writing makes us really appreciate the value of that tradition.
It's a tradition, though, that people tend to equate with slavery.

JW: Slavery is certainly there—an immense memory—in that tradition.
It describes the external condition for four hundred years. In the same way,
if you look at Spanish literature, Spanish culture, and pretend that the Moors
did not rule for four hundred years, didn't exist there, you're going to have
all kinds of problems. That's a fact that you can react to in a hundred, a
thousand different ways. That's a tension, but it doesn't constitute the tradition. It's a constituent of the tradition, but it doesn't constitute the tradition.

BT: For some people—some traditional scholars of American history—
when they talk about African American culture, they're fixated on the condition of slavery. That's all the culture they can see. They talk about "the slave
culture," but they don't really explore what the various aspects of African
American culture mean.

JW: It would be interesting—wouldn't it?—if that same kind of determinism, that same kind of reductive thinking, would be used in courses on American literature? Suppose we designed a course which looked at literature as writings from "the slaveholding culture"—which started with the premise that all American writers were part of the slaveholding culture [laughter]. Now, that's the caricature, that's the kind of trash that's sometimes thrown in people's faces—some of the charges made against "multiculturalism." But that would be interesting, wouldn't it?—to say that before you could read Fitzgerald, you had to understand that he was part of the slaveholding culture. Now I guess that might give you some interesting insights into Fitzgerald. But, on the other hand, it would also create distortions.

BT: Another equation you find is that African American culture is strictly "street culture." Of course, one doesn't have to be black to be in the streets.

JW: There's a vibrancy there. It's complicated. Because of the continuance of apartheid, one of the most vibrant places historically has always been that of the underclass, the class which has been forcibly divided from the normal routines of life of the mainstream culture. That class has been the one which has invented and preserved the counterculture. So you can't dismiss the fact that there's a real strain, a continuous strain, there. Maybe that's where some of the largest percentage of your tension might be, an important lower class tension. You have to understand what that means and why and how. That's another question. It's not a simple question of a monolithic view of African American culture as always that of the lower class, as only that.

BT: When people say these things to me about street culture, it doesn't mesh with my experience. I understand street culture, from my years in New York City, as various peoples from everywhere mixing it up—crossing paths and cultures—all the time. I couldn't quite understand how they could equate this exclusively with black culture.

JW: Also, what's nice, in a way, is to see the people who are the result of the literal biological mixing that has always been going on, between black and white, and the people who are undefinable, somewhat like the coloreds in South Africa—a mix of East Indian, Asian, African, European. They really are distinctive. It's a real trip that gives the lie to the stereotypes that Madison Avenue—in commercials, in sports—have given us. I see it happening right now. For a long time, regarding people of mixed race, the myth was that they inevitably became wasted and afloat. They were never an amalgamation of the best parts, but always an integration of the worst parts. But now they become icons, examples of amalgamation—a beautiful woman with dark skin, blonde hair, blue eyes. Where's that coming from?

BT: You make the point in *Fatheralong* about how the preferred term used to be "amalgamation" and how the racialized and racist term "miscegenation" came into use. You remind us that "amalgamation" doesn't have the same connotation.

JW: Yes, a curious switch—maybe not so curious—but curious about how these terms switched.

BT: Speaking of switching, can we get closer now to questions about the writing process. First, controlling emotional distance between the reader and characters as well as a work's implied author is a major issue for the creative writer. In terms of your writing process, how do you juggle this? More specifically, how do you manage when writing about the painful aspects of your own life? Recently, I was teaching Maxine Hong Kingston's novel *Tripmaster Monkey*. Kingston's poet-protagonist Wittman Ah Sing is walking through Golden Gate Park in San Francisco intently observing and deliberately experiencing both the attractive and unattractive sights and sounds, getting nauseated by certain things. He tells himself, "Let it all come in" and then, a couple of pages later, declares, "It's time to stop letting it all come in." Do you go through any kind of process like that in your writing? How do you handle this on a daily basis—especially "exposing" your personal life in the way you do?

JW: Writing at one level is always confession. But writing is also always hiding. I think that's the simplest answer. That's the most honest, direct answer. Writing is deceiving, writing is fiction. So no matter what it seems to somebody else, no matter how vividly I may be spilling my guts on the page, if I am a good writer, I'm spilling precisely the amount that I want to spill. It's always revealing and concealing. If I show you my bleeding hand, it may be because I don't want you to see my bleeding foot. If I show you my bleeding leg, it's because I don't want you to see my bleeding back. If it is writing that has power, intellectual force, and intricacy, then it is a craft. So what you see is not always what you get. What you get is not always what you see. I write about some things that are unspeakable. I write about them because it relieves the pressure of what is unspeakable. You can't say what's unspeakable, but you can say other things—to relieve the pressure, the burden. My life is never directly revealed on the page.

BT: You're so conscious of the mediation of experience through language. How do you decide which of your works are published as fiction and which as nonfiction? For example, given the overlapping of your Homewood material in various works, how do you know when you're writing fiction versus nonfiction? How do you sort that out?

JW: For one thing, the interface of fiction and nonfiction is a subject that I write about. The more I write about this inquiry, the more fascinating it makes the interplay and the exchange. What are the hard boundaries? So not only do I write that, but I'm involved in that, and there are only the boundaries created by the writing itself. There's the explicit commentary and explicit expression of it. I represent that play. I try to represent it in both fiction and nonfiction.

BT: Do you expect the reader to read the fiction and nonfiction books differently?

JW: I think my responsibility—and I always try to do this—my responsibility is to make my intentions clear. That's all I can do. In *Brothers and Keepers* I make it clear that I'm trying to give an accurate, factual, in a sense a documentary picture of certain aspects of my brother's life and my life. In *The Cattle Killing* I try to make it clear that there's an author inside the story like me, but if you insist on that in a literal way you're going to lose out on something. The book is instructing you to remember that you're reading it and somebody else has written it. And isn't that a kick? Isn't that weird? And don't ever take that for granted. So here you're reminded of it, here you're reminded of it again. That plays with the line between the fiction and the "out there"—fiction and real life. But it does it in the context of the ongoing enjoyment of the story, the ongoing enjoyment of the fiction. In *Brothers and Keepers* it's stated clearly that it is a nonfiction work. There may be places in it—well, there are poems in it. There are places where the author is trying to imagine what it might be like to be somebody else. It tells you that. So that the techniques and the force of fiction enter, and are represented in, what is a nonfictional work.

BT: I think this kind of writing, and this approach, requires readers to open up their thinking about what they're reading. The traditional genres elicit stock responses like, "Oh, this is fiction. I don't have to take it seriously." In fact, the traditional compartmentalizing does not really work with this kind of writing, because there's always an interplay there.

JW: It's important for one's health to be able to make judgments apart from the conventional envelopes that are given us, whether we're talking about transvestism or the news. The envelopes which used to guide us—the surface, the experiences which used to guide us—have never been reliable.

We have known this, we subject people have known this in our groins. We understand it from the ground up. From the time I was a kid I knew that there were certain ways which society dressed itself up, certain illusions it had about itself.

BT: I'd like to ask you about your virtuosity with language. When you attend so assiduously to the rhythm, the sound, the feel of language, is there a danger of being lulled by this? In other words, can't writing become a virtuoso performance—the interplay between you and the medium—which excludes the reader altogether?

JW: That's a danger, that's a danger . . . and you can also fail by plodding along in conventional ways—go dead in the water. Writing is very difficult, and there are traps in whichever form you decide to work. I myself find it increasingly difficult to read conventional narrative. The assumptions that it makes, the games that it plays, the way that it intrudes values—it seems phony to me pretty quickly and I'm just not interested in it. So, it's a kind of a dried up shell. It's interesting in an experiment like *Mason and Dixon,* this new book by Thomas Pynchon. What it attempts to do is revive an anachronistic form of the novel, both graphically and in other ways—revive an older form to recapture people's attention. So, I think that's what we're all trying to do, trying to invent something that breathes new life into the form. That means taking chances and breaking rules. That means pushing readers. And if you lose readers, maybe their children will pick it up and feel it's necessary to read something like what you're doing. So, for every one you lose, maybe you gain one. For every seven you lose, maybe you gain one. But I like that, I like playing on the edge. It's like basketball—the way the very best basketball players combine the virtuosity of individual style, blending that *me* into the long traditions of rules and patterns of the game and the team. So that you go to see Michael Jordan because you want to see a Jordanesque performance. But it doesn't destroy the continuity of the game, and it certainly enhances his particular team.

BT: When reading to an audience you have that lyrical quality in your voice that draws readers into the lilt and rhythm of the language. Whether they're listening or reading, do you ever get the sense that readers might become hypnotized by your voice?

JW: [Laughter.] Yes, mesmerized. After a reading, if somebody comes up to me and says, "That was real poetry—your writing's like poetry," well (a) I'm complimented—"Thank you." Then (b) another little voice clicks on and worries. "Does that mean that this person's kind of out there daydreaming?"

[Laughter.] You know, hearing this guy up there making these nice sounds to daydream by. I don't want that. I know that sometimes when I say that about something it means that I've lost a certain kind of acuity in my listening and judgment. You can relax into the music and miss the message. So, no, I don't want that. But, on the other hand, if somebody *really* means they're listening to it and it sounds like poetry to them, it means that the language itself is palpable—you're aware of it as a medium, what you can do with it. And that's great. That's giving the language its due. That's what's special about prose fiction. That it both tells a story—has meaning and deals with questions of right and wrong—and at the same time does it in a sensuous medium that in and of itself has value and cannot be reduced or turned into something else. It's distinctive to the medium—a particular kind of communication that's distinctive to that medium.

BT: This is a really important issue, the issue of comprehension. It's a problem when people assume that reading is mainly or only a cognitive exercise. You're talking about how through the medium, through language itself, you can both appreciate sound and other visceral qualities and apprehend what is being said. There's this important combination of thought and feeling in reading literature. There's still this assumption around that there's a split between the mind and the body. People think that to understand something is a cerebral exercise. So with most kinds of reading they don't feel the language or even try to call on their senses. The reading experience would be ideal if they can put the two sides together. Then they would be able to understand that writing doesn't have to be just one or the other.

JW: Well, think of a very powerful computer that can scan a page and turn it into a vocal report. Have you ever heard one of those mechanical voices from a computer scanner? It's a very mechanical voice. Now, think of how much the person who experiences a book that way is losing. They could take a test on it, they could tell you about the characters, they could talk about it in a very intricate, elaborate way. It would be necessary to retranslate this translation of the book made by the machine into something else to get back to the novel, to get back to the experience of the novel. When you think of these multiple translations and what's lost along the way, then maybe it's a helpful exercise to understand how distinctive is the kind of knowledge that fiction offers.

BT: Speaking of translations, and what might be lost, which other languages have your works been translated into—and are they effective?

JW: I wouldn't know because I don't know the other languages. French is the only other language I know and I don't read enough French to really

judge. *The Cattle Killing* is being translated right now—*Philadelphia Fire,
Brothers and Keepers*—into Turkish, Norwegian, German, French, Japanese,
Swedish, a bunch of languages.

BT: One high point of the recognition your work has received must have
been the MacArthur "Genius" Fellowship you were awarded in 1993. How
did you feel about getting it?

JW: The only bad thing about it was the last check [laughter].

BT: They found you, right? There was no notice, no warning?

JW: No, it's like that old TV show, "The Millionaire." It was my daughter's graduation from high school. It was great. We were all together—Judy,
my mother—all sitting around when I got the call.

BT: So your daughter said, "We knew daddy's a genius!"

JW: They knew daddy could take them out for lunch [laughter].

BT: Elsewhere you said that "you read everything." Do you keep up with
some of the contemporary American ethnic writers?

JW: I used to keep up more when I did more teaching of literature. Since
I've been at U Mass and teaching less—I only teach creative writing classes
and I use contemporary books in those—I don't keep up as much. I used to
keep up with the criticism and I used to write essays about contemporary
literature. I don't very often anymore. I don't even write reviews. I'm aware
of what's going on. But I'm not current the way I was when I was teaching
literature more.

BT: You were asked to make an assessment of contemporary American
fiction when you edited the collection *The Best American Short Stories 1996.*
How did you approach the question of literary value?

JW: I don't know exactly what you mean by *literary* value. Literary
value—well, I assume that because of my writing, my training, and my teaching, I'm just as good a judge of literature as anybody else and better than
most. What I tried to do was to be fair. For example, I know I do have certain
kinds of stories I like, but I tried to push that. If I read a work that's not
exactly my cup of tea but done very well for its kind, I wanted to be responsive to that. I didn't want to skew the process totally just simply on the basis
of my personal preference. But when you get right down to it, it was subjective.

If I had any general criteria—well, they were kind of negative. I didn't
want to know who the authors were. I wanted to get a cross-section of stories,
characters of different ages, to have some variety in kinds of language, etc.
But that's part of my taste. I like a mixture, I like diversity. I expect some

stories to be short, tight, while others will take a little more time to develop, to have more characters, more plot. But then there was also the real, practical issue that I was selecting samples of what was handed to me. So I may have wanted a whole bunch of stories about little old black men in Mississippi worrying about Martians coming and where the world's going. But then I didn't get stories like that. That's not exactly how it works, actually. I could also have done some research and looked for some stories but, frankly, doing my own work, teaching—I didn't have time to do that.

BT: Would you like to say anything about what you're working on?

JW: I'm working on a new novel tentatively called *Two Cities*. I have a working draft that I can share with an editor, at least. Then I want to work on a nonfiction book. I'm not sure about that. Some essays about what's going on now. I think basketball might be in there somewhere.

Index